The Retarded Child from Birth to Five

A Multidisciplinary Program for the Child and Family

MARVIN H. HUNTER
HELEN SCHUCMAN
GEORGE FRIEDLANDER

The Shield Institute for Retarded Children

JOHN DAY BOOKS IN
S **E**
SPECIAL EDUCATION

The John Day Company
New York

Library of Congress Cataloging in Publication Data

Hunter, Marvin H
    The retarded child from birth to five.

    Bibliography: p.
        1. Mental deficiency. 2. Handicapped children—
Rehabilitation. I. Schucman, Helen, joint author.
II. Friedlander, George, joint author. III. Title.
RJ506.M4H85   616.8'858   70-179783

The John Day Company
257 Park Avenue South
New York, N.Y. 10010
AN Intext PUBLISHER

Published on the same day in Canada by Longman Canada Limited.

PRINTED IN THE UNITED STATES OF AMERICA

Preface

In his message to the 86th Congress of the United States in 1963, President John F. Kennedy said, "Mental retardation stems from many causes. It can result from mongolism, birth injury or infection, or any of a host of conditions that cause a faulty or arrested development of intelligence to such an extent that the individual's ability to learn and to adapt to the demands of society is impaired. Once the damage is done lifetime incapacity is likely. With early detection, suitable care and training, however, a significant improvement can be achieved."

Material presented in this book makes significant contributions to the important areas of early identification and intervention, comprehensive interdisciplinary evaluation, suitable treatment programs, the process of continuing re-evaluation, and an understanding of the vital role of the family in the progress of the child. The book has the special advantage of placing its major emphasis on services for the trainable mentally retarded child, one whose special needs have been seriously neglected.

The trainable mentally retarded child, variously referred to as moderately retarded or semi-independent, is the child whose life prognosis is "sheltered living." Such living may be in a sheltered workshop, a day care center, a residential facility, or the home. The important consideration is that such children will need some type of supervision for their entire lives. Further, the presence of physical and/or mental pathology is the rule rather than the exception in this group, so that the need for extensive and highly specialized services is acute.

In 1962, the President's Panel on Mental Retardation recommended the establishment of preschool centers for the socialization and stimulation of retarded children, and for the counseling of parents relative to effective home training of the retarded. Federal legislation passed several years later provided for the establishment of special programs aimed at developing new approaches to helping preschool handicapped children.⌐

This book presents data, insights, extrapolations, and educated guesses based on many years of experience with trainable children and their families at The Shield Institute for Retarded Children. The material should be of inestimable value to all agencies and disciplines involved in setting up and conducting such programs.

Detailed descriptions of programs for training the children are included, as well as extensive guidelines for treatment programs for the families, an emphasis in accord with the recommendations of the President's Panel in connection with the role of the family in helping a handicapped child. The case histories which the book includes illustrate in detail techniques of proven value in assisting both child and family.

The truly multidisciplinary approach should be immensely helpful to all personnel working in this field. The college instructor at both graduate and undergraduate levels should find interesting factual material with which to implement theoretical approaches. Voluntary organizations and governmental agencies should find valuable practical material for planning, establishing, conducting, and evaluating programs. In addition, the families and particularly the parents are given the respect and attention they deserve, an aspect rarely given the emphasis it receives here.

The authors are to be congratulated for adding to the literature in mental deficiency a volume which so clearly defines the population worked with, the rationale for programming, suitable materials and training techniques, the results already obtained and their logical extensions and implications for the future in the all-important area of infant and preschool programs for the trainable mentally retarded child.

Chris J. De Prospo

Professor Emeritus
  The City College of New York
Past-President
  The American Association on Mental Deficiency
Professor of Special Education
  Southern Connecticut State College

Acknowledgments

This book is in itself an example of multidisciplinary cooperation. The authors particularly wish to thank the following staff members of The Shield Institute for Retarded Children who, under the medical direction of Joseph Michaels, M.D., made valuable contributions of material and ideas: Lillian Arfa, M.S., Casework Supervisor; Evelyn Boswell, R.N., School Nurse; Rhoda Ferber, M.A., Educational Director; Theresa Kellar, M.A., Senior Psychologist; George Weiss, M.D., Pediatric Consultant. Special thanks are also offered to former staff members Esther Rothman, Ph.D., and Robert Schore, M.S., for their contributions. For their past and ongoing contributions to the infant program, we wish to thank Regina Cohen, M.S., Virginia DiBonaventura, M.A., Ellen Palermo, M.A., and Arthur Roza, M.S.

The invaluable secretarial assistance of Dorothy Gluckstern, Lilyan Kushner, and Betty H. Richter contributed much to make this book possible.

We wish to thank Helaine Geismar, M.A., and Susan Weinstein, M.A., for their able assistance in the preparation of the glossary and bibliography, and Stanley Raiff of Youth Education, Inc., for his assistance.

We acknowledge with deep thanks the grants awarded to The Shield Institute for Retarded Children by the National Institutes of

Mental Health. These grants supported some of the programs which made this book possible. Finally, our appreciation is acknowledged to the Board of Directors of the Institute, the teachers, nurses, psychologists, social workers, speech therapists, and physicians, whose dedication over the years has inspired new trends in services for the mentally retarded.

Contents

CHAPTER 3

Treatment Programs for the Child   70

CHAPTER 4

Family Treatment   129

Introduction

The Shield Institute for Retarded Children is a voluntary, nonprofit organization which has served children with special needs in the City of New York since 1921. For some thirty-three years The Institute was devoted to the care of homeless children, for many of whom it was the only real home they ever knew. However, following a change in social service concepts, more and more homeless children were placed in family settings to be raised by foster parents, and the Board of Directors of The Shield Institute recognized that the need for the kind of services they were offering was diminishing. After a two-year survey of the existing areas of special care for children and consultation with many specialists in these fields, it was decided that The Shield Institute, with its many years of experience in caring for children, could make a significant contribution in helping the young, trainable mentally retarded child and his family.

When The Shield Institute for Retarded Children first began to offer specialized services to young trainable children there were virtually no guidelines to follow. The needs of these children and their families had been tragically neglected, although some small attempt had been made to help them at the community and school levels. For the most part, however, their care had been left almost exclusively to state institutions or private residential schools, which met only a very small part of the existing need. There was, in fact, no mandated education on the elementary school level for children with IQs under 50 even in a state as large as New York.

The Shield Institute, a pioneering agency in this field, accepted as its fundamental philosophy that mental retardation is a comprehensive human tragedy which handicaps the child, the family into which he is born, and the society in which he lives. In order to deal with the total problem rather than one or two separate aspects, The Shield Institute developed as an integrated, multidisciplinary service for the child and his family. A school was established, and extensive services were provided for diagnosis and treatment in the medical, psychological, speech and language, and social work areas. From the beginning, services were provided for parents as well as for the children at many levels. Individual counseling and group work at different degrees of intensity were offered to the parents as needed, in recognition of the fact that the growth of the child and the progress of the parents are inextricably interwoven. Educational and psychotherapeutic counseling programs for parents also constituted an integral part of the services.

It was in August of 1954 that The Shield Institute for Retarded Children opened its doors to retarded children aged 7 through 12, of all faiths and racial origins. There were five members in the professional staff at that time, and the first class consisted of six children. The staff was soon expanded as the number of participating families increased. The diagnostic process became geared to servicing an increasing number of children, and The Institute grew rapidly. After sixteen years of extensive experience and research, The Institute serves approximately six hundred families annually and maintains a staff of eighty professional workers. It now has two buildings. The original one has been greatly expanded, and a new one, which was completed in 1969, was especially planned and constructed for the special educational needs of retarded children.

Although The Shield Institute did not offer help for younger retarded children at first, within a few years of its inception programs were provided to 4- and 5-year-old children and their families. This preschool experience helped the children to make a smoother adjustment to the classroom when they reached school age and aided their parents in dealing more constructively with the many special problems which confronted them. The many fortunate experiences with young trainable children and their parents led the clinical and educational staffs to believe that services to the child and the family might be of even greater value if help was instituted as soon as possible after the birth of the child. With increasing experience, the conviction grew that such a program would result in maximum long-term benefits to the child, not only because of his own training gains but also because of the greater emotional stability of his family.

In April of 1958, The Shield Institute undertook to conduct a three-year program for preschool trainable children and their families under the auspices of the National Institute of Mental Health (246). The special services that were provided included a developmentally geared, clinically oriented training program for the child and therapeutic and counseling services for the parents as well. The specific aims of the project were to develop suitable school and home training programs for 3- and 4-year-old trainable retarded children, a home nursing program for severely retarded infants, and appropriate treatment programs for the parents. The major emphasis in that project was on 3- and 4-year-old children, with training procedures focused on their social adjustment, emotional development, curricular skills, and speech and language development. The curriculum stressed the development of motor skills, motor conceptual activities, self-care and self-help, safety and health activities, language, number concepts, and social development.

After training, the progress of the children was compared with their own pretraining status and also with that of comparable children who had not received formal training during the same time period. It was found that the 3- and 4-year-old children in the training programs had made real improvements over time and were also significantly superior to similar untrained children in curricular skills, freedom from distractibility, ability to attend, general emotional status, and speech and language development. At the conclusion of a specific course of treatment, provided in various forms and at different levels according to individual need, the pre- and post-therapy status of the parents were also compared. The results clearly demonstrated that significant gains had been made. The parents had become more emotionally mature and psychologically stable, better able to cope with the present and plan for the future, and more constructive and realistic in their attitudes toward the child and toward each other.

A small group of younger retarded children, ranging from several months to about 3 years of age, was also given a few services in the course of that project. Although the limited training that was provided for them at that time failed to produce demonstrable curricular gains, the infant group showed considerable improvement in the general conditions that facilitate learning. They had become significantly less hostile, negativistic, and avoiding, and their ability to sustain attention had greatly increased as their distractibility lessened. The progress made by these children and the experiences gained by the professional staff in working with them and their families served as the basis for improving ongoing services and also led to a major next step in the development of more extensive programs of help for the very young retarded child and his family. A second project, also conducted by The Shield Institute under the auspices of the National Institute of Mental Health, began in 1963 and continued through 1967 (247). This project was devoted exclusively to infant retardates and their families.

The purpose of the project for the infants was to provide the child with comprehensive, multidisciplinary training, including both direct services to the child himself and programs that trained the parents to train the child. Services were offered in the home and at The Shield Institute, where well-equipped, special nursery facilities were set up. The families were offered extensive treatment services, including psychological evaluations and treatment programs by psychiatric, psychological, casework, medical, and educational specialists on both an individual and group basis. Although the project's initial goal had been to work with fifty infants and families, the obvious need for the kinds of services that were provided necessitated almost doubling this number, and ninety-four children and their families were finally accepted for the program. After participating in this far more inclusive training program, significant post-training gains were found in the children's self-care abilities, motor skills, maturity, and level of adaptive behavior, as well as in overall language development and receptive and expressive speech. Further, there seemed to be a real relationship between the amount of improvement and the intensity of the training.

Evidence that the gains made by these children were in large part attributable to the training they had received, rather than to simple maturation alone, was found in the fact that the earlier group of comparable children, who had received less intensive training, had made only negligible gains in corresponding curricular areas. Impressive gains were demonstrated for the parents of these children as well. After therapy the parents were clearly more willing to renounce their earlier over-control, better able to plan for the future, and manifested increased stress tolerance with decreased feelings of hopelessness, depression, anxiety, and guilt. Their family relationships were more harmonious, and their attitudes toward the child were significantly less hostile and destructive. Related improvements were also reflected in their actual problem-solving behavior in the life situation.

The children who participated in the project have already been followed for some five years after its termination. Many of these children have continued in The Shield Institute's on-going training programs at home and in school, and there have been many opportunities to compare their subsequent progress with that of similar children who did not have the benefit of such early training experience. A large percentage of the project parents have also continued to avail themselves of The Shield Institute's services, providing further possibilities for comparisons. There is much to suggest that both children and parents made far more than merely transitory gains and have established a firmer foundation on which to build the future. More than ten years' experience of working with infant retardates and their families, learning from them and gaining increasing understanding of their special needs and how to meet them, has provided the basis for the comprehensive diagnostic procedures and treatment programs and the multidisciplinary thinking and action that represent the heart and core of the work at The Shield Institute. This experience has also led to the preparation of this book. It is hoped that the book will be of assistance to teachers, caseworkers, nurses, doctors, therapists, parents, and others concerned with helping young retarded children develop their limited abilities to the maximum of their potential.

Joseph V. Shostak, Executive Director
The Shield Institute for Retarded Children

The Retarded Child from
Birth to Five

CHAPTER 1

The Importance of Early Identification and Treatment

Several lines of research and clinical experience have led to the development of the concept of early identification and treatment in the field of mental retardation. Child development centers in universities and hospitals throughout the country have added to the body of knowledge of early development and have fostered an increasing interest in early training. Within the last ten years, funded research has resulted in a vast amount of literature related to the early growth and development of the normal child. Learning theory has been applied to investigations of how children learn. Emphasis on the early years of a child's life as preparatory periods for later learning has highlighted the importance of early identification and treatment of special problem areas. Studies of child-rearing practices and federal and state programs for "disadvantaged" children have pointed up the wisdom of instituting help as early as possible in the life of the child.

Earlier simplistic beliefs that retarded children act as they do merely because they are retarded have slowly given way before an increased understanding of the conditions that facilitate or hinder learning in all children. It has been gradually recognized that the retarded child's early learning constitutes the basis for his later skills, just as it does in children in general. If the effects of the past continue into the future, early identification of the retarded child's handicaps is obviously crucial. Having no margin for waste, he cannot afford the additional handicaps of false starts, needless frustrations, and lost time. Nor can his parents afford to harbor either unrealistic hope or equally unrealistic despair. Early treatment is essential not only for the child but for the family as well, and especially for the mother, who in the crucial early years is the child-rearing center of the family. The child's limited abilities are all too easily lost, and his restricted potentialities may well fail to survive a bad start. Early identification and treatment can do much to prevent him from becoming a drain on society.

There is no longer any doubt that retarded children can learn, and that their learning can benefit themselves and their society. Early training helps them to adapt, assimilate, and accommodate to their environment. However, awareness of the types of training, stimulation, and curricula that are most needed for the retarded infant is still in the beginning phases. Indeed, we are still in the process of trying to understand the retarded infant and of isolating the prognostic variables that might be helpful in estimating his social and educational future within his family and community. Progress is facilitated if the basic concepts of early identification become a working part of the philosophy of diagnosis and treatment for retarded children and their families, who comprise a sizable segment of society.

INCIDENCE

The incidence of children found to be mentally retarded in infancy or in the first several years of life is difficult to establish. Estimates of the number of newborn who will develop as mentally retarded individuals vary between 1 percent and 3 percent of the population as a whole. The prevalence figures published by the Children's Bureau in

1966 (220) predicted that approximately 3,000,000 individuals would be diagnosed as retarded by 1970. This represents a prevalence rate of approximately 1½ percent of the total population and implies that approximately 60,000 mentally retarded children are born each year. Other estimates have indicated that as many as 100,000 retarded children may be born annually. Among the many factors that make an accurate estimate difficult is the fact that most retarded children are asymptomatic at birth and develop as mildly or moderately retarded, so that their handicap may not be identified until school or even adolescent years.

Data are more available and clear cut for infants with gross anomalies. For example, Schull (242) has indicated that one pregnancy in every hundred will result in an infant with a major anomaly that can be identified before the child is a year of age. Others (179) have placed this figure higher, estimating about 4 percent for major anomalies to 13 percent for minor anomalies. The presence of an anomaly is not necessarily indicative of mental retardation, of course, although one investigation (256) reports an incidence figure of 50 percent for the development of mental retardation where there is a major anomaly such as hydrocephalus, microcephaly, meningocele, hypertelorism, or severe hypotonicity. On the basis of such data, plus evidence that suggests that approximately 20 percent of retarded children are profoundly to moderately retarded or identifiable by physical anomalies, it can be inferred that a minimum of 12,000 to 20,000 retarded children are born each year for whom early identification is possible. It is, in fact, likely that these are conservative figures, since the incidence of mongolism alone is established at 2 to 3 per 1,000 births (37), resulting in approximately 8,000 to 12,000 mongoloid children born each year.

It seems obvious that the number of retarded children for whom early identification is possible is actually quite large and that they constitute a major health and diagnostic problem in spite of the recent important developments in the area of prevention. As the Department of Health, Education and Welfare points out, it is essential to improve the effectiveness of preventive measures so as to reduce the incidence of handicapping conditions in children and prevent a marked increase in the number of handicapped in our population (105).

PREVENTION

Prevention has recently been given priority status by those of the medical profession who are working in the area of mental retardation. The impetus has been largely due to programs of medical and nursing care for low-income, disadvantaged families. Such programs can make major contributions to the field of mental retardation. Developed on a community basis, they provide early prenatal care, with strong emphasis upon maternal health in order to reduce the incidence of birth defects, prematurity, and intra-uterine difficulties. Follow-up studies of the mother can help to prevent—or at least offer early therapeutic intervention for—conditions that, if left uncorrected, might lead to a defective child. The presence of staining or periodic bleeding in a pregnant woman, exposure to viral diseases, signs of edema, toxemia, or anemia, are conditions often amenable to early therapeutic intervention. Recently, the development of the rubella vaccine has been of major help. It is also possible that prematurity and other possible causes of mental retardation may be prevented by comprehensive health programs.

Any program for total therapeutic planning for a family involves an extensive and extremely detailed approach. A major factor in such an approach is a complete case history of the family and its antecedents. Although such a family history is primarily intended to help a retarded child already handicapped, it can nevertheless contribute to prevention in many ways. The presence of tendencies toward miscarriages, spontaneous abortions or prematurity, history of endocrine disorders, blood incompatibilities, excessive smoking, drug and alcohol ingestion, or disease entities associated with mental retardation may alert the physician to make appropriate referral for further study and prompt prophylactic measures. Where there is a history of retardation or diseases related to retardation, referral for genetic analysis and counseling may be indicated. Currently, the most frequent use of genetic analysis has probably been for families with a retarded child in the primary family unit, and genetic counseling has largely been restricted to such family units where there is at least the suspicion of one member with a genetic abnormality. Geneticists have conjectured, however, that the techniques of genetic analysis may someday be as commonplace as blood tests for venereal disease and blood incompatibilities.

Increased awareness of the deleterious effects of some medications, excessive exposure to X-rays, and malnutrition during pregnancy have also contributed to prevention and helped to reduce the incidence of abnormal pregnancies and abnormal offspring. Improved practices in the fields of gynecology, anaesthesiology, and obstetrics have lessened the number of children who formerly might well have been defective at birth, while advances in medical technology have created a more benign environment for the distressed newborn, helping to reduce the incidence of abnormal development still further. In the area of pediatrics, the early detection of neurological deficits, endocrine disturbances, and metabolic disorders has permitted the pediatrician to institute appropriate treatment more quickly, before the disease process produces irreversible intellectual damage. Dietary intervention in cases such as phenylketonuria and galactosemia, seizure control medication, and prescription of supplementary glandular substances where indicated may at least aid in controlling the development of associated intellectual deficiencies. Other physical conditions present at birth may alert the pediatrician to the high risk of retardation, thus requiring close follow-up in the postnatal period. Prematurity, prolonged and difficult labor, anoxia, and jaundice are among the alerting signals that may demand frequent and extensive examination and observation. In the immediate as well as later postnatal period, conditions such as hydrocephalus may result in brain damage and mental retardation. Current techniques for appropriate medical intervention may arrest the process and reduce the possibility of permanent damage.

Although prevention remains the ideal toward which we strive, the most comprehensive program for prenatal, perinatal, and postnatal medical care, including use of all presently known preventive and remedial practices, would still leave a substantial number of retarded children to be helped. For the largest number of such children at present, the causes still remain obscure: "etiology unknown." Further, public health authorities have pointed to an apparent paradox to which the improvement in medical practice and technology and the dramatic advances in chemotherapy have led. On the one hand, improved medical diagnosis and intervention have prevented the development of mental retardation in a sizable number of children. However, the remarkable advances in life-support systems have dramatically decreased the number of damaged children who might otherwise have died at birth or in the early period of life. These children now often survive, multihandicapped and severely retarded.

In spite of the advances made in the all important area of prevention, it is apparent that mental retardation remains a major social problem. Extensive help is needed for a large number of retarded children and their families. When all appropriate medical procedures have been completed, and the impression or even the suspicion of mental retardation remains, the child and the parents should be referred as soon as possible for an intensive program of evaluation and assistance. It is the thesis of this book that the earliest possible identification is essential for the well-being of the child, the family, and the community.

PERIODS OF IDENTIFICATION

Practically speaking, the concept of early identification means *"earliest possible* identification." Mental retardation may be identified at birth, during the first years of life, at school age, or at adolescence. The actual period in which the identification is made is influenced by a large number of factors, including etiology, available diagnostic facilities, the level of retardation involved, the sophistication of the professional personnel whose help is sought, the cultural and economic background of the parents, the child's birth order, and the psychodynamics of the family unit. All too often, the formal identification of retardation is the culmination of a lengthy period of painful vacillations of parental suspicion, doubt, and hope about the status of their child. It is during this time of uncertainty that a most destructive sequence of events for both the parents and the child may well take place. The parents may suspect the presence of the disability, but perhaps through fear, denial, timidity, shame, or misunderstanding avoid seeking a confirmation that they simultaneously dread yet want. It is during this period that the most debilitating events often occur in the interaction of the mother and child.

Knowledge and certainty are preferable to anxiety and doubt. The former at least provide a realistic basis for constructive planning, while the latter merely lead to confusion and delay. However, merely giving the parents a diagnostic label without counseling or a training program for the child can hardly be regarded as a real service. Identification is only an initial step in dealing with the many problems that both the child and the parents must inevitably face.

Early identification. Identification at birth or shortly thereafter may be made by the obstetrician who delivers the child, the pediatrician during the postdelivery examination, or perhaps the charge nurse in the nursery unit. As stated previously, children in whom retardation can be identified at this point are most frequently those who have apparent physical anomalies—among the more obvious cases of this is mongolism or Down's Syndrome, which is present in about 1 of every 500 children. Macrocephaly is also easily identifiable in some instances, although it is not necessarily indicative of mental retardation. Physicians may, even in the absence of physical anomalies in the child, have grave suspicion at the time of birth that mental retardation is a possibility. Prematurity, anoxia, low Apgar ratings, asphyxia, and various types of birth difficulties may all contribute to a reasonable suspicion of future difficulties.

The presence of such factors raises very crucial questions for the physician, such as, "Do I tell the parents?" "When do I tell them?" "Do I tell the mother or the father?" and "How much do I tell them?" The answers to these questions and many others must be individualized for the particular parents, the disability of the child, and the nature of the relationships involved, including the relationship of the physician to the parents. The communication of such basic or primary information cannot but result in questions on the part of the parents, which the physician may not be equipped to answer adequately. Nevertheless, experience suggests that, when reasonable certainty of the condition exists at birth, it is advisable for the parents to be informed of the situation by the physician who best knows the family. He is in a good position to consider the nature of the family carefully and to answer such questions as which of the parents should be told first, or whether it would be wiser if both were informed at the same time.

It is quite likely that the informing physician's approach to the problem will be essentially subjective. He may, for example, offer the parents the advice he believes he would follow if the child were his own. According to many parents, the physicians who informed them of the child's condition have been both highly emotional and often quite authoritative. In fact, some parents report that the physician's advice has been given almost as a command. The parents may be told, "The child should be institutionalized at once." Sometimes the mother is advised not even to see the child, and to "forget about him; pretend he never existed; out of sight, out of mind." However, experience with numerous parents of immediately institutionalized children indicates that "out of sight" is not always "out of mind." The following case history from the records of a center servicing retarded children and their families is illustrative:

> Mrs. A. came to the initial appointment with the social worker without her husband, explaining that he "would be very angry at me if he knew I was here." Three weeks earlier, she had called for an appointment to talk about Mary, her eleven-month-old mongoloid daughter, who had been placed in an upstate nursing home. Mrs. A. stated that she had been married three years before, when she was 38 years old and her husband was 45. It was her first marriage and his second. Prior to the marriage she had been a bank teller, and her husband was a sales manager at a large textile company.
>
> Mary had been a great disappointment to her husband, who had looked forward to having a family. He had had no children by his first wife, who died in an automobile accident. He had been told that Mary was a mongoloid on the day of her birth, and he had told his wife on the following day. She reported that she was shocked on hearing this, since

she had already seen Mary and had noticed nothing wrong with her. However, her obstetrician, who was a friend of her husband's family, visited her that day and explained Mary's condition to her, adding that the child "would never be cured," and "would be a burden to her parents for the rest of their lives."

The obstetrician strongly recommended that Mary be institutionalized immediately, since the parents might otherwise become attached to her if they took her home and would find the inevitable separation much harder later on. Mr. A. was strongly in favor of following the advice, and with his wife's passive permission he arranged for Mary to be placed in a nursing home. Mrs. A. said at first that she had not seen Mary since the day she left the hospital. Nevertheless, she talked fondly about the child and seemed to be very aware of her progress. When asked about this, she admitted that she had gone to see her daughter several times, without her husband's knowledge. She had also established a relationship with the attendant who cared for Mary and corresponded with her regularly. She began to cry when she produced a photograph of Mary that had been taken by the attendant and sent to her.

When Mrs. A. regained her composure, she said she had really come to the center because she wanted to get her daughter back, and wondered if there was some way in which she could be helped to regain the child. Mary was apparently scheduled to be transferred to a state institution within a few months, and Mrs. A believed that once this was done Mary would be lost to her forever. The mother responded with evident anxiety and distress to the social worker's suggestion that her husband would have to be involved in the decision. She told of several unsuccessful attempts to speak to her husband about Mary in the past and said that she was certain he would not even agree to a joint interview. However, she did promise to approach him that evening, and a tentative appointment was made for the following week with both Mr. and Mrs. A. and the social worker.

Mrs. A. called the next morning to report that her husband had agreed to the interview. She asked the social worker, however, that her visits to Mary be kept confidential. The worker agreed but did suggest that Mrs. A. should talk to her husband openly about her feelings at the interview. When the parents arrived together Mr. A. was obviously resentful, and made it quite clear that he had come to satisfy his wife and saw no point in discussing what he regarded as a closed issue. The social worker remained silent as Mrs. A. began to speak. For the first time since the birth of Mary, Mrs. A. began to talk to her husband about some of her real feelings. Mr. A.'s initial attempts at aloofness were quickly replaced by a genuine concern for his wife. He began to express feelings of tenderness toward her, although he retained his total rejection of their retarded daughter.

The first session with both parents ended with their mutual agreement that the problem of Mary could no longer be ignored, and that more thinking and talking about it were essential. For the following ten weeks, Mr. and Mrs. A. met with the social worker once a week for two hours. At these sessions the parents discussed the period since Mary's conception in some detail. Their hopes for a family, their disappointment in their defective baby, the feelings of urgency and failure, and their attempts to repress their feelings and forget the child were brought up and considered. The critical point came in the eighth session, when Mr. A. agreed to accompany his wife to visit Mary at the nursing home.

Mr. and Mrs. A. went to see Mary together and met with the worker next day to discuss their reactions. At this session Mrs. A. was initially silent and Mr. A. started the discussion by saying that he was surprised to find that he had felt quite warm toward Mary and had not experienced the anger and resentment he had expected. He had not seen her as the monster he had somehow pictured in his mind. He struggled unsuccessfully to find words to express his feelings and then, turning to his wife, said he was glad he had gone to see his child because it had lifted a great weight from his shoulders.

Mrs. A. remained silent until the end of the session, when she began to speak softly about her own feelings. She said that when Mary had been so precipitously taken from her, she had had no chance to realize what her feelings really were. She was grateful to her husband for the feelings he had just experienced, which made her believe, for the first time since Mary was born, that he really loved her and was not rejecting her for having borne him a defective child. Then she spoke of doubts about her own ability to raise Mary and anxieties about her adequacy as a parent. She also spoke openly about feelings of shame about the child. Despite these doubts, she said she was certain she would not be able to live with herself if she did not try to be a real mother to Mary.

At this point, Mrs. A. asked her husband to bring Mary home. There was a long pause as Mr. A. looked at his wife in silence, anguishing over the decision. Finally, he said simply, "Yes." Mary came home four weeks later. She and her parents are now actively involved in a home training program for retarded infants and their families. Mr. A. participates occasionally in training sessions with the child and in joint sessions with his wife and the social worker. They are both greatly relieved at having arrived at a reasoned, thoughtful, mutual plan about Mary, instead of their hasty and precipitous initial decision.

The question of institutional placement is a highly individual matter, neither "right" nor "wrong" in itself. It should be decided on as realistic a basis as possible. However, it can hardly be hoped to avoid considerable emotional repercussions. Feelings of guilt and recrimination may last for long periods after a child has been placed in an institution, especially when the placement is made shortly after the child's birth and there has been little or no time for careful consideration. These feelings may increase when the parents see the progress of other retarded children who have been kept in the community. As Slobody and Scanlan (255) have pointed out, while early placement of a retarded child in an institution may appear to be the most suitable method of dealing with the problem, it will sometimes have unforeseen and disastrous consequences for the child and the family. In those cases where special family circumstances do indicate the need for immediate placement, the collaborative support of a professional team which includes an appropriate level of psychotherapy for the parents can aid immeasurably in placing the separation on as realistic a basis as possible. This may well minimize possible aftereffects of guilt, rejection, and despair.

Sometimes the physician is tempted to put off the ordeal of informing the parents, "explaining" the delay on the grounds that he is not entirely certain of the diagnosis or that the child may outgrow his evident handicaps. Many parents have described this painful period of uncertainty, during which they grew more and more suspicious and concerned about the status of their child and suffered increasing anxiety and confusion. Often this situation results in extreme resentment on the part of the parents, who had hitherto looked confidently to their physician for guidance and assistance. Further, the uncertainty often prevents parents from seeking the aid that might help them to think more constructively about the problem and become more realistic in their own attitudes toward it.

The physician who is well informed about available community resources and the kinds of specialized services they offer is in a better position to inform the parents with reasonable confidence than is the physician who depends almost entirely on his own medical knowledge of the problems involved. In addition to the lack of such necessary factual knowledge, however, there may be a number of other inhibiting circumstances. The difficulties of informing the parents even when the diagnosis is reasonably clear-cut may, for example, be exacerbated by inadequacy of communication between the parent and physician. The parents' tendency to utilize denial will contribute to making communication difficult. Even parents who have apparently been accurately informed of the child's status sometimes complain later that they "really did not know." Anxious parents are often poor listeners and are very likely to misinterpret what is told to them. They may be resorting to denial as a mechanism to defend themselves against overwhelming anguish. They may misunderstand the terms used by the physician. They may believe that he implied the child's condition was temporary or perhaps amenable to medical cure. On the other hand, they may also believe that his words meant that all realistic hope is impossible.

There are other sources of potential interference with the communication process between the parents and the physician that can totally distort the message the parents receive, leaving them bewildered and impaired in their ability to think constructively. Even where the diagnosis is correctly received, subsequent questions that the parents ask may remain unanswered: "Will he ever be normal?" "Will he go to school?" "Will he be dangerous?" "How will he affect our other children?" Even though such questions can often not be answered definitively, parents need to discuss them with someone who has some relevant information and experience. Providing the parents with a diagnostic label or a diagnostic impression, then, should not be regarded as more than a first step in what should become a more extensive counseling process.

Parents who are told of the child's diagnosis at birth are likely to show different reactions from parents whose retarded child is identified at a later stage of development. Although the former initially may experience a state of shock and anxiety, they will frequently be quicker to seek practical assistance, feeling frustrated and disappointed in the absence of concrete help. Lack of support during this period may also contribute heavily to the parental discord so often observed when the child is older. While some parents draw closer to one another in the face of their common tragedy, mutual accusations are all too frequent and often intensify in time. Defenses have not yet become rigid at the beginning, however, and the parents are usually still open for therapeutic intervention. They have not yet acquired a body of myth, misinformation, and misunderstanding, nor have they been subjected as yet to the uninformed and often contradictory advice so freely given by friends and relatives. Some of the more favorable outcomes with parents have, understandably enough, been obtained when they received counseling before the child was six months old.

Later identification. First to be identified, then, are those children with obvious physical anomalies, the profoundly retarded, and/or those whose circumstances of birth or early infancy are sufficiently alarming to alert the physician to the need for detailed study and observation. Other children, however, who lack gross anomalies and whose birth histories are unexceptional, may nevertheless exhibit signs of slow development in the basic gross motor activities, such as rolling over, supporting the head, or sitting with support. Still others may lack alertness or awareness of their environment, failing to respond to their parents as most babies do, or exhibiting lethargy in sucking and feeding behavior. Reports from parents that the child is "too good" or "too quiet" or, conversely, "too excited" or "too active" may also be clues which, taken together with other factors, may indicate potential difficulties. Understandably enough, the physician confronted with his own or parental suspicions based largely on equivocal facts is often unwilling to alarm parents needlessly, preferring to adopt a "wait and see" attitude. This decision is often bolstered by the belief that there is nothing to be done now anyway, so there would be no point in upsetting the parents at this time. In the experience of many parents and professional workers, however, such temporizing is frequently more harmful than beneficial. The parents all too often harbor silent suspicions that they are unwilling to verbalize but which nevertheless undermine their relationships with their child, with the physician, and with each other.

Failure of the physician to state his suspicions may well lead to a pact of silence that may hinder appeal to more definitive diagnostic procedures and seriously delay available treatment for both the infant and the parents. For example, the infant may receive excellent general physical and medical care, but failure to explore openly his delayed development might deprive him of participation in a program of early perceptual care and stimulation. Parents of children who have been identified as retarded several years after birth often report a frustrating and anxiety-provoking series of encounters in which they were told, "It is just a stage he is in," "He'll grow out of it," or "It's too soon to tell." Such answers to parental doubts are, of course, appropriate in many cases. However, when they are applied indiscriminately, they may result in the neglect of the special needs of the child for several years, with accompanying deterioration of relationships in the family. The kinds of risks inherent in delaying identification and treatment are well illustrated by the case of Mark, which is summarized below.

> Mr. and Mrs. S. were married for seven years before their first child was born. The delay was due in part to Mr. S.'s wish to complete his education before incurring major responsibilities. While employed as a part-time insurance salesman, he completed college and then law school. Mrs. S. worked as a legal secretary until the birth of her son, Mark. She was quite anxious and apprehensive about pregnancy and more than willing to delay it, since her older brother was mongoloid and she was afraid that she might have a mongoloid child. When Mark was born, Mrs. S. was 29 and Mr. S. was 30. He had passed the bar examination and was working as a partner in a well-established law firm. Mrs. S. had stopped working in her third month of pregnancy, and the parents had moved to a larger apartment near the home of Mr. S.'s mother, with whom Mrs. S. had established an affectionate but dependent relationship.
>
> The pregnancy was full term and essentially normal, although Mrs. S. reported intermittent staining in the third month of the pregnancy and nausea throughout. A forceps delivery was necessary, but the baby's Apgar rating and pediatric examination indicated a normal newborn. Several months had passed uneventfully, and Mrs. S. was enormously relieved as she began to believe that her fears of having a defective child were unfounded. However, she did experience considerable difficulty in caring for Mark. He was her first child, and she had little previous experience with such responsibilities. She was comforted by the physical and moral support

of her mother-in-law, who actively participated in raising the child.

The mother's first serious doubts about Mark's development occurred when he was 4 months old. While she was feeding him he seemed to stiffen and momentarily roll his eyes back. She mentioned this to her mother-in-law, who dismissed it as merely reflecting irrational anxiety, a conclusion which the pediatrician reinforced. Shortly afterwards, Mrs. S. developed a pneumonia which required a brief stay in the hospital, and Mark was cared for by her mother-in-law. When Mrs. S. returned home she resumed the major care of Mark, but resented the attachment he had formed to her mother-in-law in her absence and began to care for him by herself. By the time Mark was 14 months old, she had become increasingly alarmed about him. Though largely unaware of normal development milestones, she felt that "he did not crawl enough," and was concerned that he made no attempts to stand. She was, however, fearful of consulting the pediatrician about this, still hoping that she was merely an overanxious mother.

Nevertheless, Mrs. S.'s anxiety about Mark increased daily. She finally reached a point of irrational distress and began to believe that she was somehow responsible for Mark's difficulties. She insisted that he often failed to respond when she called him, though he did seem to respond to his father. She also felt that Mark was more irritable with her and often cried when she picked him up. At length she was in such a state of inner turmoil that she began to find that staying at home alone with Mark was intolerable. When Mark was 17 months old she returned to work on a part-time basis, leaving Mark in the care of baby sitters. She attempted to justify this decision on the grounds that, since Mark reacted better with other people, she was "doing the right thing for both of them" by returning to work.

When the parents finally came for help, Mr. S. confessed that he had thought his wife had been exaggerating Mark's problems until, as a result of her return to work, he spent more time with the child himself. At this point he, too, became concerned. As Mr. S. put it, the child "just didn't seem right." At the age of 23 months he was still crawling and made no attempt to stand or walk. He had also become increasingly irritable and had developed very erratic patterns of sleep, often dozing for short periods during the day and staying awake until very late at night. Baby sitters were beginning to find him difficult to manage, and one after another declined to stay with him. Mrs. S. now regarded herself as a totally inadequate mother.

In despair, Mrs. S. invited her mother-in-law to live with the family and assume full responsibility for caring for Mark, a task which she no longer felt competent to handle. For the next 4 months, Mrs. S. limited her own contact with Mark largely to the weekends, having returned to work on a full-time basis. She was deeply disturbed because Mark seemed increasingly lethargic and failed to respond to her almost entirely. She interpreted this as total rejection. Contact between Mrs. S. and Mark became minimal. His behavior and his slow development seemed to her proof of her own inadequacy, and she could hardly bear to be with him. Meanwhile, her mother-in-law justified Mark's slow development on the grounds that his father had been "a slow walker" and did not talk until he was almost 3 years old. She also cited her personal physician, whose son did not begin to walk until even later.

When Mark was 28 months old he began to stand independently, and took some tentative first steps. He also began to use word partials, although he did so inconsistently and erratically. However, he continued to be an irritable child and difficult to manage. He often cried for no apparent reason and showed general diminished interest in his surroundings. He did not seem to notice his mother when she came home from work, and she reacted by staying away and working overtime several nights a week. The subject of Mark's behavior was discussed decreasingly by the parents as time went on. In fact, conversations between Mr. and Mrs. S. became increasingly rare and quite artificial.

When the boy was approaching his third birthday Mr. S. had clearly recognized that Mark had real difficulties. He tended, however, to attribute them entirely to his wife's neglect. He therefore urgently suggested that she leave her job and devote herself to her son. His insistence threw Mrs. S. into panic. She could not, as she put it, "live with her own failure." As the choice between working or caring for Mark became more imminent, her anxiety increased and she became overtly depressed. This was apparent to her employer, with whom she had established a warm and understanding relationship. One especially tearful afternoon, she confessed her fears about Mark to him, along with her own feelings of personal failure. Her employer had previously worked with an association for parents of retarded children, and he suggested to Mrs. S. that she contact them for advice. Mrs. S. was shocked and angrily rejected the idea that Mark might be retarded. However, she did agree that he should be examined by a specialist. She discussed this with her husband, who made an appointment with a neurologist whom their pediatrician recommended.

Mark was seen by the neurologist when he was 36 months old and this examination brought the child to a specialized center some two months later. The neurologist's diagnosis was one of petit mal seizures with delayed development. At the center Mark was described as mildly retarded, with indications of cerebral dysrhythmia, the latter being confirmed by detailed neurological and EEG findings. Mark's greatest limitations were found to lie in the areas of speech and gross motor behavior. The diagnostic findings were communicated to Mr. and Mrs. S., and a program of medication, training, and stimulation for Mark combined with counseling for the parents was quickly initiated.

The real extent of the tragedy inherent in the situation of Mark and his family came to light during the counseling sessions with the parents. Mrs. S. cried almost continuously during the initial sessions. She was initially relieved to find that her inadequacy as a mother was not the basic cause of Mark's slow development; however, this was considerably offset by her guilt about not having insisted on treatment earlier. A reasonably good outcome was eventually achieved in this case, with both Mark and his parents. Mark responded well to medication, became much less irritable, and began to learn from stimulation and training. Mrs. S. stayed home to care for him for a while, finding his increasing responsiveness to her more and more rewarding. However, she also wanted to return to work on a part-time basis, to which Mr. S. no longer objected. A warm, reliable baby sitter was found, who quickly established a good relationship with Mark and his parents. Although there will be many future problems for this family, and many difficult decisions to make, they are getting off to a good though belated start. However, the parents went through much emotional distress which earlier identification and treatment for Mark might have avoided, and the possibility remains that Mark may have suffered additional damage as a result of the delay.

In the absence of significant and fairly obvious medical findings the period of suspicion and suspense may be prolonged for a number of years. This is frequently needlessly time-wasting, especially where multidisciplinary diagnostic evaluation centers to which the child might be referred are available. In communities where these centers are lacking, different patterns of referral, diagnosis, and treatment may be anticipated. Under such circumstances, middle-income families usually confer with their pediatrician about the child's delayed development. When and if he becomes at least fairly certain of retardation, he may refer the parents to other medical specialists, such as a psychiatrist or a neurologist in private practice or associated with a clinic. It is often this medical specialist who informs the parents of the child's status. Unfortunately, many of these specialists, though highly trained in their own fields, are not sufficiently familiar with the various types of services available in the field of retardation. As a result, parents may be given a diagnosis of the child's condition but no information about a possible treatment facility. Low-income parents, on the other hand, are more likely to seek help at a Child Health Center or similar agency. In terms of informing parents of the child's handicaps such agencies are sometimes more immediate and may also be more familiar with available services for the retarded provided by voluntary or public agencies.

The degree of the child's retardation is also a major factor in determining when the presence of the mental handicap is likely to be found. The identification and diagnosis of the mildly retarded child is often delayed until he reaches school age, and the requirements of academic performance and increasing behavioral control point up the child's special deficiencies. This frequently entails a series of frustrating rejections from inappropriate class placements, before the realistic educational needs of the child are recognized. Many years that might have been spent in a suitable training program can be wasted in this way, to the detriment of both child and family. The time lag between suspicion, identification, and treatment is currently a serious problem. If needless tragedy is to be avoided, identification should be sufficiently prompt to prevent or at least greatly shorten the painful period of suspicion and doubt. However, identification must be only an initial step in planning programs of help for the whole family.

FAMILY PERSPECTIVE

Mental retardation is a problem for the diagnostician, the school, and the community. The most personal and salient consideration in many cases, however, is for the child's parents. Parental reactions to the birth of a retarded child may range from deep depression through passive resignation to the kind of active, realistic acceptance that is, understandably enough, relatively rare. In attempting to understand the reactions of particular parents, detailed and intensive consideration must be given to the whole family constellation, the socioeconomic and cultural background, the values, interests, and ambitions of the family, the status and number of previous children, the age of the parents, whether the retarded child was wanted and additional children are hoped for, and many other factors. Such considerations are all part of the background against which the period of pregnancy and its culmination in the birth of a retarded child must be evaluated.

Some relevant questions related to the prenatal period involve a history of possible abortions or miscarriages and the attitudes of the mother during the pregnancy: whether the pregnancy was welcome, passively endured, or actively resented. These and other questions concerning prenatal care, illness, and nutrition will all affect the attitude of the parents as they await the birth of the child. The actual delivery is a serious medical event that affects the entire family. There are life and death implications for mother and child, and while families generally approach the delivery with feelings of relief and optimism, these are often mixed with anxiety and even dread. Procedures that the mother does not understand during labor and delivery may be viewed with suspicion and later used as an "explanation" for a condition the child may have. Mothers whose minds are still clouded by medication and anaesthesia have grossly misreported statements by doctors in the delivery room or nurses in the early days of the child's life. Fear that something is wrong with the child may assail the mother unless she can see him immediately. The mother, and to some extent the father and family as well, are often in a highly tense and vulnerable state at this crucial point in the newborn infant's life.

INITIAL REACTIONS

Periods of shock, bewilderment, and disbelief are common immediate reactions to the recognition of having a retarded child. This may be followed by a time of parental vacillation between unrealistic despair and equally unrealistic hope. Some parents race from one expert to another, searching for an authority who will deny the bitter fact of retardation in their child. Other parents will hunt frantically for someone to provide them with a magical cure. Among such sources of false hopes are various mechanical devices, untested surgical procedures, and a variety of injections, all of which imply that the problem can be cured.

The parents' ego strengths and weaknesses play an important role in this phase of the long-range adjustive process. Those parents who tend to be self-depreciating, anxious, and guilty in other aspects of living usually find the birth of a retarded child a severe blow to their self-esteem. In fact, greatly increased feelings of worthlessness may reach the point of suicidal fantasies. The retarded child may be perceived as a living demonstration of the parents' inferiority, and given such intense and intolerable feelings, parents may desperately try to ferret out an explanation for the tragedy that will absolve them from guilt. Sometimes a past illness or accident is blamed, becoming a source of anger and preoccupation in spite of all evidence to the contrary. Sometimes the blame is projected onto someone who handled the infant and might have damaged him.

A more serious possibility from the point of view of family cohesiveness is the tendency of parents to blame each other. This leads to endless recriminations, accusations, and counteraccusations. At best, most marriages include some oversensitized areas and psychic sore spots, and the birth of a retarded child all too often becomes the focus for preexisting mutual antagonisms. Anger between the parents tends to feed upon itself, and within a relatively short period of time a highly complicated framework of suspicion, fear, and hostility can achieve mammoth proportions. The case of Mr. and Mrs. W. outlined below illustrates this kind of parental reaction.

> Bruce, Mr. and Mrs. W.'s retarded child, was the younger of two children. Both parents were teachers, but Mrs. W. had not worked since the birth of Anne, her first child, who was three and a half years older than Bruce. Mr. W. had suffered considerable distress and depression about Bruce's condition, feeling that he might be responsible for it since he was an adopted child and knew nothing about his original family's background. Mrs. W. denied any serious illnesses in her own family and was angry and resentful that "this awful thing should happen to me." She also remarked, quite bitterly, "My brother's children are fine, and we both came from the same parents."

By the time Bruce was two years old, Mrs. W. had begun to refer to the children as "my daughter" and "his son." This was actually encouraged by Mrs. W.'s parents, who had opposed her marriage to someone "without a real family." When Anne entered first grade, Mrs. W. decided to return to work, despite her husband's objections that it was not fair to Bruce to leave him in the care of a housekeeper. Mrs. W. obtained an excellent but demanding position, which she could not keep because she could not find a permanent housekeeper who could manage Bruce. At the age of two and a half he was an extremely hyperactive, irritable, and "difficult" child.

The initial diagnosis of microcephaly had been later confirmed by a neurological consultant, who prescribed medication for Bruce which, however, had little effect. Nevertheless, it was Mr. W.'s contention that Bruce's behavioral problems were the result of being "deserted" by his mother and had no connection with his organic deficits. Mr. and Mrs. W.'s relationship deteriorated to the point of almost constant bickering about Bruce. Despite their sophistication, they did not understand the developmental and behavioral nature of Bruce's disability, perhaps because of their own neurotic investments. Mr. W. alternated between self-doubt and anger at his wife for blaming him for Bruce's condition. Mrs. W., angry at being burdened with an atypical child, became more and more accusing and resentful of her husband. By the time the parents turned to an agency for help, it was as much to save their marriage as to find help for Bruce.

A MULTIDISCIPLINARY CENTER

A special diagnostic and treatment center for the retarded child and his family has many advantages. The health and welfare of the child are only one aspect of a total program of help. The education and counseling of the parents can help them achieve more realistic goals and a better understanding of the many problems that confront them and thus serve as a potent force in the future growth and development of the child. Even the simplest aspects of retardation may need clarification in order to avoid potentially harmful misunderstanding. Many parents have "shopped" in so many medical and diagnostic facilities that they are confused even at the level of simple terminology. Their own values and the particular directions that their wishful thinking takes tend to add to this confusion. For example, the simple statement, "My child is mentally retarded," may imply to some parents that he will never go to college, while to others it means that the child is not so bright as his brothers and sisters; to still others, the statement signifies that the child will never be able to learn anything that might enable him to remain in the family. Words like "educable" and "trainable" have proved to be similarly ambiguous. The term "IQ," in particular, is open to mistaken interpretations. Parents may have been told, for example, that the norm is 100 and their child has an IQ of 50. From this they will sometimes conclude that their child has half the intelligence of an average child and will continue to develop at half the average rate. One of the many needs that the multidisciplinary center can meet is to help the parents clear up the misconceptions that may well be adding to their problems.

A major need for the child that the multidisciplinary center can meet is teaching the parents how to stimulate and focus the child's learning as early as possible. Parents who are raising average children do not usually give much thought to structuring the learning process that goes on during the child's early growth. It is more or less assumed that he will draw sufficient stimuli from the environment and use, integrate, and assimilate them automatically in the growth process, without the need for external direction. The retarded child, however, is limited in his ability to learn on his own initiative, and he needs direction from the beginning. If a retarded child is not diagnosed at birth, the limited results of natural maturation generally become apparent in such signs as nonresponsiveness, nonawareness of the environment, and failure to meet simple milestones of growth at the expected ages. The anxieties of the parents as they realize that their child is not developing the way other children do and their lack of awareness of the special training techniques he needs can become highly destructive in terms of his future development.

The multidisciplinary center can do much to allay parental anxiety while training the parents to train the child. Special "how to do it" programs are often provided, individualized for each child. These programs spell out in detail many facilitating activities, not only in terms of the child's needs but also with regard to the dynamics of the family. Careful consideration is given to the home and to the economic situation and the particular social, ethnic, and religious background of the family. These considerations are undertaken with the primary therapeutic goal of appealing to the healthy core of the parents and the family, so that the family unit can be provided with a sounder basis on which to continue on its own.

CHAPTER 2

The Diagnostic
Process

The comprehensive evaluation of a child suspected of mental retardation is best undertaken through an integrated approach by a number of specialists: pediatricians, neurologists, psychiatrists, nurses, psychologists, social workers, and experts in special education and communication skills. Although these specialists attempt to evaluate the child as a complete, functioning individual, each one nevertheless employs the observation techniques, organizational skills, and analytical tools of his particular discipline. The impressions of the child and family gathered by members of different disciplines are often quite similar. The psychologist and the physician may, for example, note a mother's overprotectiveness or perhaps her more overt hostility. Nevertheless, the insights provided by a particular discipline usually make special contributions to the whole picture. It is the physician who is competent to establish a diagnosis such as hydrocephalus, while it is the psychologist who is trained to distinguish among specific perceptual disabilities.

As a result of a team approach, then, a multidisciplinary diagnostic evaluation differs markedly from a strictly medical examination. Beyond simply determining the fact of the child's retardation and attempting to identify its causes, the team seeks to gain a total picture of the child and his family. Such a diagnostic process obviously does not focus solely on the child. It also considers the whole family—the parents, brothers and sisters, grandparents, and other relatives in the child's life situation. At another level, it also considers the mores of the larger community as they affect the family's attitudes. By collaborating in obtaining an extensive evaluation of the family's strengths as well as weaknesses and the child's potentialities as well as his pathology, the diagnostic team lays the foundation for an individualized program of stimulation and training for the child and appropriate help for the family.

THE INITIAL INQUIRY

The parents' first contact with a center is usually a telephone call or a letter inquiring about available services and requesting further information. Perhaps the family was referred to the center by a hospital, or heard of it from an acquaintance or a friend. Sometimes the initial inquiry is made on behalf of the parents by a social agency, a hospital social service department, or a child health center. When the initial inquiry is made by the parents, the response should be free of any assumptions about the requests they will subsequently make of the center. In some cases, especially with infant retardates, the parents may have had no previous diagnostic evaluation of the child, while others may want the results of a previous evaluation checked with the hope of modification. Some parents may be under the misapprehension that the center is a residential agency for the child, while others may know of their child's retardation and are contacting the center for help for themselves. Except for simple factual information about the center, many questions will have to be postponed until a personal interview with a professional worker is set up. It is often clear, however, even at this early stage, that many parents who apply for diagnosis and treatment of the child are also interested in obtaining help in their own relationships, which may be strained by the multiple difficulties of coping with the child.

In response to the initial inquiry, the parents are usually sent a formal application for services. The application form asks for basic family information, such as names, ages, occupations, and educational status of the family members, and the names and addresses of physicians or agencies who have previously seen the child. The form also generally asks the reason for making the application. Representative responses to this question include answers such as, "To find out why my baby is so slow," "The doctors told me my child needs special attention," "I have a mongolian baby and I want to cure him," "I was told my baby is brain damaged and nothing can be done. I hope you can help," or "I think my son is not developing well, but my husband says he is. Could you find out who is right?" Responses range all the way from a high level of sophistication to obvious naïveté about the whole field.

The next step in the admission process is the initial interview, generally with a caseworker. This meeting is not scheduled until the application has been filled in and returned. Some applications are returned very quickly. Others may not arrive for weeks or months, and still others, about 10 percent, are never returned. Experience suggests that the speed with which an application is returned is a fairly good indication of the degree of parental motivation for service. In a follow-up study by one agency, for example, twenty parents who had not returned applications after a period of three months were contacted by the center, but only two eventually came for an interview. The remainder had either placed the child elsewhere, refused services because of transportation difficulties or family problems, or decided the child did not need the kind of service the agency provided. Five felt that their child was really normal, and of these, four reapplied several years later for enrollment in the school program.

In reflecting upon her failure to apply for service previously, one mother mentioned her sorrow and extreme sensitivity in even discussing her child's handicaps, a problem that the passing years had lessened. Another stated that her husband had insisted that their child was perfectly normal, and that she was "looking for trouble." A third mother explained her motivation for delay at a later counseling session, when she revealed her intense guilt and her belief that she had caused her son's retardation by an early attempt at a self-induced abortion. She had told no one about this, and the possibility of exposure had frightened her so much at the time of her first inquiry to the center that she had temporarily dropped the matter. Even the later application had been made only at the insistence of her husband, who could not understand her reluctance to seek training for their child, now four years old. In subsequent counseling sessions, this mother was able to speak openly, discuss her feelings, and gain some relief from the acute sense of guilt she had secretly harbored since the birth of the child.

Growing experience with parents highlights the need for sensitivity in the case of even the most routine procedures of a diagnostic and treatment center. Even a telephone inquiry or the completion of an initial application for services can often be major steps in the recognition of the problem and in the search for a solution.

THE DIAGNOSTIC TEAM

The following discussion of the potential contributions of each discipline to a comprehensive diagnostic picture of the child and family represents more of an ideal than a practical set of requirements for many agencies servicing infant retardates. Many will have to do with less, and hopefully there will be some that can offer even more. However, a diagnostic team such as the one described here is necessary for an initial work-up that offers a solid basis for initiating a meaningful program of comprehensive help. The procedures that are mentioned below represent but one pattern for a well-functioning and effective multidisciplinary center.

The social worker. Each inquiry about the program at the center is referred to an intake social worker who conducts the first meeting with the parents at the center. Although both parents are asked to attend the first interview, the mother frequently comes alone. The social worker obtains a medical and social history of the child, siblings, parents, and other relatives. In order to establish a constructive relationship during the interview, the worker takes his cues from the parent's comments and avoids forcing a line of questioning that may seem threatening. Failure to respond to the parent's feelings or to probe for information the parent is not yet ready to offer may result in data with little dynamic significance, and, even more importantly, may undercut the parent's trust and willingness to cooperate.

A good treatment relationship established at the first interview requires that the parent be an active participant in a process of discovery about the child and family. Too often, these parents have been treated essentially as psychiatric patients, which tends to increase anxiety and guilt and to lessen the potential benefits of a mutual partnership of honest exploration between parent and professional worker. At this early stage, the social worker must remember that most parents' factual information about mental retardation is quite limited. They may make many inaccurate statements, often reflecting popular mythology or incorrect interpretations of previous professional consultations. The social worker can help to reassure the parents and to aid them in understanding the significance of retardation by at least clarifying definitions and concepts to some extent. It is therefore essential that the social worker conducting the interview has had considerable special training and experience in the area, so that the information given the parents is both accurate and honest.

The social worker may also be able to help allay some of the parents' uncertainty by describing the services that are available at the center and explaining their goals. The social worker may, in fact, show the parents the facilities in operation, if possible. If they can see the school their child will attend and the children engaged in activity, parents will begin to imagine what their child's activities might be. This must be done with consideration for the level of retardation of their particular child. The parents of a profoundly retarded child, for example, might be unrealistically misled by observing the activities of a class of moderately retarded children, perhaps concluding that their child will function in a similar manner as the result of participating in the training program. It is the social worker's responsibility to avoid engendering false hopes as much as to lighten unwarranted despair.

Perceptive answers by the social worker to the parents' questions can do much to add a new dimension to the family's understanding and to encourage their emotional readiness to participate in the program. Practical as well as theoretical information may be helpful in meeting these important parental needs. A parent may ask, for example, about the toys and training equipment in the office, providing the social worker with an opportunity to explain how certain activities may improve a child's coordination and contribute to a better adjustment at home. It should also be remembered that at the time of this first contact, the emotional adaptation of the parents tends to be quite unstable. Many parents who have only recently discovered or suspected that their baby is retarded are overtly depressed and anxious. During the first interview, however, they are likely to talk exclusively about the problems of the child, avoiding any discussion of their own feelings. Some parents may make obviously contradictory statements. For example, a parent may tell the social worker that the child's early development was normal, while mentioning several developmental milestones that represent quite delayed achievement. It is usually unwise to respond to such inaccuracies or self-deceptions at this point, since little would be gained by premature attempts at confrontation or correction. Frequently, these deceptions help to protect the parent against too direct intrusions of reality which might well overwhelm them at the time. Such protective devices, then, should be carefully respected during this initial phase.

Some parents are aware of their need for counseling or guidance at the time of the first interview and may express it by direct or at least fairly transparent requests for help. Sometimes it is clear to the social worker that the parents are actually more interested in help for themselves than for the child, even though their conversation may center around him. Other parents will ask openly for help for themselves, while simultaneously indicating that they are actually strongly resistant to therapeutic intervention. The perceptive and experienced social worker will listen carefully to everything the parents relate or imply, learning as much as he can from them without disturbing their equilibrium or threatening his relationship with them.

When parents do touch on their own feelings during the initial interview, the most frequent subject to be brought up is the guilt they experience. This is a highly sensitive area and one that has all too frequently been handled by extensive recourse to displacement and projection. For example, a parent may focus on some source of real or imagined neglect of the child, a belief in a faulty genetic background, an attempted abortion, or a number of adverse parental conditions, in an attempt to avoid his own guilt feelings about the child's condition. Denial of the parents' underlying resentment is also common. The case of Mr. and Mrs. B. illustrates these characteristics:

> Mr. and Mrs. B. were referred to the center when their retarded son Jay was two years old. They had two older children who were developing normally. Mr. B., who attended college for one year, was a self-employed electrician. Mrs. B., a high school graduate, was a secretary before her marriage. When her two older children began school, Mrs. B. enrolled in several courses to complete college entrance requirements. When she was first interviewed at the center, she had finished the equivalent of three years of college through day and evening classes. However, since the birth of Jay, the retarded child, she had been unable to finish the courses necessary for a degree.
>
> Mrs. B. expressed a great deal of conflict and guilt about Jay. She had not planned this last pregnancy. She had not, in fact, wanted another child, and had taken some unsuccessful steps to induce abortion. She was deeply concerned that she was responsible for Jay's retardation but had no idea that she was bitterly resentful of the child because she felt that he had upset her own educational plans. She presented herself as a self-sacrificing, devoted mother, inclined to be overprotective, perhaps, but totally committed to "doing all the right things" for her son. At this point, her underlying anger was carefully concealed, and its presence was betrayed only by covert means and very indirect expressions.

Even in the first interview with the parents, the social worker can begin to estimate how well they will adapt to and assist in the various aspects of the child's projected training program. There is great variation in this area. In spite of strong feelings of their own inadequacy and failure in caring for the child, some parents may be unwilling to leave his care to others, or reject child-rearing advice that conflicts with practices in which they believe. On the other hand, where there are acute feelings of failure, it may sometimes be necessary to limit parental participation in the early phase of the child's training. The case of Mrs. P. illustrates some of the initial problems that may arise in parental participation:

> Mrs. P. was self-referred, and her presenting request was for help in training her brain-injured daughter. The mother, now 21 years old and born in Boston, at the age of two had been placed for adoption following her parents' divorce. Mrs. P. said she felt lucky that she had been placed with a family that was so wonderful to her, and had loved her and raised her with strong feelings of closeness. Soon, however, obvious questions were raised about this reported "ideal" relationship. Following her adoptive father's death in Mrs. P.'s early teens, she had rebelled against her adoptive mother and began truanting from school and staying out late at night.
>
> Mrs. P. had given birth to an out-of-wedlock child, who was placed for adoption. She later regretted this decision, found herself brooding about the baby, and attributed her decision to relinquish the child to the pressures of her family. She then began seeking out her own natural mother, and her adoptive mother's willingness to allow this helped her to resolve at least some of the conflicts she was facing in this regard.
>
> Mrs. P. was a high school graduate, completing her education after the birth of her first child and then working as a secretary. She described her present marriage as a happy one, referring to her husband as a person with whom she "can talk things over." He knew of her out-of-wedlock child but his family did not, and she was afraid of their rejection should they ever find out. She said she was subject to many episodes of depression and also suffered from severe headaches. In discussing her brain-injured daughter, Mrs. P. stated her belief that this child's condition was "a fitting punishment" for her surrender of her first child, and for her evasiveness with her husband's family. She had also come to suspect some connection between her overprotective role toward her daughter and these sources of guilt and anxiety.
>
> Because of the evident intensity of Mrs. P.'s distress, the social worker felt that this mother would be unable to participate in the child's training program without some prior alleviation of her guilt feelings and the deeply debased self-image she so openly expressed. It was therefore recommended that the mother should not participate immediately in the child's training, but should wait until she attained greater feelings of personal worth and more realistic goals to direct her future decisions.

This is but one of many possible examples of the importance of recognizing the particular needs of individual parents in terms of emotional status, aspirations, and special areas of tension and frustration. This process is a necessary step in setting up a program that will help to identify and develop the strengths the family possesses, and draw upon them to improve the parents' relationships with each other and with the retarded child. One of the social worker's final considerations in the initial interview is to prepare the parents for the diagnostic procedure to follow, by describing the different steps that comprise the multidisciplinary evaluation and explaining how they will contribute to an individualized program of help for the child and the family.

The medical evaluation. The medical aspects of an adequate diagnostic procedure benefit greatly from the combined services of a pediatrician, a psychiatrist, an ophthalmologist, a dentist, and a nurse. Other specialists may be called on for consultation as indicated, and laboratory procedures requested when necessary. The medical evaluation thus becomes a collaborative effort to arrive at a total picture of the child's health and general physical adaptation. The medical diagnostic procedure, like other aspects of the total evaluation, is a search for assets as well as liabilities; a search for whatever potentialities the child may have that can serve as a basis for achieving more efficient functioning. Although the physician is concerned with delineating the pathology, he must also recognize that the most valuable findings in terms of the child's future lie in the identification of his remaining strengths. This includes all the sensory and motor potentialities that can be used for the child's later training and future development.

It is unfortunate that many physicians who are inexperienced in dealing with the specialized treatment and training of retarded children equate mental retardation with hopelessness, and once having made the diagnosis, fail either to identify the child's strengths, or to look for other handicaps that may be limiting him still further. The following case material highlights the importance of identifying such additional problems:

John D., a 20-month-old mongoloid boy, was brought to a special center for retarded children by his parents, on the recommendation of friends whose child attended a preschool program there. Mr. and Mrs. D. had been informed of John's diagnosis shortly after his birth. They had brought the baby home, and subsequently joined a parents' association for retarded children, which had been of great educational and emotional benefit to them. The parents were primarily interested in having an educational evaluation of the child, with a view to eventual placement in a special nursery school program. John was their only child, and they had lavished a great deal of affection and attention on him. They had themselves instituted an individual program of training and stimulation for the child, utilizing techniques they had learned at lectures and through reading.

The parents stated that they had come to the center because they felt that it was time for John to be exposed to other children. When their request was discussed in some detail it was found to have greater urgency than was immediately apparent. Mr. and Mrs. D. were well aware that mongoloid children vary greatly in intelligence and were concerned because they suspected that John was "more handicapped" than many other mongoloid children. The evaluation at the center was, in fact, the child's first formal specialized diagnostic evaluation. He had been under the medical care of a patient and attentive pediatrician, who, however, did not specialize in the area and was not familiar with the available agencies for help. Aside from his report, the only other medical data available were found in the child's birth record, which referred to the premature birth of a child with Down's Syndrome but gave few details.

John had weighed four pounds, seven ounces, at birth, received resuscitation, and spent three days in an incubator. His Apgar rating was seven, and he was discharged after eight days. Fortunately, Mr. and Mrs. D. were excellent observers and well able to describe John's progress when questioned specifically about his developmental milestones. The general impression, based upon the history and the results of the pediatrician's physical examinations, was of a moderately to severely retarded mongoloid infant. However, the observations of the parents indicated certain atypical features. There was, for example, considerable irritability, a suggestion of eyelid blinking and loss of eye contact, and a history of unusual periods of lethargy alternating with hyperactivity.

The observations of these parents pointed to a need for a complete neurological evaluation for John. The results indicated an abnormal electroencephalogram, with clear indications of a seizure pattern. Further review with the parents of the child's behavior indicated the presence of seizures even more clearly. They now reported behavior that they had not mentioned previously because they had thought these aberrations were part of "being a mongoloid." The parents recalled that, on four occasions, John had begun to twitch and had subsequently fallen asleep for short periods of time. It now seemed highly likely that the child had had at least four seizures and quite possibly more that had gone unrecognized. Since his seizures were not controlled, it was quite possible that additional injury to the brain had been incurred.

Following the diagnostic evaluation at the center, John was immediately placed on medication for controlling future seizure activity.

John's case illustrates the unfortunate fact that, even with sophisticated parents and good but standard pediatric care, additional handicaps may be overlooked in the light of the primary diagnosis. A specialized, multidisciplinary center can be particularly helpful in this respect. The special training of the staff and the special evaluation tools that are available may well combine to uncover additional problem areas that might otherwise remain unnoticed, and therefore uncorrected or uncontrolled.

The basic pediatric examination at a specialized center is conducted in much the same manner as the average child's annual checkup, though with certain differences and a number of additions. One major goal of the examination is the establishment of a medical diagnosis and etiology, both of which, however, may remain undetermined even though the fact of retardation is apparent. Nevertheless, a review of the child's medical history and a thorough physical checkup can offer a wealth of relevant information. The medical records obtained from hospitals and from physicians who previously examined or treated the child are extremely important in contributing to the diagnostic process. The hospital birth record is perhaps the single most important piece of secondary information. Sometimes it is also possible to obtain detailed nursery observation of the postnatal days. A careful study of these and subsequent medical reports will often yield a diagnostic impression that can then be confirmed by actual examination of the child. An analysis of the longitudinal sequence of medical findings is particularly helpful in the case of children suffering from petit mal, grand mal, cerebral palsy, and other disorders that may have a slow or insidious onset.

If a public health nurse is part of the team, she can be of great help in the pediatric examination. She can greet the mother in the waiting room, take the family history for the pediatrician's reference during the examination, and escort the mother and child to the examining room. Often the parent is very apprehensive about the examination, and the nurse can do much to allay such fears with kindness, reassurance, and an understanding acceptance of the child. A sensitive nurse can, in fact, make a real contribution to making the whole examination situation more positive and less threatening.

As the actual examination of the child begins, the pediatrician notes the child's stance and gait. Does the child hold his head erect? Can he sit, stand, walk, and run adequately in relation to his chronological age? The pediatrician also notes the child's facial expressions and apparent changes in mood, also looking for signs of differential awareness of parent, examiner, and nurse, and the extent of his interest in his surroundings, as indicated through eye movements, eye contact, and body movements, as well as verbalizations. The child's reactions to the examination itself are carefully observed, and any inappropriate or tantrum level crying or unusual behaviors noted. Generally, the pediatrician evaluates the child's overall mood, as well as his mood fluctuations. Is he essentially apathetic, phlegmatic, interested, irritable, hyperactive, distractible, impulsive, aggressive, passive, easily distracted or relatively focussed? All such characteristics and behavioral reactions may reflect neurological abnormalities or other handicaps that may require more thorough investigation.

Neurological impairments sometimes resulting in bizarre behavior characterize many mental retardates. These disorders may be caused by pre- or postnatal infections such as encephalitis and rubella, by lead and other types of poisoning, or by anoxia or trauma. Cranial and peripheral nerve palsies, or altered reflexes and sensory nerve changes with resulting neuromuscular defects, may be the residual effects of brain damage. Other neurological symptoms that may be evident to the pediatrician include different forms of dysrhythmia, such as episodes of staring, lip twitching, convulsions, or other strange and unusual movements. A complete history of the child's dysrhythmic patterns is very useful to the examining physician. Unfortunately, it is often impossible to obtain, since parents may ignore or fail to recognize petit mal seizures manifested merely by erratic eye blinks or head jerks. If such symptoms are suspected by the pediatrician, skull X-rays and an electroencephalographic recording may well be suggested. While neither negative nor positive electroencephalographic findings necessarily distinguish normal from retarded children, such studies may nevertheless help to detect certain neuropathological conditions often associated with mental retardation, such as various types of epilepsy, brain damage associated with cerebral palsy, or possible lesions or tumors.

The data gathered during the neurological examination may indicate referral to another specialist. Further, the absence of positive neurological findings does not rule out the possibility of organic brain damage, which may, in fact, be reflected chiefly in mood and behavior disorders. Nevertheless, the neurological phase of the medical examination can provide much invaluable information. Basic reflex patterns are carefully evaluated for the possible presence of neurological abnormalities. Specific reflexes are usually studied, including the following:

The Moro reflex, a specific "startle" reaction, is a response to a loud noise or sudden movement. It is present in the newborn child and generally persists until about the fifth or sixth month of life. Either the absence of this response in the newborn infant, or its presence after the seventh month or so of life, may indicate possible neurological impairment.

The tonic neck reflex is present in early infancy and usually remains until the seventh or eighth month of life. It is elicited by turning the infant's head to one side while he is lying on his back. The infant will then automatically extend his arms in what has been described as a "fencing" position. The presence of this reflex beyond the eighth month or so may be a questionable sign.

The neck righting reflex generally occurs after the tonic neck reflex disappears, usually before the child is a year old. Now when his head is moved to one side there will be a movement of the child's upper torso in the same direction. Failure of this reflex to appear may give rise to suspicions, and aberrations in its appearance may be associated with disorders such as cerebral palsy.

The stepping reflex occurs when the infant, supported in a standing position, makes rhythmic "stepping" movements. This reaction usually disappears in the first six weeks of life. Its undue persistence may raise suspicions about the baby's cortical activity.

The palmar reflex may be seen in children under two months of age. The child automatically closes his fist on objects and holds on quite strongly. This reaction does not usually continue beyond three to four months.

The plantar reflex is an automatic reaction in which the toes curl over an object placed under them. Normally, this reflex disappears before the child is 12 months of age.

In *the Babinski reflex*, the large toe is extended upwards upon appropriate stimulation. Failure to elicit either reflex in the young infant, or conversely, their persistence in the older infant can both be indications of possible neurological abnormalities.

The parachute reflex generally appears when the child is about 13 months of age. The child will place his arms over his head when he is lifted up and suddenly lowered to the floor. Its absence may be a suspicious sign.

The rooting reflex tends to disappear in normal children at about one year of age, but may persist for several years in retarded children. This reaction is elicited by slight finger pressure on the baby's cheek, following which he will then turn his head to the finger and open his mouth.

These reflexes are evaluated not only for their presence or absence, but also for the quality and symmetry of the response. Deviations may require referral for special laboratory procedures and/or more extensive neurological investigation.

In evaluating body development the pediatrician weighs the child and measures his height and his head and chest circumferences. Using a percentile scale based on the general population at the child's age for each measurement, the pediatrician checks the ratings of each of these measurements in relation to each other, in order to determine possible discrepancies. For example, a child in the 3rd percentile for height and the 98th percentile for head circumference is clearly abnormally proportioned. These measurements are also considered in terms of standard deviations from the mean for the general population at the child's age. An interval of one standard deviation to either side of the mean includes approximately 68 percent of the population; an interval of two standard deviations includes 95 percent; and an interval of three, 99.7 percent. Consequently, measurements within one standard deviation of the mean may well be normal, while those which deviate from the mean by one or more standard deviations are likely to be questionable.

In his examination of the child's head, the pediatrician looks for disproportion of the face and skull, which is characteristic of many syndromes related to mental retardation. The pediatrician must consider many possibilities in connection with distorted head shapes. Premature closure of one or more of the sutures may be involved. Microcephaly or hydrocephaly may cause early or delayed closure of the fontanelles, the spaces between the bones in the head. Observations may well have to be supplemented by X-rays, since deviations from the normal, even when they are quite extreme, are sometimes deceiving.

The pediatrician examines the child's vision, since visual defects can impair psychomotor development and impede progress in training. Visual problems are difficult to determine in infants, but if any such impairment is suspected the child can be referred for a special ophthalmological examination. Besides studying the child's actual visual function, the pediatrician checks for specific abnormalities in the eye areas, such as the epicanthic folds characteristic of mongolism, strabismus, drooping lid, or lens cataracts of one or both eyes which may result from maternal rubella infection during the first three months of pregnancy. Inside the eye, an eyeground examination may reveal retinal inflammations or degeneration, perhaps indicating serious metabolic disorders sometimes associated with mental retardation. The presence of areas of depigmentation in the iris, perhaps in the form of Brushfield's spots, may be noteworthy. Measurement of the space between the child's eyes is also important in this phase of the medical examination. Deviations in this respect, particularly when accompanied by cleft-lip, cleft palate, or other facial disfiguration, are often associated with pecific syndromes often characterized by retardation.

The pediatrician also tests the child's hearing acuity, and, if possible, determines the cause of auditory defect. This area, too, is of vital mportance to the child's future training. Hearing deficiencies may esult from either nerve deafness or structural defects of bones of the middle ear. The pediatrician is equipped to do adequate screening in audition, but an audiologist or otolaryngologist may be needed for a more detailed study. The child's ears are also examined by the pediatrician for anatomical deviations sometimes associated with mental retardation. Possible signs include ears that are prominently protruding, disproportionately small or large, poorly formed, or noticeably low set.

Particularly when accompanied by other abnormalities, peculiar nasal features may be associated with certain syndromes characterized by mental retardation. One of the commonest examples is the broad, flat nose with depressed bridge so characteristic of the mongoloid. A markedly pursed mouth is also frequently associated with mongolism, while an underdeveloped lower jaw is more characteristic of other syndromes associated with mental retardation. The pediatrician also looks inside the child's mouth for evidence of a highly arched palate, a cleft palate, or immobility of the soft palate. A thickened tongue may be associated with cretinism, while a rough, cracked tongue is often found in the mongoloid. The child's teeth are also of concern, since their condition may jeopardize his general health and interfere with his speech. A child with decayed, ground down, or badly stained teeth may need referral to a dentist. Teeth that are poorly developed, crowded, misshapen, or irregular may also have diagnostic significance.

An examination of the child's neck, too, may be of special relevance to possible mental retardation. For example, a short, wide, webbed neck may be associated with various chromosomal abnormalities, especially when other abnormalities are also present. Puffy or thickened skin may be a symptom of cretinism, while dry, rough skin of mongolism. Various skin lesions may also be associated with certain relevant syndromes.

Anatomical defects of the arms, hands, and feet are particularly noted in the pediatric examination, since bone structures are often affected by genetic, metabolic, and endocrine factors. The pediatrician looks for peculiar creases on the palm, such as the simian line, checks to make sure all of the bones are present, and looks for the obvious anomalies, such as webbed fingers, as well as the more obscure irregularities. The heart is one of several organs that can be affected by genetic defects or maternal infections during pregnancy. The pediatrician listens for murmurs and checks the child's heart for enlargement, both symptoms being signs of possible congenital heart disease. Enlargement of the liver and/or the spleen may point to metabolic disturbances, while maldevelopments of the genitalia may be associated with various types of genetic or endocrine defects.

After completing the physical examination, it is most helpful for the pediatrician to discuss the child's condition with the parents. He sometimes finds that, although a parent may already know the major medical findings, he has little or no awareness of their implications. For example, parents who have been told that a child has "weak legs" may interpret this as a justification for carrying him and not allowing him to walk by himself. The child then walks poorly due to lack of exercise and restricted learning experience. Similarly, parents who have been told that their child's chewing and swallowing functions are impaired may react with panic at the child's slightest cough while he is eating. They may, in fact, keep him too long on baby food, limit his nutrition, and infantilize him and overrestrict his experience. Such misconceptions can often be discovered and dispelled through open discussion with the pediatrician. A post-examination session also enables the pediatrician to discuss medication and related problems with the parent, such as the types of drugs the child has been taking and the frequency, consistency, and duration of treatment. A reexamination of drug therapy, with changes in type and dosage, is often in order.

Laboratory procedures. The findings of the pediatric and neurological examination may frequently indicate the need for specialized laboratory procedures to help establish and uncover additional handicaps and special problem areas. These highly specialized tests are usually performed in a hospital setting to which the child is referred.

Perhaps the most common of such procedures are an electroencephalogram, urinalysis, skull X-rays, and a blood count. The electroencephalogram is useful in detecting convulsive disorders. Urinalysis can aid in detecting other disorders. Skull X-rays may confirm diagnoses related to cranial abnormalities, while blood analyses may indicate the presence of lead poisoning and other defects. Additional laboratory procedures, such as pneumoencephalogram or chromosomal analysis, may also be appropriate if pediatric examination or the medical history indicates their use.

The nurse's visit to the home. A public health nurse can offer the family further help in addition to contributing to the ease of the medical examination. She may escort the parent and child from the examining room and make an appointment with the mother to meet at the center or at the home to discuss the family history and the child's development in more detail. In their own home, the parents may be more willing to present and discuss material that they were not ready to disclose earlier and in an unfamiliar setting. Completing the medical history at home also gives the parents time to consult other family members and to think of additional information. The home setting, then, has many special values for the nurse's visit.

The primary purpose of the nurse's visit to the home at this stage is to obtain a more detailed medical history of the family, including an account of the mother's prenatal status, delivery, and postnatal care. Also reviewed is the child's early development, including his past illnesses, diet, and physical capacities. During the visit, the nurse can also observe how the mother, the child, and other family members interact. She can note the materials available in the home for providing stimulation for the child. Further, she can compare the child's actual behavior with his reported behavior, and discrepancies in this respect are not infrequent. Sometimes a mother reports, for example, that the child can use a spoon for feeding, but during the home visit the nurse may see that it is the mother who actually handles the spoon, while the child merely puts his hand on hers. The whole tone of the mother-child relationship should concern the nurse during this visit. She notes, for example, how the mother holds, carries, and assists the child, as well as how the child communicates with the mother and other family members.

In a very real sense, this visit can provide a more accurate and better integrated impression of the child's total functioning than do observations made in the artificial atmosphere of an examining room. However, whether the information is obtained at the home or at the center, the medical history that the nurse obtains should be quite comprehensive for maximum benefit. Some parents tend to speak more freely about medical problems to a nurse or a physician than to a social worker. The nurse may thus be able to clear up some of the contradictory information obtained in the initial interview. The nurse may also be able to explore certain medical problem areas that were insufficiently covered previously. For example, the parent may have reported that the child was seizure free, actually meaning only that he did not have grand mal seizures. The nurse may ask further questions, such as, "Does your child sometimes stop playing, and just sit and stare?" "Does he ever suddenly drop toys, and seem unable to grasp anything for a little while?" "Do his eyes blink a great deal?" "Were there ever times when he suddenly stiffened?" Such specific questions can be quite helpful, since many parents had not previously associated such behaviors with seizures. This kind of information, much of which only the parent can supply, is often very important in considering possibilities such as seizures.

The sleep pattern of the child also requires careful evaluation and questioning. Although bizarre or unusual sleep patterns are unlikely to go unnoticed by the parents, they may be reluctant to mention those they know about, regarding them as reflections of parental inadequacy. Some parents may also tell the nurse about their "good" babies who sleep deeply and take frequent naps, without realizing that the child is abnormally lethargic. The possibility of neglect or abuse of the child is also considered by the nurse during the visit. Retarded infants require considerably more care than do normal children. This can be perceived by the parent as an unfair burden, and some may react by providing the minimal physical care that the child requires, without attending to his social and affectional needs. There may even be deliberate physical neglect or actual abuse of the child, particularly by parents who are excessively resentful of the retardation. In these situations, the nurse might report her findings to the social worker, who in turn may subsequently consult a psychiatrist to help determine the best course to follow with the parents.

As part of the developmental history, the nurse questions the mother in great detail about the child's self-care progress. Specific information about sucking, swallowing, and feeding behavior is relevant. A parent may realize that the child is deficient in these areas but assume that the problems are entirely due to his retardation. However, delayed achievement in some of these areas may be more of a reflection of the parental reaction to the retardation. The parent may assume, for example, that the child is incapable of feeding himself, continuing to feed him, and depriving him of the opportunity for the development of feeding skills. Similarly, recognizing the child's limited abilities for coordinated physical movements, a parent may not permit him to crawl, thus further limiting his experience with his body and with the environment. Such problems may be amenable to guidance from the nurse and other treatment personnel, as part of the therapeutic program for the child and family.

The psychological evaluation. The special area of the psychologist is behavior. When a psychologist evaluates a child he studies his behavior clinically, analyzes it qualitatively through the use of some instruments, and measures it quantitatively through the use of others. He attempts to identify the causes of the child's behavior and tries to predict how the child will behave in the future. The psychologist is interested in normal as well as abnormal behavior. In fact, he must be exceedingly familiar with normal behavior, because the chief way in which he can identify the abnormal is by comparing it with the normal and realizing that it is different.

"Normal" and "abnormal" behavior are meaningless terms apart from the age of the child. The behavior the child manifests can be considered retarded only if he has reached an actual age when it should have been outgrown. Behavioral norms vary both qualitatively and quantitatively from year to year, and in the case of very young children, from month to month, and even from week to week. At each age level, the norm consists of those abilities that most children of that age have developed, and the types of behavior that they manifest. Behavioral deviation consists of what fewer children do at that particular age, and extreme deviation consists of those behaviors that the smallest number of children exhibit.

It is safe to say that no child, retarded or otherwise, either differs from other children of his age in all respects, or is like them in all ways. It is the psychologist's function to identify both the child's similarities and his differences. For this purpose, an adequate psychological evaluation of a retarded child cannot consist merely of giving him tests that result in an IQ score. A comprehensive psychological assessment aims at adding to the understanding of the child's individual growth and development processes and to the overall quality of his responsiveness to his environment, as well as at obtaining a picture of his particular pattern of abilities and disabilities.

Although the psychologist has available a large number of mental and motor tests for children, one of the chief values of these instruments lies in the opportunities they provide for close observation and clinical astuteness. Evaluation of the infant retardate is likely to be more dependent on the ability of the evaluator to be alert to subtle clues than on the actual tests that are given or attempted. In infancy, inferences concerning the child's intellectual status are based largely on evidence of physical growth and development. Since developmental progress is dependent on interaction between child and environment through assimilation and accommodation, an important factor is to assess the degree of the child's awareness and responsiveness. As yet, there are few if any objective instruments for measuring "input" (receptivity) and "output" (behavior) for children whose ability to respond is severely limited. In order to obtain what information he can, the sensitive clinician notes even mere reflex responses, such as eye blinks at loud sounds, eyelids closing to light, or unusual startle reactions.

For the child who is capable of giving adequate response, the psychological examination includes a series of specific, age appropriate tasks that permit detailed observation of the child's responses in many areas. In the case of older and/or less retarded children, reactions to real or imagined failures may also be noted. The child's test performance also provides a pointed and detailed record of how the child uses his resources, as well as what resources he has. The extent of his curiosity, spontaneity, protest, dependency, and relatedness to things and people can be observed. The psychologist can also note the child's characteristic problem-solving approaches and method of coping with new situations. These data contribute to a comprehensive picture of the child's overall functioning at this time: his strengths, his weaknesses, his difficulties, and his attempts at dealing with them.

The child's physical appearance, shifts of mood, physical movements, awareness of objects and people, reactions to familiar and unfamiliar faces, and his particular likes and dislikes are all considered in the attempt to reach as full a description of the child's behavior as possible. The psychologist notes whether the child looks toward sounds, reaches out for things, and is capable of sustained, goal-directed activity. Does the child, for example, imitate sounds and activities, shake a rattle or kick a ball, or respond to his name? A mere list of what the child can and cannot do is clearly inadequate. A far more detailed analysis is needed to assist other members of the diagnostic and treatment team. The simple statement "the child walks without assistance," for example, covers too wide a spectrum of abilities to be very useful. The child may actually walk quite poorly, even though he does walk without help. The psychologist must therefore provide a more exact description, such as "the child walks unassisted, but with a broad and clumsy gait, and arms held out to the side."

The administration of suitable tests, where possible, enables the psychologist to study the child's behavior in areas where problems might not otherwise be detected. It is the overall pattern of the child's responses on these tests, rather than his quantitative scores, that is of paramount importance in contributing both to the diagnosis of retardation and to the identification of his particular strengths and weaknesses.

A psychological evaluation sufficiently extensive to be of real assistance in these respects must include a variety of tests, since no one instrument is likely to be either sufficiently accurate or sufficiently inclusive to permit valid inferences about the child's future behavior. Through judicious use of all or part of different tests, the psychologist can often obtain enough information about the individual child's abilities and disabilities to help form the basis for a broad picture of his present and potential level of functioning.

The use of a battery of tests suitable for the particular child can provide at least some indication of how he stands in relation to other children of his age, and what level of training is likely to be most appropriate for him in view of the relative strengths and weaknesses he demonstrates at the time. Instruments that are appropriate for a particular child should minimize the effects of possible limitations imposed by additional handicaps. For example, some instruments are designed with special regard for the perceptually handicapped child, while performance tests may be more suitable with children from foreign-language backgrounds, or those with little or no speech. Tests requiring minimal motor dexterity may be used with those whose motor coordination is poor.

Psychological tests are available for children of all ages, with items suitable for the different age levels. Tests for infants consist largely of simple perceptual and motor items, with prevocalization measurements and indices of rudimentary social development for those still well below a year of age. Language development, elementary reasoning, and simple number concepts can be investigated in the normal child around the age of three. Test emphasis on reasoning increases with the age of the child, the items becoming more abstract as he grows older. Thus, tests at the youngest age levels stress tasks such as following an object with the eyes and head, attending to a voice or bell, or lifting the head. With increasing age, more complex manual tasks are employed, involving manipulation of blocks, peg boards, and eating utensils. At a still more advanced level, the child is required to name objects, or at least to point to objects named by the examiner. At each age level, test signs of retardation become more meaningful as the discrepancies between what the child should do and what he does do increase in number and magnitude.

The child's abilities can be studied in terms of his past accomplishments or achievements, his present level of skills, and his aptitudes or potentialities for future development. In addition to those that measure abilities, tests for children are available in many other areas of behavior, ranging from those that investigate fairly narrow segments of functioning, such as interests, beliefs, values, and attitudes, to those that attempt to study personality structure and function more globally. Such tests may be quite helpful in the case of older, less severely retarded children. It is rare, however, that they are applicable to young trainable children. In fact, tests that are appropriate to the chronological age of a retarded child are usually much too difficult for him. If he is severely or profoundly retarded, he may require tests that are actually intended for infants, even though he is at school age or even beyond.

There is obviously little point in merely giving a child a series of tests that are beyond his abilities. Once the nature and extent of his disabilities have been established, tests are needed to identify whatever areas of ability remain. Some retarded children, particularly the young and more severely impaired, may be so inaccessible or so distractible that formal testing is impossible. One can still arrive at some estimate of the developmental progress and functioning level of such children through the use of instruments administered to an adult who is thoroughly familiar with the child. Such an informant, often the mother, can be asked a standard series of questions designed to provide a picture of the child's development in areas such as self-care, locomotion, playing, socialization, and communication. Tests of this kind provide some insights into the development of the child and also help the psychologist to understand the parent's view of the child, estimate the extent of parental willingness to discuss the child openly and without defensiveness, and uncover discrepancies between the child's actual progress and the parent's perceptions. Information of this kind is particularly useful in planning treatment for both the child and the family.

Special tests have also been devised for assessing parental attitudes toward the retarded child. Such tests can be especially helpful in estimating the level of assistance that might be most beneficial to the parent. Another valuable technique is to have a parent describe a typical day in the child's life, discussing his behavior on awakening, eating, and during play activities. During the parent's description, the psychologist can ask questions in an informal, conversational manner, avoiding the more specific type of questioning, which the parent might find more threatening. For example, instead of asking directly, "Can your child wash his hands without your help?" the psychologist can follow up leads in the parent's self-directed narrative, asking the question as it arises naturally in the context of the description.

In addition to his more general observations, the psychologist should be especially alert to environmental factors in the child's development. It is often quite difficult to separate biomedical from environmental factors, since they interact with one another so closely. Thus, a parent who believes that his child is "unteachable" will often fail to provide the stimuli necessary to encourage developing the child's abilities to their fullest potential. In cases of gross developmental failure or severe performance lag, the psychologist must also consider the possibility of actual sensory deprivation: tactile, visual, auditory, or motor. The child may not have been provided with sufficiently interesting toys. Perhaps the mother rarely talks to him, cuddles him, or exercises his body, because the child does not respond with the usual smiles and cooing behavior that she expects and wants. More extreme environmental deprivation may result when the mother leaves the child alone in a bare room, or when he shares a crowded room with several brothers and sisters.

The psychologist also notes the social and interpersonal deficits the child may have. Is his behavior overdependent, essentially passive, or overtly aggressive? Such reactions may sometimes be initial signs of behavior disorders that will interfere with the child's subsequent training. Astute observations at this point can contribute significantly to the structuring of an educational program that will minimize the adverse effects of the child's special emotional, experiential, and physical handicaps.

A major problem in differential diagnosis is the frequent behavioral similarity between retarded and emotionally disturbed children. The distinction is obscured still further by the fact that retarded children are unlikely to escape emotional disturbances, and in many ways do behave like the emotionally disturbed. Some of these problems may originate in the child's organically based restlessness, his difficulties in attention and concentration, and his factual experiences of instability. However, primary problem areas tend to decrease his frustration tolerance, disrupt his relationships, and interfere with his learning. His actual life experiences, too, may lower his functioning efficiency still further. After repeated experiences of failure, combined perhaps with unrealistic demands of the parents and an unstimulating environmental setting, there is little doubt that a retarded child will develop emotional problems.

During the entire psychological diagnostic evaluation, the relationship between the child and parent emerges as a major factor in the child's life. Actually, it is highly artificial even to attempt a diagnosis of the child as a separate entity, since his whole emotional and behavioral life is so intimately dependent on his interaction with the parents. The psychologist can often only sense or guess at how the child's behavior is related to parental needs and demands. However, as the psychologist gains more and more insight into the nature of the parent-child relationship, a treatment plan can be formulated that aims at improving their interaction at many levels.

The psychological evaluation, then, should include appropriate tests that permit comparisons between this child's development and that of other children of his age. More importantly, however, the evaluation aims at obtaining as complete a picture as possible of the child as he functions at that particular point in time. The assessment includes a detailed account of his positive resources as well as his limitations. It also provides an estimate of how he learns, copes with new experiences and stimuli, obtains information from the environment, and integrates and utilizes the information he obtains. Such a comprehensive psychological evaluation helps in setting up suitable programs for the child and the parent and provides an essential baseline with which the later progress of both can be compared.

The educational evaluation. Although the infant retardate is hardly ready for education in the standard sense, an educator trained in child development can be a valuable member of the diagnostic team. Since he understands the course of normal growth and development, he can offer highly specialized assistance in delineating specific levels of retardation. He can also help in distinguishing mental retardation from delayed developmental processes in an otherwise normal child. In his assessment of the child, the educational developmentalist studies the learning behavior and related characteristics of the young retardate in order to identify special areas of potential learning weakness as well as those that represent potential learning strengths. Learning in this context is obviously not restricted to academic achievement. The educational process is present in every facet of the child's day-to-day living. Incidental learning, spontaneous associations, and potential for transfer occur with each new experience. The child's past learning is a vital part of his present learning behavior. A nine-month-old child who habitually throws a spoon on the floor may have learned, for example, that someone will pick it up. Similar types of learning take place from the time the child wakes up until he goes to sleep at night. The trained educator can observe many clues that enable him to build up a picture of the child's overall learning level, including past influences and future potentialities.

The educational study and diagnosis of the infant retardate may reveal areas of unexpected strengths to be taken into account in designing an appropriate training program for him. The educator may also detect special problem areas that indicate hitherto unsuspected handicaps. The educational diagnosis should cover both, arriving at an individualized educational profile that permits the projection of the child's abilities to learn and maintain skills. For a retarded infant or young child who is still lying in a crib, the educator notes whatever simple infant abilities are present in formulating an educational assessment. He provides a series of suitable stimuli, such as a teething ring, a bottle, a rubber ball, or a dangling toy, and records the child's responses to them. He notes whether the child responds to one toy in particular, and how he responds to it. He observes the child's reactions to smiles, bright lights, and loud noises, and also to positional changes. He looks carefully for the child's quality of functioning in each sensory area and notes any lack or excessive use of a particular response.

With a child who is somewhat older and more physically mature, the educational diagnostician can utilize a larger variety of materials to study sensory responses and investigate abilities to perceive and react to sensory stimulation. For the child who has already developed rudimentary social awareness, exposure to a group of peers in a classroom setting is particularly useful for purposes of educational diagnosis. In this environment, the child's method of making contact with the other children, his ability to share with them and with adults, and the capacity to tolerate noise, movement, and physical contact can all be noted. The child's particular methods of communication can also be studied in this setting. His alertness to his home environment can be inferred from observations of his responses to simple housekeeping equipment, such as a stove, a sink, a bed, and dishes, all scaled to his size.

Tricycles, walking boards, and slides can be used to test total body coordination in the older and more physically developed child. The educator can gauge the development of fine finger coordination by having the child work with a large peg board and string beads. The use of materials of this kind may also reveal the level of visual-motor coordination that the child has achieved, since his reach and grasp can be studied. Clues to his characteristic problem-solving approaches, of particular importance in considering a suitable training program, can be observed and recorded. Large cube- and pyramid-shaped blocks, brightly colored on some sides and drab on the others, can be used to determine the child's awareness of differences in shape and color and to help assess his incidental learning. The educator can also investigate areas of functioning such as motor and perceptual-motor acuity, and study the child's progress in self-care and health, safety, language arts, number concepts, and social development.

The use of developmental milestones in diagnosing retardation is a standard procedure and one with vital relevance for education. The absence at appropriate ages of developmental behaviors such as smiling, rolling over, reaching for and holding objects, sitting, pushing, standing, and teasing may be associated with mental retardation. Many factors may inhibit the development of these activities; a lack of head movement, for example, may be the result of poorly developed musculature, a neurological or visual defect, or emotional apathy. The educational diagnosis attempts to establish the causal factors for such developmental failures as clearly as possible, since problems that induced them may handicap the child's future learning as well.

During the course of his examination, the educator studies the child's minute reactions to sensory stimuli, his awareness of environmental changes, and his responses to people and things. Temperament, personality traits, and behavior patterns are noted, since children who are quite similar in physical abilities as such may differ greatly in their actual achievements as a result of differing interests, levels of perseverance, and curiosity and treatment. It is not primarily gross distinctions, but rather the more minute, detailed, and specific differences among retarded children to which the educational diagnostician should be sensitive. Such detailed observations are particularly important in an evaluation of the infant retardate, whose deficits may restrict the responsiveness of others to him. Thus, a child who does not smile or babble may be infrequently picked up and held less by his parents. This lack of stimulation, in turn, may severely affect the development of the child's motor abilities and also interfere with his later social relationships and learning behavior.

The interaction of the infant and his environment is, in fact, of major importance in understanding the child's patterns of response and in estimating his learning potentialities. In his attempts to make such an estimate, the educator uses his own observations and also the reports of other members of the team to help in identifying the particular combination of factors that influence the child's responses. A genuinely useful educational diagnosis and prognosis for later training include insights into the child's entire daily life, his routine schedules, sleeping arrangements, feeding techniques, exposure to other people, and many other facets of his actual life experience.

The educational program that will be developed for the retarded infant will emphasize self-care and socialization, in order to help him make the best possible adjustment to his family and community. A first essential step in formulating a long-range treatment program for him is a careful diagnostic evaluation of the level of skill the child has already achieved, including an assessment of his learning style, self-motivation, determination, responsiveness, and general functions. The educator must actually try to understand the nature of the infant's world, with its sounds, sights, movements, and textures. The process of maturation involves a set of predispositions whose development is facilitated or hindered by environmental conditions. It is the totality of these conditions that the educator attempts to describe and analyze in his diagnostic study.

The speech and language evaluation. The communication behavior of the retarded infant and preschool child covers a wide range, extending from primitive grimaces, gestures, undifferentiated noises and sounds to symbolic utterances of word partials, words, and groups of words. These categories are not mutually exclusive, so that the performance of many children involves several forms of both non-verbal and verbal production. For the child with neurological, sensory, perceptual, environmental, intellectual, or psychological problems, an exact timetable of expectancy levels in communication behavior and abilities cannot be expected. Therefore, a single available assessment instrument or procedure cannot serve to evaluate the child's language level adequately. For an adequate evaluation of his speech and language levels, the examiner must usually devise special materials to test sensory input areas, integration, retention, retrieval, and observable communication behavior.

A specialized interview of the parents by a specialist in communication is often a valuable first step in the speech and language evaluation process. For example, the parent may be asked specific questions concerning the child's awareness of visual and auditory stimuli, the nature of his responses to nonverbal and verbal stimuli, and the degree to which such responses are vocal and understandable to family, peers, and strangers. From the case history and the medical and pyschological evaluations, the examiner in speech and language development can obtain information that may aid in determining possible reasons for some of the child's handicaps in language development and also in estimating which procedures would be most helpful for evaluation purposes.

An awareness of the social and emotional status of the family assists the speech and language specialist in assessing the values within the family that may contribute to the amount and quality of language stimulation which the child receives. The pregnancy and birth data assist him by providing possible reasons for considering physical, neurological, and maturational factors related to the child's language status. The physical examination and growth data give him needed information about the child's sensory integrity, especially as it involves vision and audition, as well as the status of his articulatory organs, the development and growth of his sucking, swallowing, and chewing, and his adaptive behavior as he interacts with his environment. The patterns of the child's auditory awareness and response, and also of his sound production and language development, present a much needed background for an adequate evaluation of his speech and language function.

The first direct source of information about the child is observation of his actual language behavior in a number of different situations. The experienced speech and language specialist will look for first clues as soon as he meets the child and the parents, perhaps in the waiting room. There he can observe the ways in which child and parent relate to and communicate with each other. He can also speak to the parent about the examination that is to follow and prepare him to participate appropriately in the examination procedure. Unless the child has to be carried into the room and placed in a crib, one can note how he enters the examination room, and how he separates from the parent. These factors can be observed both in action and attitude. The manner in which he conducts himself in relation to the room, the materials, and the examiner offers valuable information about him. A number of relevant behavior areas can be evaluated in this context. The examiner notes, for example, whether the child demonstrates any unusual physical activity. Are his actions related or unrelated to the tasks presented to him? How does he secure information about the materials used?

Does he communicate with the examiner? Is his communication non-verbal or verbal? Is it essentially echolalic or perseverative? Are his verbalizations appropriate or deficient in content and/or clarity? Is there any evidence of a possible hearing deficiency that would require further investigation?

The incidence of hearing disorders among young mentally retarded children cannot be ascertained with any degree of accuracy. However, there is general agreement among authorities that the hearing problems of the retarded are substantially greater than those of normal children. It is imperative, therefore, that every effort be made to assess the general hearing status of the retarded infant who is to be involved in a program of speech and language development.

In the infant retardate, gross hearing may be tested by noting his responses to mother-child interaction sounds, such as kissing and clucking, and his reactions to "approval" noises made by the examiner from beyond the child's range of vision. The examiner can note, for example, if the child smiles at the sound or gives other signs of awareness, such as attempting to seek out the source of the sound. A pure-tone screening test of hearing is suitable for the preschool child who can respond to the procedure appropriately. If there is evidence of a possible hearing impairment, the child should be referred for a full-scale audiometric examination. The speech and language specialist can, however, note whether the child is able to attend to specific procedures and materials, and what his responses are to success, failure, and frustration. How does he react to the concluding of the examination? What are his attitudes and actions on leaving the room? What took place when he returned to the parent?

The speech and language examination also provides an opportunity for observing the physical aspect of the child, his general development and nutrition, evidences of possible sensory deficiency, obvious anomalies, drooling, tics, and minimal signs of seizure activity. The child's general movement around the room and the way he works with blocks, pegs, beads, and puzzles can give valuable indications of his gross and fine motor functions. Problems of movement, gait, and manipulation may point to organic impairment that may be responsible for or contributory to the child's communication difficulties.

A physical examination of the child's articulatory organs is part of his medical examination. However, it is in the speech and language evaluation that these organs are seen in actual use, and their scope and ease of movement evaluated. Various physical conditions of the lips, tongue, the hard and soft palates, the pharynx, and the mouth and jaw occlusion are areas for medical and dental specialists and should be referred to the proper specialists, as indicated. However, this aspect of the overall diagnostic process can help to evaluate the child's ability to secure verbal and nonverbal information, to interpret and integrate it, and to respond to it verbally and nonverbally. Special tests devised for retarded children and examiner-created instruments generally become part of the repertoire of every experienced diagnostician in speech and language areas. The following areas can be assessed fairly readily:

The child's ability to identify real objects can be studied by noting his reactions to common objects in his environment, such as a rattle, a ball, a bottle, a cup, and the like. Visual material, such as colorful and interesting toys, jungle gym objects, and the like, may help to mobilize the child's visual attention. He may even reach toward and attempt to use such materials. Objects of different textures can also be used to obtain tactile response. In all of these areas, the examination focusses on the ability of the child to attend to and use, in whatever way he can, the stimuli that exist in the normal environment of children. The child who through attention, curiosity, and mobilization of potential can use these materials as input stimuli is usually the child who is ready to use basic sensory material for later growth. It is important that even fleeting signs—smiling, grimacing, cessation of activity, or the beginning of activity—be observed and evaluated. These may be the only responses that can be elicited at this time and are noteworthy in the identification of infant abilities.

For the older child, paired sets of objects and pictures can be used, the child being asked to point to or name the object depicted, depending on the level of his communication skills. The ability to comprehend speech can be assessed by giving him commands that range from simple through more complex requests. The child can be asked, for example, to "Open the door." At a more complicated level, he can be asked to perform more than one activity sequentially, such as, "Pick up the blocks, and put them on the table." These requests should be made without accompanying gestures if verbal comprehension is being evaluated. If no responses are forthcoming, varying degrees of gestures and other nonverbal indications may be introduced, to determine the amount of nonverbal aids necessary to induce the child's comprehension.

A series of actions may also be requested verbally, such as, "Show me the bottle and put it on that table." If the child fails to respond to the verbal request "Show me," he can be presented with the object utilized in the action among a group of articles and shown in pantomime the action that is performed with it. For the older and less retarded child, verbal responses can be elicited by presenting him with statements from which the key words are missing, to be supplied by the child himself. Items might include, for example, "You sit on a ____." "You see with your ____." and "You put your hat on your ____." To assess the child's imitative abilities and auditory memory, he can be asked to repeat words of increasing complexity, beginning with "boy," "girl," and "baby," and extending to more complicated words such as "telephone" and "airplane." Phrases can also be added, again beginning with simpler ones and extending to the more difficult. Simple phrases such as "I eat candy," and "I play ball" are suitable for the beginning of a series that can easily be extended to increasing levels of difficulty.

The preschool child's association skills can be evaluated through many techniques, including matching, sorting, and categorizing. To evaluate his matching abilities, he can be shown, say, three objects or pictures, two of which are related. Such a series might include a pencil, a piece of paper, and a cup, or pictures corresponding to these objects. Other items might consist of a cookie, a glass of milk, and a knife, a comb, a brush, and a cup, and so on. The series can readily be made more complex if the child's abilities warrant an upward extension. Some simple sorting tests are available and others can easily be made. Simple sorting features, such as color or shape, are most suitable.

Categorizing objects by usage is a simple procedure for assessing another dimension of the child's associative skills. If he has already developed some degree of verbal skill, some appraisal of his intelligibility should be made. For the younger or more retarded child, the appropriateness and consistency of his nonverbal communic .tion can also be estimated in play activity.

When the child's medical, psychological, and developmental, as well as speech and language data, have been collected, an individual treatment program in language development can be delineated. Obviously, the program should begin at the level where some success can reasonably be anticipated, with successive steps planned in accordance with the child's potential for future growth in communication behavior. This diagnostic clinical approach requires constant reevaluation and planning. However, an initial prognostic statement may be included in the examiner's first evaluation, subject to periodic reassessment of the child's progress. The first diagnostic report describes the child's total performance, characterizes his level of comprehension, charts his proficiency in sound production, and makes a tentative prognosis for future speech development. Two examples of such an initial evaluative process are briefly summarized below:

A. was a 29-month-old mongoloid son of American-born parents. Upon examination, it was ascertained that he was aware of sounds and could also localize them. An inspection of the oral mechanism revealed no anomalies. There was mild drooling. The child successfully pointed to six common objects but could neither match nor name them himself. He could follow simple, single verbal requests well. His spontaneous vocalization was considered as moderate in quantity, with some jargon and a few simple word partials. He was evaluated as a mild to moderately retarded child with an 18 to 21 month overall language level, and characterized as alert and available for stimulation in language areas. Prognosis was considered good.

B. was an 18-month-old son of Puerto Rican parents. The medical diagnosis was cerebral palsy. He was found to be aware of sounds, but he did not localize them by turning his head or moving his eyes in their direction. His vocalizations consisted of gross noises and grunts, with no vowel sounds. He did not communicate his needs except for crying. An inspection of the oral mechanism revealed the absence of teeth. There was no drooling. He did not point to nor match objects. B. was judged to be a severely retarded child, with a language level below six months. Prognosis was considered poor.

THE DIAGNOSTIC STAFF CONFERENCE

A staff conference held at the conclusion of the various phases of the diagnostic process is one of the best ways of pooling information and reaching viable decisions. Such a conference has two basic purposes: to formulate a total diagnostic picture of the child, and to project a treatment program for the child and family. In some cases, it may be desirable to refer the family elsewhere for the most suitable treatment programs for them. Such referrals can be decided on at the diagnostic staff conference, the center accepting the responsibility for placement and follow up. At some centers, the medical director of the center serves as chairman of the diagnostic staff conference. At other centers, the chief social worker, pediatrician, psychologist, or another staff member may lead the meeting. The leadership may rotate or be fixed, depending on the way the center is set up. All members of the diagnostic team, each with a written report of his evaluation of the child, should attend the conference, as well as treatment staff members, professionals from other centers that are involved with the family, and perhaps staff members from other centers, for whom the conference may provide some specialized professional training. Procedures for conducting the conference will vary from one center to another. The one outlined below is but one of many possibilities. It is, however, one that has proved to be particularly helpful.

First, the social worker summarizes the initial interview with the parents and makes some tentative treatment recommendations. Next, the medical director reviews all previous medical and related evaluations and summarizes the previous findings and clinical impressions. Then, the pediatrician, nurse, psychologist, speech therapist, and educator present synopses of their respective evaluations and give their recommendations for suitable treatment or training in their special areas. After these presentations, the medical director proposes a tentative diagnostic impression of the child for group discussion. The standards of both the American Association on Mental Deficiency (141) and the American Psychiatric Association (85) are used in the attempt to arrive at a formal diagnosis. Often it is easier to agree on an impression of a child's level of functioning than it is to assign him to a specific diagnostic category and to determine the precise etiology of the disorder. In fact, perhaps the most frequent diagnostic statement is merely "chronic undifferentiated brain syndrome, etiology undetermined." Sometimes additional laboratory examinations may clarify the etiology further, but unless a progressive deteriorative process in the child or a genetic defect in the family is suspected, further pursuit of etiological factors may be largely academic for purposes of formulating a tentative treatment program for the child and the family.

While there is often some disagreement among the staff members on diagnostic issues, the child's level of retardation and a reasonable educational prognosis are questions that are even more likely to arouse controversy. The members of the diagnostic team may arrive at different prognostic impressions from very similar examinations of the infant. One member of the team may, for example, emphasize the child's physical disabilities, which may be of a kind commonly associated with severe retardation. Another may note the beginning of babbling and verbal play, which more often indicate moderate retardation. While such differences of opinion rarely amount to more than a half-step on the five-point scale of profound, severe, moderate, mild, and borderline retardation, they are quite important in developing a fair picture of a child's present level of functioning, and in estimating his potential for future training.

The tentative treatment program decided on during the discussion may range from one involving active stimulation and training for a moderately retarded infant to an extremely limited program suitable for the profoundly retarded with severe neurological impairments. The program may also involve the services of other centers, particularly in the areas of medical care and physical therapy. The parents, and particularly the mother, must sanction the program and cooperate in many of its aspects, since progress in the child's training is heavily dependent on her willingness and ability to participate. It is often the social worker's responsibility to raise these issues with the parents and also to communicate the staff members' recommendations to them in the informing process that follows the diagnostic staff conference.

The following case material briefly illustrates the general procedures and kinds of data presented at the diagnostic staff conference as described above:

> Mark R. was 18 months when he was first brought to the center. The family had been referred by a large city hospital where Mark was born. His parents were American born, of Italian extraction.
>
> Mrs. R. was 27 years old at the time. At the initial interview with the social worker her manner was open and pleasant, and she gave information spontaneously and cooperatively, showing concern and sincere interest in Mark. She was apparently in good health, and her health history was essentially unremarkable. She had completed two years of high school and was employed as a saleslady during the early years of her marriage. Her father was alive and active at the age of 70, and few significant problems were reported in connection with members of his immediate family. Mrs. R.'s mother, a diabetic, was 67, and suffered from a number of physical difficulties. One of her maternal aunts had suffered an involutional depression, and a distant cousin had borne a mongoloid child. Mrs. R., the third youngest in her family, had three brothers and four sisters, all living, married, and parents of healthy children.
>
> Mr. R. was 30 years old, a high school graduate who had spent ten years in the armed services and was subsequently employed as a plumber. Although unable to join his wife at the initial interview because of an upper respiratory infection, his general health history was reportedly good. His wife described him as active, energetic, a hard worker, and a warm and interested husband and father. She mentioned that his mother had been killed in an automobile accident at the age of 41, and his father had died of a brain tumor at 53. One of his maternal nieces was epileptic, and his paternal grandmother had reportedly committed suicide. Mr. R. was the third oldest child in his family. One of the pair of twins born before him had died in infancy, while the other was now married and the mother of two healthy children. Another married sister was childless, and there were also two unmarried brothers. The living siblings were presumably in reasonably good health, and nothing remarkable was noted in their health histories.

Mrs. R.'s first pregnancy had resulted in the spontaneous delivery of a boy now 29 months old and in good health. The delivery had been uncomplicated, but Mrs. R. reported some eight weeks of intermittent vaginal bleeding afterwards. Mark was her second child. There had been no pregnancies in between, and Mark was a wanted child. Mrs. R. had continued to work until the sixth month of pregnancy and had suffered little discomfort throughout. However, there had been intermittent bleeding for some five days before the delivery. According to Mark's birth record, labor had lasted 11 hours and 10 minutes, and there was a report of "partial separated placenta, with previous vaginal bleeding." Delivery was at term, and the infant weighed 5 pounds and 9 ounces. The mother and child were both reported to be in good condition at the time of his birth and also on discharge from the hospital.

Mrs. R. told the social worker that she had suspected "something was wrong" during Mark's first month of life, because he sometimes "got stiff and his eyes seemed to stare." He was returned to the hospital and studied at the child neurological clinic when he was three months old. An electro-encephalogram taken at that time was described as "abnormal, indicating cerebral dysfunction greater on the right side." He was diagnosed as mentally retarded, placed on medication to control seizures, and subsequently followed in the outpatient department of the hospital. His first major seizure was noted when he was eight months old, and thereafter he reportedly suffered eight to ten seizures daily despite the prescribed medication. Mrs. R. said that he had made very slow developmental progress. At 18 months, he was still unable to sit or chew, had a very weak grasp, and was barely able to hold his head erect.

In the medical examination at the center, Mark was described as a poorly nourished child, weighing 15 pounds and 12 ounces and measuring 26½ inches in height. His head circumference was only 42 centimeters. The anterior fontanelle was open, measuring approximately 2 x ½ centimeters. His left ear was set noticeably lower than the right. There was a left external squint with nystagmus, and the ophthalmologist reported several visual defects that would require corrective lenses when Mark was older. He had nine poorly formed teeth, a short neck, and simian line on his left palm. His general musculature was hypotonic, and the anal sphincter reflex was absent. He seemed to be barely aware of the environment, reacting largely with a startle reaction and much eye blinking. No autonomic abnormalities were noted. At one point in the examination, there was a tonic spasm of the left half of the body, which lasted about two minutes. The head was turned to the left, with the upper and lower extremities completely extended. This episode was followed by a coarse nystagmus to the right side.

Mark's poor muscle tone was also noted by the psychologist, who described the child as having the physical appearance of a 3-month-old infant. His head balance could not be maintained, and his head drooped to the left. He could not maintain a sitting position even with support, and there were only slight indications that he might be aware of sound. He did not react differentially to his mother and to strangers, and seizure activity was noted in the course of the examination. On the Vineland Social Maturity Scale (90), with the mother as informant, Mark achieved a social age of about 3 months and an approximate Social Quotient of 27, suggesting grossly inferior social development. On the Cattell Infant Intelligence Scale (71) his IQ was estimated at 20, pointing to severe retardation. His chief attempt at adaptive behavior consisted of vague, raking movements of his left hand. Similar behavioral descriptions, notations related to apparent seizure activity, an essentially vegetative level of reaction, and evidence of severe mental retardation were also noted by the educational specialist. No vocalizations were heard in the course of the examinations nor reported by the mother.

In the summing up of the data from the various phases of the diagnostic evaluations, it was noted that, although there was some evidence of congenital malformation such as the child's displaced left ear and the simian line, etiological factors that would account for Mark's evident brain damage were not conclusively demonstrated. While consideration was given to the reported premature placental separation prior to Mark's birth, it could not be ascertained whether sufficient oxygen deprivation had occurred to produce clinical brain damage.

The consensus that the diagnostic team reached was that the prognosis for Mark was quite poor, and that the center's efforts would be best directed toward helping the parents adapt to the child's condition realistically and arrive at as constructive a resolution as possible. The issue was raised that the considerable amount of time and attention that Mark required might deprive his brother of needed attention, since the mother had mentioned that the boy had frequent temper tantrums and seemed to be a difficult and unhappy child. It was further suggested that Mrs. R. be advised to undergo a thorough obstetrical examination before any subsequent pregnancies, in view of her past obstetrical history. The final diagnostic impression arrived at for Mark was of severe mental retardation, organic brain syndrome with convulsive disorder, mixed type, petit mal and grand mal, and congenital abnormalities; etiology undetermined.

Cathy T. was a 27-month-old mongoloid child, who was referred to the center by a parent organization to which her mother had gone for advice. Mrs. T., 25 years old and of American-born parents, was a high school graduate and had been employed as a secretary prior to her marriage. Her manner during the initial interview was described by the social worker as suspicious, evasive, and secretive. When she gave information it was obviously guarded and carefully edited. Mr. T., who accompanied his wife to the interview, was 27 years old. He was also a high school graduate and was now employed as a television repairman. His father was born in Scotland, and his mother in the United States.

Mrs. T.'s mother had died at the age of 51, reportedly of a "heart attack." Her father, aged 59, was living and in good health. She was an only child. Mr. T.'s parents, both in their middle 50's, were alive and active. He had three younger siblings, two brothers and one sister, all of whom were living, healthy and unmarried. No other significant family history emerged during the interview. Both parents were reportedly in good health, with nothing remarkable in their own health histories. Cathy had a younger sister who was a year old at the time. Her birth was without significant incidents, and she was apparently doing well. No other pregnancies had intervened between that birth and the conception of Cathy, who was a wanted child.

Mrs. T. stated that she had had considerable difficulty in walking at the beginning of the last trimester of her pregnancy with Cathy. In about the thirty-fourth week of the pregnancy Mrs. T. was admitted to the hospital, where Cathy was born prematurely after some four hours of labor. No complications were reported related to the delivery. The infant had weighed 3 pounds and 10 ounces, and mongolism was noted at the time of the birth. Mr. T. was notified of this shortly afterwards, and Mrs. T. was told of it before she left the hospital. Neither parent had apparently considered institutionalization, although both wanted additional opinions and more information. The hospital had referred the parents to a pediatric evaluation service when Cathy was 10 months old, where the diagnosis of mongolism was confirmed. In describing the child's developmental progress, Mrs. T. reported that Cathy had rolled over at 4 months of age, sat at 12 months, and stood with support at about 20 months. She could now feed herself although somewhat awkwardly, and she was not toilet trained.

When she was examined at the center, Cathy was described as a blond, brown-eyed mongoloid-appearing child, with fair nutrition. She weighed 18 pounds and 6 ounces, and measured only 28¾ inches in height. Her head was small: 42½ centimeters in diameter. The chest measured 47 centimeters, and the intercanthal distance was 2¾ centimeters. A mildly flattened occiput was noted. The interior fontanelle was still open about 1 x 1 centimeters. The eyes slanted inward, and there was a mild bilateral epicanthus. Seven irregular teeth were present, two lower and one upper incisors and four molars. A systolic murmur of the heart was noted which was not transmitted. She had a short, in-turned fifth finger on both hands, with a single palmar crease. A gap was noted between the first and second toe on both feet. Joint mobility was marked with generalized hypotonic musculature. She could stand with support and even take a few uncertain steps; lack of confidence seemed to be adding to her difficulties in ambulation. Nevertheless, her overall mood was cheerful, and she appeared to be reasonably related to and interested in her surroundings.

The psychologist was quite impressed by the extent of Cathy's relatedness and inquisitiveness. She made extensive attempts to communicate, using sounds and gestures and even an occasional word. She could imitate some demonstrations, though immaturely, and evidently enjoyed doing so. On the Vineland Social Maturity Scale, with the mother as informant, she achieved a social age of 14 months and a social quotient of 59, suggesting mildly retarded social development. On the Cattell Infant Intelligence Scale her mental age was approximately 11 months and her IQ was estimated at 46, indicating a moderate degree of mental retardation. Form, color, and size had little or no meaning for her as yet, and her fine motor development was below age expectations and there was only the beginning of a pincer movement. Gross motor coordination was also described as inadequate. Overall, she seemed to be developing at a moderately retarded rate and was judged to be available for training in self-care, socialization, and language stimulation.

During the educational evaluation, it was noted that Cathy showed some tendency to favor her right hand, although this was not entirely consistent. It was further observed that she often underreached for objects, sometimes by a rather wide margin. She would, however, generally persist until she achieved her objective. The infantile nature of her fine finger coordination and also the awkwardness of her general gross motor coordination were again noted. The educational specialist reported that Cathy seemed to be able to mobilize her abilities and energy toward achieving what she wanted, whether it be crawling, turning over, exhibiting negativism and resistance, or gaining possession of a toy. It was felt that this characteristic might be directed so as to become a distinct asset in training. It was also noted that Cathy could bite cookies and chew fairly well, and that her attempts to drink from a cup were moderately successful.

In the speech and language evaluation, Cathy was noted to communicate largely through facial expressions and gestures, as was also stated in other phases of the overall study evaluation. However, her potential for future language development was considered as good. While she related warmly and spontaneously to adults, she was still relatively unresponsive to children. It was, however, the impression of the educational specialist that Cathy would be available for a nursery school program within several months. It was suggested that, in the meantime, interim training should emphasize the development of more adequate motor skills as the most pressing training need.

As is the case with many mongoloid children, Cathy did not present a serious diagnostic problem. The diagnostic impression reached at the conference was one of a moderately retarded mongoloid child. Among the questions that were discussed at the conference were the attitudes of the mother and the extent of her actual involvement. It was not the impression of the staff that she was available for guidance and counseling at that time, although it was agreed that such services should be offered to her if she indicated a desire for them now or in the future. Currently, it was felt that discussions with the nurse and other involved staff members would probably be most helpful to her and might also be the means for making her more accessible for further assistance later. As for Cathy, it was the unanimous staff opinion that she would respond well to a brief period of home training with subsequent participation in a nursery group program and eventually in a full day program at the center's training school.

THE INFORMING INTERVIEW

The basic purpose of the informing interview is to clarify the conclusions arrived at in the diagnostic staff conference to the parents. Often it is a social worker who conducts the interview, explains the diagnostic findings, and places them in the context of the projected treatment program for both child and family. Hopefully, the social worker is one who has had an opportunity to develop a trusting, supportive relationship with the parents during the intake interview and, perhaps, in other prearranged interviews or casual meetings with the parents when the child was scheduled for diagnostic evaluations.

For the informing interview, the social worker needs a comprehensive understanding of diagnosis, etiology, and prognosis. Partial information, or a poorly organized or hasty presentation, may both confuse and disturb the parents unnecessarily. It is helpful to have both parents attend the interview, in order to eliminate the possible distortion of secondhand information, to encourage an open exchange between the parents about their child's retardation, and to establish attitudes of shared responsibility. Occasionally, another member of the family may be included at the parents' request—for example, a grandmother living with the family who carries a major responsibility for the child's care. Usually, however, it is not wise to include a third person unless the parents are separated or divorced. Additional family members may be brought to later sessions, if their attendance is indicated.

The informing process usually requires several sessions. Being informed that their child is retarded often carries an emotional impact that rules out constructive planning with the parents during the first session. The intensity of their emotional reactions depends on many factors: the age of the child, the parents' prior knowledge of the child's condition, and whether he is a first-born or an only child, among other considerations. The parents' readiness to accept information must determine the rate of the informing process. If parents are given a hasty technical summary of the findings and a list of authoritative recommendations, they may respond initially with frightened acquiescence but later express confusion and rejection of the diagnostic information and proposed plans. Occasionally parents will react to the diagnostic information by denying the presence of any handicap in the child. However, particularly with encouragement, most parents are willing to speak of their doubts and questions about their child's abilities and bring themselves to reasonably direct recognition of the symptoms of retardation. In fact, the social worker can sometimes begin the informing process by confirming or substantiating the parents' observations with material in the team's reports and examples of selected tasks that the child could not perform. Such functional descriptions of the child's behavior are preferable to diagnostic labels and technical terminology.

The use of professional jargon does not usually help parents to understand their child's problems, and may even damage their self-confidence by making them seem even more bewildering. Nor is it generally wise to deal with some of the questions the parents may raise about the child's future, especially if the questions are not relevant to the present situation. Questions about adult employment or adolescent sexual activity may be largely reflections of the parents' current generalized anxieties, and it is probably wise to refocus the discussion to the present and reserve such questions for later sessions. Indeed, prognostic statements should probably not be projected beyond the next three or four years of the child's life at most. This kind of discussion can perhaps be handled most constructively by stressing what the child may be able to accomplish in that time with proper training and stimulation. Later sessions may include more specific estimates of the child's future functioning level, if reasonable evidence emerges on which they can be based.

There may be a temptation for the social worker to minimize the extent of the child's retardation, particularly with parents of a profoundly retarded child. There may also be an inclination to soften the diagnosis in order to reduce the parents' anxiety and dismay. Whatever the motivation, minimizing the problem can lead only to later disappointment and further misunderstanding. Although the parents need not be confronted immediately with the whole picture, the diagnostic impressions of the team should be given to them with sufficient accuracy to foster the development of a healthy pattern of adaptation to reality. The social worker may find that the most natural way of informing the parents is to follow their own questions. "Will he ever walk?" can lead into an exploration of the skills and developmental levels required for walking, and the staff's impressions of the child's current abilities in these areas. This, in turn, may promote a discussion of the kind of training program that would encourage developing these abilities further. The social worker may also plan future conferences for the parents with the nurse, psychologist, or educator, to explore these questions and other pertinent issues more fully.

The most constructive emphasis for the informing interviewer is that the diagnostic conclusions are not an end, but rather a beginning step in the development of a treatment program for encouraging the child's development and the family's well-being. There will, of course, be some parents who refuse to accept the proposed help either for the child or for themselves. Others may attempt to utilize the diagnostic information given them to reach an impulsive resolution to their conflicting feelings and attitudes. For example, parents who have been considering institutional placement for the child may try to resolve their conflicts overhastily, in order to experience the relief of making a decision one way or another. Even if the parents are eager to make a quick decision, a series of subsequent meetings should be planned, if possible, to discuss the realities of the situation and the possible effects of the decision on the family. Direct advice should be avoided in the informing interview, and, in fact, in subsequent sessions as well. Only the parents can really make the actual decisions about what to do with their child. They are entitled, however, to all the information available to help them form a realistic appraisal of the situation and to help them in the decision-making process.

Some parents object specifically to certain aspects of the information given in the informing interview. They may state, for example, that the child was frightened during the examinations and did not perform as well as he does at home with his family. At this point, such reactions do not represent a challenge to be met and overcome. Achieving a shared understanding may require a number of sessions which emphasize open discussion rather than authoritarian insistence. The degree of success of the informing process can be measured by the extent of the parents' realistic acceptance of their child's retardation, and their hopes for at least some reasonably constructive solution to the child's problems and their own. Increasing awareness of the child's specific strengths and weaknesses is best achieved through the parents' involvement in his actual training and in later counseling and guidance sessions. The informing interview, like the diagnostic process itself, is merely a beginning phase in helping the child develop whatever abilities he can and assisting the parents to accept the tragedy of retardation as realistically as possible.

CHAPTER 3

Treatment Programs
for the Child

The development and implementation of a suitable treatment program for the retarded infant is based on a series of interrelated assumptions about human development. It is assumed, first, that maturation is not a simple unfolding of genetic potentialities, but a process that is intimately involved in the interaction of the developing individual and the external and internal environment. The view that maturation is solely or even primarily dependent on endowment has recently come under severe criticism, and the prevailing viewpoint emphasizes the essential contribution of environmental input to the achievement of maturational or developmental milestones. This emphasis may be somewhat less important for the normal than the retarded infant, since the former can generally utilize the usual stimuli in the environment to obtain much of the stimulation he needs. However, the retarded infant, because of defective motor or perceptual abilities, cannot do so. His development must be carefully fostered, nurtured, and stimulated.

The rationale for setting up a training program for the retarded infant also rests on the assumption that a crucial period of learning is the first three years of a child's life, the foundations for future achievement being laid in infancy. The infant must therefore be provided with the kinds of experiences on which subsequent learning can be based. The specific kinds of experiences that are most facilitating for learning as well as maturation in the retarded infant are still insufficiently understood. We can only assume that the best course is to provide him with the kinds of stimulation that approximate the level of stimulation the intact infant receives. This presents numerous problems and requires a highly individualized approach, since the retarded infant may suffer from a lack of the necessary stimulation for many different reasons.

The retarded infant's basic perceptual mechanisms may be defective, thus limiting the stimuli he can receive. This, in turn, may result in failure to instigate motor responses that would, if present, elicit stimulation from the environment. For example, a child who cannot visually integrate his perception of his mother's face, or who cannot blink or coo or babble in response to her, may not be touched and picked up as often as the necessary level of stimulation for him would require. Sometimes the child's perceptual mechanisms are intact, but his motor responses are defective. This, too, can have much the same limiting results, delaying or even preventing the child from reaching the usual developmental milestones. The interaction between the infant's faulty sensory and motor mechanisms may also hamper or prevent these achievements. Walking, for example, is a basic motor response that may be seriously delayed because of inadequate perceptual feedback.

These and other considerations predicate that a suitable program of training and stimulation for the retarded infant should contain many stimuli in perceptual and motor areas, presented to the child with more than average intensity and frequency. In order to achieve this, both the child and the environment must be actively manipulated, so that the input resembles that which the normal infant receives as closely as possible. The detrimental effects of understimulation of the normal infant are already well known and documented. The effects of understimulation of the retarded infant can be catastrophic.

While an appropriate program for the retarded infant needs to be planned and supervised by professional personnel, it is still the parents who are the infant's chief teacher, since it is through them that the child's program is primarily conducted. The parents are thus the most important members of the treatment team. Quite often, they will require professional help to enable them to assume and maintain this role. Part of their therapy may be their actual involvement in the child's training, their conferences with the members of the treatment team, and, more directly, participation in individual or group psychotherapy. Appropriate treatment for the child involves many areas, including medical, nursing, communication, and educational assistance. However, educational guidance and group or individual psychotherapy should also be available for parents and siblings where necessary, if the overall goals of the program are to be achieved.

In many cases, it is the infant's parents and siblings who can be regarded as the primary patients, particularly if the child is profoundly retarded, with a poor prognosis for future development. Since training for such a child will very probably meet with only minimal success, the major therapeutic goals are often best directed toward helping the family adapt realistically to the child's severe limitations and unpromising future. Since every child and every family has distinct needs, every program must be unique. The individualized plan for treatment first projected at the diagnostic staff conference must undergo a continuous process of modification as the child's abilities increase, the parents' needs change, and new decisions about the child's future are made or old ones are reconsidered. With adequate planning, coordination, and flexibility, a multidisciplinary treatment program based on the special needs of the child and the family can do much to increase the well-being of both. Such a treatment program is described in this chapter.

MEDICAL TREATMENT

The retarded child needs the general health care that all children require. However, in the sections that follow such general health considerations are largely omitted because of their easy availability in the pediatric literature. More technical information is also not included because of its highly specialized nature. The emphasis here is therefore on some of the special medical needs of retarded children.

The most effective form of medical management and treatment for the mentally retarded child generally includes a regularly scheduled pediatric examination and review at least twice yearly. Etiological factors that may be uncovered will sometimes point to the most effective forms of therapy: for example, whether medical or surgical procedures are indicated. At these examinations, the results of previously prescribed medication and treatment can also be evaluated and modified, as indicated. In addition, if a nurse is conducting the child's home training program she can participate in these pediatric examinations, becoming more familiar with his medical status and thus better able to understand the limiting effect of the pathological factors he exhibits upon his development. A sound on-going health program for the child, in which his physical strengths as well as his physical weaknesses are identified, can be established, reviewed, or brought up to date at these times.

Guidance to the parents on problems of feeding, growth, development, training, and discipline is often of primary importance. Minor and major illnesses must be considered. Poor dietary or hygienic care must be corrected in order to help prevent subsequent illnesses. Possibilities such as uremia, obesity, malnutrition, acute or chronic infections, and possible metabolic disturbances must be identified and treated.

Immunization procedures should be instituted, but with the precautions recommended by the American Academy of Pediatrics (222) carefully observed. These precautions can be summarized as follows: Cerebral damage in the infant warrants delay in starting immunization. If there are severe febrile reactions, with or without convulsions, active immunization procedures should not be initiated until after the child is a year of age. Single antigens rather than the usual multiple antigens are recommended, and fractional doses should be used.

Drug therapies. Retarded children are, of course, subject to the usual childhood illnesses, and in some instances they are even more vulnerable than the normal child. Now, however, there are available treatment procedures for some of their areas of special weakness. For example, leukemia and upper respiratory illness, which occur more often in the mongoloid child than in the normal, are now treated effectively with antibiotics and other newer drugs, as well as blood transfusions. Medical treatment for cases of lead or other metal poisoning that might lead to mental retardation is being increasingly used successfully. The judicious use of drugs affecting the behavioral reactions of retarded children has also been most helpful. For example, a common disturbance in such children is hyperactivity, which is sometimes associated with hyperkinesis. In treating a hyperactive child, the physician may prescribe "tranquilizers" from various categories, such as anti-histamines, which may have a sedative action, or perhaps even stimulants such as amphetamines, which, in some instances, have the paradoxical effect of lowering the child's activity level. The results of such treatment can vary from the negligible to the dramatic. The relatively rare occurrence of adverse side effects does not constitute a serious deterrent to therapy of this kind, although the possibility does imply that close observation and management are needed.

Medical treatment is also quite effective in treating convulsive disorders, which are encountered so frequently in retarded infants. Currently, the physician has many drugs available for this purpose, ranging from the ubiquitous phenobarbital to the more sophisticated anti-convulsants with more specific goals. The type of medication to be prescribed for the particular child depends upon the nature of the convulsive disorder—whether it is associated with infantile spasms, petit mal, or grand mal. Sometimes combinations of drugs, as well as methods and times of their administration, are varied systematically until the optimum combination and dosage are established. An additional guide may be the electroencephalogram, which may reflect the neurophysiological status of the child. However, his own responses are still a major criterion for judging the efficacy of particular medications. Obviously, the management of a convulsive disorder is best left to a physician trained and experienced in that particular area of neuropathology. Many young children are highly resistant to taking medication by mouth. This may be a particular problem with a young retarded child, since it is not possible to explain the necessity of taking the medication in a way that is meaningful to him. There are, however, several practical approaches to this problem by which it can be overcome. The medication can, for example, be concealed in some form of food or liquid that the child particularly likes, or he can be offered a special delicacy or preferred treat of some kind as a reward for taking it.

Special dietary regimens. Recent research in inborn errors of metabolism has uncovered a number of previously undiagnosed metabolic disorders, some of which are treatable by special diets. In some cases the diet is monotonous and even unpleasant, and the child is apt to become resistive, so that management can be quite difficult. However, the results, as in phenylpyruvic oligophrenia (PKU), have sometimes been rewarding. Hopefully, the eventual solution for this category of metabolic disorders will be found in genetic research and prevention. In the meantime, however, the physician must rely on chemical and physiological findings that may point to dietary and medical therapies.

Surgical procedures. For some diagnostic categories associated with retardation the newer surgical developments offer helpful procedures to alleviate or improve the status of the child. The recent strides in heart surgery, for example, have been especially helpful to children with septal defects which do not heal spontaneously, pathology that is relatively common among mongoloid children, and those with multiple congenital defects. Reparative or plastic surgery can often correct such congenital defects as cleft palates and lip and ear deformities. Surgery can also eliminate or at least improve some cranial or craniofacial malformations, such as microcephaly, owing to premature closure of sutures, and can be used to arrest or correct some forms of hydrocephaly and meningocele formations associated with spinal column malformations. Other special types of surgery are frequently employed to assist an afflicted child. An ophthalmological surgeon may be able to correct muscle imbalance or remove congenital cataracts. Other less frequent forms of pathology, such as bone and muscle disabilities, may also require corrective surgery or orthopedic intervention. Nor in the light of these newer and sometimes more dramatic procedures should one forget the importance of older and more common ones, such as tonsillectomies or herniorrhaphies.

Ophthalmological procedures. An annual eye examination is strongly recommended for the older retarded child. If glasses are prescribed, it is important to make sure that they are comfortable and that the child actually wears them. It is wise to order two pairs in case one is broken and to fit them with elasticized bands that fit around the child's head. If the child resists wearing the glasses, it may be because the frames are too tight across the bridge of his nose or perhaps behind his ears. Most mildly or moderately retarded children with poor eyesight quickly realize how much the glasses improve their vision and are therefore willing to leave them on. The more severely retarded child, however, may need to be trained to wear glasses by having them put on for short periods during which he is carefully watched. Gradually, the periods are increased in frequency and duration. Optometric training is a technique that has proven of value for some older and less retarded children, but this approach, which involves special perceptual training, has not been made applicable to the younger and more retarded child. There are also some indications that while this kind of specialized training may be of value for certain diagnostic categories associated with retardation, it may perhaps not be suitable for retarded children in general.

Dental procedures. A dental appointment is advisable at least once a year for the somewhat older retarded child. Dental treatment for retarded children is often a difficult process. It is frequently necessary to hospitalize the child and put him under general anesthesia, a procedure that tends to make the family quite apprehensive, especially if the child has cardiac complications or brain damage. The parents may fear that the child will suffer further brain damage, have seizures, or even die. A discussion of the procedure and the actual extent of risk involved is usually indicated to minimize undue parental anxiety. A discussion of proper dental hygiene with the parents is also advisable. For many reasons, retarded children often have poor teeth and gums. Many parents find cleaning the child's teeth and stimulating his gums properly quite difficult to do regularly, and the child's own skill in this respect is apt to be very limited at first. He may swallow the toothpaste, be unable to use the toothbrush correctly, and have trouble rinsing his mouth. Sore and swollen gums are sometimes a side effect of certain medication he may need, so that brushing his teeth may be a painful procedure for him. Other dental problems needing special attention may result from continued soft diets or the phenomenon of tooth grinding, which is fairly common among retarded children.

Further corrective procedures. Of considerable importance in the therapeutic regimen prescribed for many retarded children is the use of special prosthetic appliances and the services of ancillary medical personnel. Prostheses may include corrective lenses, hearing aids, dental devices, hip and leg braces or harnesses, to name but a few of the more commonly employed devices. Physical therapy is particularly important in cases where there is evidence of neuromuscular imbalance. In such instances, abnormal muscular tone and deformity may be actually prevented by proper physical therapy. Correct posturing of the child may also avoid or at least considerably reduce the extent of deformities.

Genetic counseling. A complete treatment program for parents of a retarded child should include chromosomal analysis and genetic counseling for families where these procedures are applicable. If the physician believes that the child's retardation may be associated with a disorder of genetic origin, he can refer the parents to a specialized genetic counseling facility if the center does not offer such services itself. There are relatively few such facilities at present, their waiting lists are often long, and the costs are apt to be high. Nonetheless, such services are valuable where they are relevant. Even when specific genetic analysis is not available, it is still possible for the physician to counsel parents on the basis of the family history, the nature of the child's disorder, and the health status of the parents.

Parents of retarded children are understandably anxious about the implications of their retarded child's disorder for their own future children and for their grandchildren as well. The question of additional children is often a crucial decision for them, especially if the retarded child is their firstborn. This subject must be approached with great care and sensitivity by the physician. While some causes of retardation have a genetic basis, too often parents erroneously assume that their child's retardation is hereditary and have regretfully limited the size of their family because of their unwarranted fears. Many distortions and much misinformation may have entered into the decision. For example, one parent may actually blame the other's family for the supposed or real hereditary defect, which can easily lead to severe marital difficulties. For many parents, even the most careful reference to a genetic fault carries with it an implication of guilt and condemnation, creating feelings of revulsion and despair. Genetic information, then, must be very clearly and accurately stated, leaving as little room for misunderstanding or misinterpretation as possible.

Some parents harbor silent fears of a genetic or hereditary "taint," even though all the available evidence points to etiological factors arising during pregnancy, birth, or afterwards. Such fears can sometimes be allayed during a competent informing interview. In some cases it can clearly be stated that the child's disorder is *not* genetic, so that the parents need not be afraid of transmittal to future children or grandchildren. On the other hand, some disorders, such as Tay Sachs disease, phenylketonuria (PKU), and Hurler's syndrome, are genetically related. Probably the most frequent condition that involves chromosomal abnormality is mongolism. Recent research has isolated at least three distinct forms of chromosomal abnormalities, each of which has different implications for genetic counseling. In the most common form, the possibility of occurrence of the condition in a future child is as low as one in two hundred. In less common forms, such as translocation, the possibility of having a future child who will be similarly afflicted may increase to one out of three, with the additional possibility that, even if the child is normal himself, he may carry the translocation factor and affect his children. In view of the present limited availability of genetic laboratories, chromosomal analysis is hardly a routine procedure and should probably still be reserved for those parents who, on the basis of history or previous births in the family, can be considered "genetically suspect."

One of the more recent developments in the area of genetics is amniocentesis, a procedure which consists of studying cells obtained from the amniotic fluid to assess the unborn child's chromosomal status. If a genetic defect is found, the mother can be offered a therapeutic abortion in geographic areas where such procedures are legal. While chromosomal analysis, amniocentesis, and genetic counseling are basically techniques for the prevention of mental retardation, they also offer the physician an important treatment opportunity for advising and counseling the parents. Judicious use of the findings and the implications of the genetic studies can often help to allay unnecessary anxiety, replacing it with hope and constructive action.

The physician in the team. The physician can be particularly effective as a consultant to the nonmedical members of the interdisciplinary team. For example, it is often important for a teacher to consult a physician in order to understand the medical and behavioral problems of a particular child before he is placed in an educational setting. The teacher may also need to be fully aware of the child's physical abilities and disabilities before planning a suitable training program for him. A sound understanding of his physiological limitations can often help to avoid the frustrations inherent in trying to teach him tasks for which he is not ready. Further, an accurate appraisal of his physical status can also help to avert overprotection. For example, misunderstandings about the significance of a heart murmur may result in an unnecessarily restrictive program for a child who is quite capable of physical exertion, and who would actually benefit from it.

It is also most helpful for teachers to be aware of the specific symptoms of particular disabilities that they are likely to encounter in their retarded pupils. For example, children with cerebral dysrhythmias sometimes react to their internal discomfort with behavioral disturbances such as rocking or head banging. Overconcern on the part of the teacher may reinforce the child's self-destructive behavior and perhaps establish it as an attention-getting device or a way of showing rebelliousness and resentment. On the other hand, given adequate information and experience, an alert teacher is often the first to notice a child's petit mal seizures and report them to the physician, since the parents may have become accustomed to the child's slight tremors, eye blinking, shoulder shrugging, and momentary lapses into quiet, and consider such episodes as unimportant, if not actually normal.

Teachers of retarded children should also be reasonably knowledgeable about epilepsy, since it sometimes occurs in association with retardation. A teacher who has read about grand mal seizures but has neither seen them nor discussed them with a physician may bring a great deal of misinformation and mythology to her first direct experience with them. She may, in fact, dread the possibility of such an incident occurring in her classroom. Although it is perhaps impossible to eradicate this initial apprehension completely, the physician can help to allay it by showing the teacher the proper steps to take, thus giving her some feeling of control of the situation as well as teaching her how to help the child. In cases of uncontrolled laughing, crying, or screaming, the teacher may have to permit the seizure to run its course, concentrating on preventing the child from injuring himself or others. During such an episode the child may begin to throw things quite violently, push his fists through a window, or beat them against the walls. Verbal commands to the child are useless under these circumstances, since in such seizures, unlike the temper tantrums that they resemble, the child has temporarily lost his self-control. Afterwards, he may be so exhausted that requests and instructions will still fail to reach him. After the seizure, he should therefore be permitted to lie down and rest or sleep as long as he wishes.

It is especially important that the teacher is specifically told about each child's medication schedules and their possible side effects. She should, in fact, keep a daily record of the behavior of a child who is receiving medication, particularly noting changes in alertness, motor abilities, bowel and bladder control, or mood and energy level. This record is a valuable guide for the physician who is prescribing the medication. Many drugs for children with, say, dysrhythmic activity or metabolic disorders, are administered largely on an empirical basis, and only detailed observation of the child's behavioral reactions can gauge the actual effects of the drug. On the basis of a carefully written report by the child's teacher, the physician may want to change or alter the dosage of the prescribed medication. Sometimes the medication can be gradually diminished and perhaps entirely eliminated, if a progressive report of his behavior warrants it. Good behavioral reporting on the teacher's part can also prevent the child from continuing on medication for which he has poor tolerance or which is ineffective.

The psychiatrist is among the medical specialists who can make a significant contribution to the child's training program. The teacher can function best in her more therapeutic role if she has an adequate understanding of the psychodynamic factors involved in the interactions of the child and his whole environment. It is in helping to formulate these psychodynamic constellations that the psychiatrist, as well as the psychologist and the social worker, can render major service to the retarded infant and his family. Psychotherapy can perhaps be considered chiefly as a possible treatment modality for the older and higher functioning retarded child. However, for the younger and lower functioning child, a well-trained, dedicated teacher is often more effective, since she can offer the child a small group setting, in a suitable environment and with a special set of activities carefully adapted to his special needs. The setting, the frequency of the meeting, the level of mutuality, the nature of the involvement, and the position of the teacher in the situation are all potential therapeutic tools.

The most comprehensive approach to therapeutic help for the retarded child, as with all children, emphasizes working with the family. In some centers such services for the parents are provided by clinical psychologists, while others utilize social workers working under psychiatric supervision. Still others employ the psychiatrist for conducting the therapeutic activities with the parents. Further, in situations where medically oriented implementation and supervision of individual and group therapy is indicated, the psychiatrist can make a substantial contribution to the mental health of the family. It is evident that no one discipline can hope to acquire all the knowledge and skill necessary to deal adequately with the retarded infant and his family, giving maximum benefit to both. Success will, in large measure, depend on the judicious use of all available diagnostic and therapeutic resources, from the chemical laboratory to electronic devices, from the geneticist to the pathologist, from the teacher to the physician, and from all members of the team to one another.

THE HOME TRAINING PROGRAM

The basic emphases in a practical home training program for the retarded infant are on his physical needs and developmental achievements. The core curriculum stresses basic child-care techniques such as feeding, bathing, and dressing, adapted to the needs of an infant who requires special maturational assistance. It would perhaps be best to have this program carried out by a registered nurse who has a background in public health nursing and training in developmental psychology, and who works under direct medical supervision. It would be particularly helpful if this nurse also assisted at the medical diagnostic evaluation and accompanied the parent and child to the subsequent medical follow-up examinations. The chief function of the nurse in carrying out the infant home training program is to provide a systematic plan for training and stimulating the child, with guidance for the parents in implementing the specific training procedures. It should be noted, however, that while the person who conducts the home training program is designated as a nurse in the sections that follow, other possibilities are discussed later.

Planning the program. The parents, as the primary teachers of the infant should, if possible, become skilled in specific training exercises for the child. The nurse must offer the parents support and encouragement in this difficult undertaking, giving them precise and detailed instructions while helping to minimize their anxiety. For example, a parent may be reluctant to conduct the exercises that are prescribed to develop the child's muscles, fearing that he may be injured or demonstrate the actual extent of his disabilities. Through actual demonstrations with the child, supplemented by sensitive encouragement, the nurse can help the parent participate more comfortably in the training program, despite the inevitable frustrations and disappointments.

The home training program for the retarded infant needs to be planned with limited goals set for each visit. For example, one session might emphasize holding the child correctly. Another might focus on presenting a toy, and still another on associating sound with the toy. A series of short-term goals are thus established, to be achieved on a step-by-step basis. The family's willingness to work consistently with the child, and their patience with very slow and limited results, are vital to ultimate success and are often dependent on their hopes for future achievement possibilities. These positive expectations can be self-fulfilling, since the child's smallest response may provide the reinforcement needed for the parents to participate with more enthusiasm in training. This, in turn, can result in further gains. It often facilitates these gains if the nurse encourages the parents to establish a routine of frequent, planned periods of interaction with the child. The mother who follows planned routines will find them quite similar in content to the care required by a normal child who is, however, considerably younger than the retarded child whose training she is conducting.

When the retarded child is fed, the mother holds him, talks to him, and cuddles him like a newborn infant. Frequently, the retarded child does not demand as much attention as does a normal child of the same age. Instead of crying to be held, for example, he may remain quiet and willing to sleep through much of the day and night. The mother may therefore need active encouragement to help her understand the need to provide extra stimulation to this infant who, in this formative period of life, must be introduced to the world outside the crib. The mother may have to bring the child into the world of sounds, textures, movements, objects, and people. The child may need to be held, rocked, cooed to, played with, tickled, rubbed, and stroked quite frequently, so that he becomes aware of external sources of affection and pleasure. The mother may, for instance, facilitate this awareness by placing a string of attractive toys over the child's crib. She may play records, carry the child around the house, or talk to him as she handles him during the daily activities. Learning depends on growth, development, and experience. The retarded child needs to have external stimuli patiently presented to him again and again, to help him achieve even the very beginnings of conceptual development.

A major factor in developing an individualized home training program is an adequate understanding of the attitudes of the family members toward the retarded infant. A parent may, for example, recognize the infant's need for stimulation in the development of cognitive or perceptual skills but be unaware of his affectional needs. All children need a warm, affectionate atmosphere for optimal development of their potentialities. Such an atmosphere represents the necessary emotional climate for maximum growth. Without such positive interest and concern, the child is deprived of many important learning experiences and fails to develop trust in his surroundings. Without consistent encouragement, stimulation becomes haphazard and fragmentary. All infants depend on those around them to bring the world to them. Failure to present a sufficiently stimulating environment to the retarded infant, in particular, can be a severe deterrent to his emotional and physical development.

Child-rearing practices. The family's existing child-rearing practices need careful study to help in the development of the training program. Parents' techniques vary as widely as do their attitudes. Many family child-rearing practices are the products of cultural tradition, economic necessity, parental emotions, neighborly advice, and often superstitions as well. Often, a parent jumps to inaccurate conclusions. For example, if one child was successfully taught a particular skill in one way, the parent may apply the same instructional process indiscriminately to other children, without consideration of their different needs and abilities. Specific home training procedures to be instituted must therefore be carefully and fully reviewed with the parents, the type and depth of the explanations depending on their particular intellectual level and cultural background. One mother, for example, may have a real need to understand the theoretical bases of child development, while such explanations would be more likely to bore or confuse another mother.

The visits of the nurse to the home should be leisurely enough to allow the parents sufficient time for discussions of whatever problems they may want to raise. One mother, perhaps, may wonder how best to explain the retarded infant's condition to an older child, or possibly to a neighbor. Another mother may be concerned about spending too much time with the retarded child, to the neglect of the other children in the family. Questions are sometimes raised that are best handled as leads toward a therapeutic relationship for the parent with a psychologist, social worker, or psychiatrist at the center. It is often the nurse who forms the bridge to this type of service to the parents.

Feeding and nutrition. The infant's world centers around feeding and other aspects of physical comfort. He senses love, acceptance, anger, and irritation in terms of responses to his demands for food and general physical care. While special feeding problems may result from the infant's retardation, they may also reflect the parents' emotional problems in dealing with him. Helping the parents understand the importance of their roles in meeting the child's needs, and assisting them to provide sufficient emotional support as well as proper feeding and nutrition, is one of the most important goals of the home training program.

Working under pediatric supervision, the nurse provides a major source of help by setting up a sound nutritional program for the child, whose early feeding may well be complicated by abdominal spasms, seizure patterns, vomiting, and swallowing and sucking difficulties. The pediatrician determines whether medication or food supplements should be prescribed in order to facilitate feeding and balance the infant's diet. The nurse explains their purpose and possible side effects to the parents. She also asks about changes the parents may notice. For example, sudden weight gain or increase in fluid intake and urination may be symptoms of metabolic disorders and should be brought to the pediatrician's attention. An undernourished child also needs pediatric study, perhaps resulting in a change of formula or a supplementary feeding schedule.

The mother's state of mind as she feeds the child is of utmost importance. A mother who is suffering from a sense of despair because of her baby's retardation may be reluctant to come into close, affectionate physical contact with him. She may, for example, want to feed him while he is lying down. The nurse may then have to explain that feeding is easier for the mother and more reassuring for the child if she holds him in her arms, keeping his head raised and supported. The child's "feeding personality" may be quickly apparent to the nurse. Some infants are obviously hungry, suck rapidly, finish quickly, and cry for more. Others will dawdle and suck intermittently. It is generally wiser and simpler for the mother to adapt to the child's feeding style, rather than insisting that the infant conform to her own preferences. Progress is facilitated if the child's needs are met at each step, helping him to proceed to the next.

The child who can suck and swallow may be introduced to a cup by first being spoonfed his milk. Adding cereal to the milk gives the formula a thicker consistency and makes the process easier to handle. Often a retarded child can be given strained baby foods, cereals, fruits, and vegetables at about the same ages as a normal child. Even when the child has no teeth, his gums are usually hard enough for him to begin eating strained junior foods when he is chronologically ready. Dietary suggestions, however, must take the family's cultural and economic background into consideration. Some parents cannot afford items such as strained meats. Others may be reluctant to feed the child foods they themselves dislike, and religious dietary laws may forbid giving certain foods to him. Sometimes a mother will object to giving the child a particular food if an illness actually unrelated to it happened to occur when the child had eaten it on a previous occasion. Individual factors such as these must all be given due consideration in dietary planning and advising.

Generally speaking, new food textures are most easily introduced during the first two years of the child's life. Later on, the child's preferences and habits are apt to be too rigid to change easily, and he may react to new tastes and unfamiliar foods with great resistance. A hungry child, of course, is more receptive to new foods, and it may even be necessary to deprive a child to some extent of his accustomed soft diet in order to introduce harder foods and help him learn to chew. Sometimes the child can be helped to improve his chewing by imitating his mother as she shows him how she chews, while moving the child's jaws in a chewing motion with her hands as he watches.

Parents of retarded children often continue to feed the child themselves well beyond the time when he could be successfully taught self-feeding. A mother may fear that the child's attempts to feed himself will be too messy and time consuming. She may also be afraid that the child will choke, or otherwise injure himself. Children who can sit without support are usually ready to begin feeding themselves. They may begin by eating dry cereal, chocolate, pieces of bread, toast, raisins, pretzels, or carrots with their hands. To teach the child to handle a spoon, the mother should sit next to him, since he may find it difficult to transpose the actions of someone who is facing him. With the mother alongside him, it is also easier for the child to "help" her dip spoon into the cereal, lift it by placing his hand on his mother's, and finally put it into his mouth. Slowly the child learns to imitate these actions, and finally to perform them himself.

There will, however, be many accidents. It is essential that the family recognize and accept the fact that spilling and splattering are part of learning self-feeding, and that punishment or obvious displeasure will merely discourage the child from trying to improve. It may be better for the family's morale to have a child who is just learning to feed himself eat in advance of the rest. In this way discomfort and criticism are minimized, and the mother also has a chance to give the child maximal assistance. At first she should be reasonably available for help throughout the feeding period. She should not, however, constantly hover over the child as though she were always expecting the worst. It is best for her to be near but to occupy herself with other things, allowing the child to experiment and learn by doing, but be ready to help him when necessary. When the child has developed sufficient feeding skills, eating with the family has the advantage of fostering a sense of social participation. The first experiences of eating with the family can be made more successful for everyone if the child is given foods he has already learned to manage successfully, thus minimizing the chances of accidents.

Overweight in a retarded child is often the result of poor diet combined with lack of proper exercise. Careful dietary regulation is the beginning of effective treatment in such cases. A "snack" diet of ice cream, cookies, and soda is all too frequent with retarded children, since it avoids the time-consuming and often quite difficult task of instituting normal eating habits. However, such a diet interferes seriously with good nutrition. Observing small groups of children at mealtime at the center is a useful way to introduce the mother to better feeding techniques. There are also some parental attitudes that foster overfeeding. For example, some mothers may actually be unaware that obesity in infancy and childhood is undesirable. Some cultures, in fact, equate "fat" with "loved" and "well-nourished." However, overfeeding is a harmful practice with any child, regardless of how it may be interpreted. Clarifying issues such as this is part of the nurse's function in working with the mother.

Exercise. Retarded children are not necessarily more fragile than other children. Nevertheless, their neurological and physical impairments tend to induce parental fears that exercise and even locomotion and exploration will cause further damage. Consequently, many retarded children are needlessly deprived of necessary opportunities to use their bodies effectively. They therefore remain sedentary and passive and fail to develop the motor coordination needed for crawling and walking. This limits even further the variety and intensity of environmental stimulation that they receive. Many retarded infants need planned exercise and continual encouragement to help them develop the physical abilities that will, in turn, permit more active exploration of the environment. A practical daily program of suitable physical activity to develop musculature and encourage movement must be planned for the child with special regard for his particular problem areas. Some retarded children have localized physical impairments, such as weakness or paralysis of arms or legs. In others, the tongue and muscles involved in chewing and swallowing may be affected. Specific exercise of the affected areas may strengthen the muscles and avoid atrophy. Such exercise programs can often be successfully carried out by the parent with the guidance of the nurse.

Exercises suitable for the retarded infant are necessarily simple. The mother may, for example, merely encourage the child to thrash about while she gently massages his arms, legs, back, and abdomen. More specifically, with the child on his back and his arms lifted above his head, the mother can stretch his arms up, bring them gently down to his sides, extend them out sideways, and place them across his chest. With the child still on his back, she can also stretch his legs out straight, gently push them against her arm, and then release them. The child's legs can also be bent back in a knee-bend position, then pushed out, pulled up, and pushed back again. The child's ankles can be gently rotated. His head can be carefully moved from side to side, forward and backward, and rotated slowly. The mother can also massage the child's neck and provide support for his head when he is sitting up.

Sitting. Eventually, most infants will be able to hold their heads up without support. When the child has reached this stage, he is usually ready for a series of exercises that teach him the movements needed for sitting up alone. With the child on his back, the mother can hold both his hands, slowly pull him up to a sitting position, leave him in this position for a moment, and then gently lower him again. It may be necessary to continue to support the child's head for some time after this exercise is introduced. When the child is able to sit without support, he can be encouraged to remain sitting by placing attractive and interesting toys within his easy reach. His own preferred toys are best for this purpose.

The ability to sit alone is an important developmental achievement in the series of successive stages in which the child becomes increasingly involved with his environment. By sitting up and reaching out, he has increased the range of his world and achieved a broadened visual field which can slowly encompass larger and larger areas. The ability to sit unsupported is often acquired quite late by the retarded child and much slow, careful, and patient work with adult help may be needed before it is definitely established. Even when the child seems to have developed the skill, the next step should not be introduced for a while. Regression may be frequent. Even if the child finally succeeds in sitting up unassisted, he may be quite incapable of doing so on the following day. Each achievement needs to be practiced repeatedly before work on the next sequential step is begun.

Standing. Children who can continue to sit unassisted after being positioned by the adult are generally ready to use some initiative of their own. To encourage this, a low, steady bar, within the child's reach while he is sitting, may provide the stimulus needed for his own first attempts at standing alone. The mother can help to train him for this step by taking his hands while he is sitting and gently pulling him to his feet, allowing him to contribute as much to the action as possible. Later, he may try to stand without parental support. Most parents correctly consider standing a major achievement. The child's reaction, however, may be quite different, since children who can stand are often incapable of the coordination needed for sitting down again. The child may therefore be terrified by finding himself in this new and precarious position, and the mother may find him screaming with fright. To avoid this, she need only hold the child's hands and help him down slowly, bending his knees as he goes down. Alternately, she can put the child's hand on the bar, if one has been provided, and assist him in lowering himself. Sitting down may well require more practice than standing.

Crawling. A child who can sit unsupported and has some confidence in his ability to balance will usually try to broaden his areas of exploration spontaneously by developing some form of locomotion, usually crawling. Crawling methods vary widely. The child may "swim" on his stomach, propel himself by pulling up his knees and pushing himself along on his elbows, or bounce along on his buttocks. Some children will use hands and knees, moving the right arm and leg forward simultaneously, followed by the left. More advanced crawling, with the left arm moving with the right leg and the right arm with the left leg, tends to develop spontaneously in a child with good neuromuscular integration. Most retarded children, however, must be taught to do it. In training for it, the mother moves the child's arm and opposite leg simultaneously in practice sessions, until the child adopts this form of crawling himself. Meanwhile, the parent should not insist upon any particular crawling method, since such limitations might seriously hamper the child's exploratory movements.

A child uses locomotion to get somewhere, to do something, to see something. This independent curiosity and the use of action to satisfy it can be encouraged by allowing the child to use his own locomotive technique, awkward though it may seem. The crawling period also presents excellent opportunities for teaching the child body awareness and for developing basic spatial language concepts. The child crawls *under, around,* and *over* things. He puts his hands *into* things and takes them *out of* places. These activities, many of which need to be assisted by the parent in any case, can be used still further to help the child to associate words with actions and places. Where the child can associate words with activities, the mother may find that his activities can be directed by words. Instead of pulling the child to his feet, lifting him off a chair, or dragging him away from the stove, the mother may eventually be able to substitute directions such as "stand up," "get down," and "stop."

Walking. The next step is walking, at least for the child who has no serious skeletal or neuromuscular disorders and who can use objects such as a chair or a bar to pull himself to his feet. His first attempts may be quite spontaneous. If he is standing and wants to move toward a nearby object, he may cling to a piece of furniture and slide or shuffle toward his goal. This initial effort is his first attempt to walk unassisted. A retarded child is taught to walk in the same way as a normal child: the adult holds the child's hands to provide balance and encouragement. However, this is a difficult process even for a normal child and becomes an extremely complex learning experience for retarded children. Their frequent visual, motor, and spatial dysfunctions make walking a skill that requires many months of training and practice. Every small variation, such as stepping over a small object, is a new ability to be practiced and finally mastered.

The parents must be very patient during the learning-to-walk period and willing to let the child work unassisted in spite of frequent tumbles. He will develop self-confidence only by trying, failing, and finally succeeding on his own. The walking stage is one in which many retarded children become very hesitant, lacking in self-confidence, and painfully shy if parental sanctions overly limit their actions. Overprotectiveness in connection with the child's attempts to walk may also hamper further motor activity and development. Parental fears that the child may become too active and harm himself may result in confining the child too often and too long to a carriage or a crib. Other essentially distructive parental attitudes include regarding the retarded child as a helpless baby, and thus reflecting unconscious or sometimes even conscious desires to keep him dependent. Some parents may feel inadequate to cope with an active child and encourage passivity, believing that caring for the child will be easier if he retains a simple, restricted daily living pattern. Walking is thus seen as a threat to parental control and comfort. Some parents, in fact, may confine the child to a small area long after any such restrictions are necessary.

Common sense dictates some limitations on any child's locomotive exploration, and all parents are wise to put valuable possessions, drugs, poisons, and sharp objects out of his reach until he has learned that he can safely play with certain things and not with others. However, children like to explore drawers, closets, and cabinets, and safe play objects put within easy reach in a particular place in the house show the child that this is "his place," where he can explore freely. When he has learned this, he may be ready to be taught to put his things away after playing with them.

Verbal reinforcement. Throughout all activities, the mother is encouraged to talk to the child. Even when the accompanying words may have little or no effect on the actual performance of the activity, verbal contact with the child is still important. It is often particularly helpful if the mother accompanies some activities with a few related descriptive words. The importance of such verbal reinforcement is illustrated by the following brief description of this phase of a home training program:

> Charles S., a 26-month-old mongoloid boy, had most of the characteristic physical stigmata of mongolism. His musculature was flaccid, his grasp was loose, his sucking was poor, his head did not turn easily, and his tongue drooped from his mouth. His special home training program was designed to bring the environment to him in an ordered, even, and patterned manner, suited to his particular problem areas.
>
> Mrs. S. understood that training for Charles must emphasize awareness of the environment and provide him with a repetitive pattern of situations with rewards for appropriate response. Verbal descriptions were continually coupled with the actual activities to which they referred, such as, "Charles sits up," "Charles lies down," "Charles gets washed," and "Charles eats lunch." She propped the child in a sitting position and brought toys directly to him. She placed his hands around various objects and deliberately made different sounds near him. Each successful action he made himself—for example, inserting a peg in a hole—was rewarded with a hug and words of praise. This "programmed" instruction helped him to relate to his environment, and to ready him for participating in a group program at the center.

Supplementary group instruction. The specific procedures that are set up in a home training program for the retarded infant are often tedious for the family, and the meager results are frequently discouraging. The mother, on whom the major burden usually falls, may be further distressed by fear of depriving her other children and her husband of their fair share of her time and energy. It is particularly difficult for many families to maintain the high level of motivation that such a program demands for a long period of time, perhaps for years. Sometimes a sense of isolation and martyrdom sets in. The use of group teaching is often a viable and practical antidote to such reactions. Though most of the training is still conducted in the home, it may be advisable to schedule regular group sessions at the center, where groups of four or five mothers can meet with the staff for further help in handling their children.

Group participation will often dramatically decrease the parent's sense of isolation and offers considerable support and practical help as well. Mothers who have already solved a specific problem with their own child can describe and demonstrate the techniques they used, thus helping other mothers who are faced with a similar situation. The atmosphere of the group itself can be positive and helpful. To achieve this, however, it is important to select the members of the group very carefully. The basic selection variables found in one center to be most useful for this kind of training group were the age and level of functioning of the infant, since the parents of children who are comparable in these respects have similar training problems. These groups may also pave the way for subsequent parent therapy groups conducted by a social worker, psychologist, or psychiatrist. Meanwhile, the sessions represent a valuable adjunctive service to the home training program, helping to maintain motivation, stimulate ideas, and decrease feelings of isolation.

Frequency of home visits. An important consideration in the development of a home training program is the frequency and intensity of services that will be most helpful to the child and the family. This can be determined only on the basis of individual need, plus such practical considerations as the best use of professional time and the availability of the family. The comprehensive goals of the overall program require considerable time on the part of the mother in particular. The parents may also be asked to meet with the social worker and speech therapist at the center and make periodic visits to various staff members for reevaluations and reconsiderations. Specific emergencies and a number of special problems may require additional meetings. The home training program thus requires a great deal of professional as well as parental time.

In considering how best to allocate staff time, it can generally be said that specific clinical treatment services for the child should be maximum for the mildly or moderately retarded infant and minimum for the severely or profoundly retarded child. Usually, the most effective overall program for the latter involves relatively few professional home visits, a limited number of sessions in speech and language training for the child at the center, and major concentration on help for the family. The size of the family and the ages of the siblings are important considerations in planning for this, since the mother with other young children, for example, frequently has less freedom to keep appointments. On the other hand, if the siblings are older and mentally and emotionally available, their participation in a special educational or counseling group for brothers and sisters of retarded children may well be very helpful for the family as a unit.

Personnel for a home training program. While a registered nurse with the special training described previously is probably best suited to take charge of the home training program, there are other possibilities. In fact, no single discipline is prepared at present to cope with all of the activities involved in the conduct of such a program. The ideal person would, in fact, be part physician, nurse, educator, psychologist, and social worker. Regardless of the person's initial discipline, then, special training in allied fields is necessary. Further, specialists in education, psychology, social work, speech and language development, and medicine must be available for consultation and supervision, when needed. The problems facing the retarded child and his family do not respect strict boundaries of traditional professional practice.

There are a number of possible alternatives to a nurse as the key person in the home training of retarded infants. A nursery school teacher with some knowledge of and experience with the physical problems and care of the retarded infant, for example, might be highly suitable. It might even be possible to train paraprofessionals for the purpose, provided the training is adequate and sufficient supervision is maintained throughout. The term "infant instructor" (23) has been coined for one who is specially equipped to carry out such special programs. New specialties of this kind may well arise under the impetus of increasing need.

Possibilities of operant conditioning. Recently, considerable interest has been directed toward the application of operant conditioning techniques for retarded children. Though these techniques are hardly new, recent research has suggested that a particular systematic application can result in a more effective training program. Most of the work in this area has been done in residential settings, where it is more feasible to achieve the patterned control of the environment required by this technique. Psychologists have also developed techniques that show some promise of success with severely and profoundly retarded children similar to that which has been achieved with the moderately and mildly retarded.

Conditioning techniques have not been so successfully adapted to infant and preschool retarded children who are living at home and being treated at a day training center. There are some indications, however, that some techniques for the control of specific symptoms such as head banging and biting may prove successful even in the day treatment situation. For this, the active and consistent cooperation of the parents is required. They must participate in a carefully controlled series of responses designed to reward the child for the desired behaviors and extinguish the undesirable ones. Such programmed responses may sometimes conflict with the more natural and affectionate parental inclinations, particularly if procedures require denial of reward or punishment as well as positive reinforcement, but the conditioning program must be adhered to in a systematic manner. Research in this area is continuing, and it is possible that in the near future a greater systematic application of at least some of the techniques of operant conditioning may well be available for retarded infants.

THE SCHOOL PROGRAM

Classroom education for the young retarded child is in many ways a continuation and extension of his home training program. However, the classroom situation provides the child with a new learning environment, offers more formal training in basic skills, and emphasizes group experiences. In preparing the child for the transition to the classroom, the nurse can be particularly helpful if she brings the child to the center with increasing frequency toward the latter part of his period of home training. After this preliminary orientation, the child is prepared to progress through a series of planned steps in frequency of school attendance ranging from twice weekly to daily for half a day and finally to full-day classroom sessions.

A suitable school curriculum for the young retarded child is based upon many factors, including his age, level of maturity and adaptation, ability to separate from parents, verbal and nonverbal communications skills, distractibility, kind and degree of special impairments, and level of physical development. A program must be individualized as much as possible and designed to build upon each child's unique methods of coping with a variety of environments. One of the important considerations is the composition of the school group.

Group composition. The selection of children who can form an organic functioning educational group is a highly complicated and often largely an intuitive process. Careful consideration must be given not only to the characteristics of the individual children, but also to the physical structure of the group setting, such as the size and location of the classroom in the building, the maximum length and frequency of the sessions to be conducted, the optimal size of the group, and the number, background, and qualifications of the educational personnel to be involved.

The following are examples of four types of groups that have been quite successful with young retarded children at one center. A teacher trained in early childhood education and a teaching assistant were assigned to each of the groups, which included from two to seven children, some of whom attended three times a week and others daily:

1. *The A Groups* were organized around a nucleus of children who had previously been exposed to a modified group experience. Their members ranged in age from 29 to 48 months, with IQs from 43 to 70. They had the potentiality for eventual placement in special classes in public school, and many already communicated verbally. Gross physical de-

fects and severe coordination problems were minimal. The children were aware of each other and looked forward to school attendance. They had few major behavioral difficulties and responded well to an organized program consisting of a variety of nursery school routines. They were relatively independent, pleasant, easily involved with objects, and eager to involve other children in their play.

The initial *A group* goals included achieving awareness and development of good self-care habits. Musical and rhythmic activities were emphasized to encourage the children in using their bodies. These groups made considerable gains in toilet training and other aspects of self-care. They also became more aware and considerate of each other, sharing their toys without teacher supervision and expressing concern when one of their members failed to appear for class. They participated eagerly in special events such as birthday parties and could be taken to visit children in other classrooms. They could also join older groups in general school activities, taking short trips to the store, seeing motion pictures, and attending group "assembly and roundup" to watch children performing songs and dances.

2. *The B Groups* consisted of children similar in age and intellectual and social potentialities to those in the A groups, but quite different in tone and temperament. The *B group* children were hyperactive and hyperkinetic. Their frustration tolerance was low, they were extremely distractible, and they responded poorly to shifts in routine and changes of pace. They were difficult to manage as a group and needed a great deal of adult structure and firmness. Many of the *B group* children presented the familiar clinical picture of the "organically damaged." The curriculum for the *B groups* was organized around sensory stimulation, visual-motor coordination training, perceptual training, and verbal activities.

The total *B group* program was based on sequential and developmental stages of growth in these interrelated areas. It was necessary, for example, to provide these children with gross motor coordination activities such as climbing, hopping, pulling, and pushing. These activities led naturally to training in spatial and perceptual areas, which, in turn, helped to prepare for cognitive development. As the children became ready for this level of achievement, more refined "table work" was provided for them. As the *B groups* progressed, a rather intangible quality, which might be called "cohesion," developed. The group structure no longer seemed so disjunctive, and there were many more moments of quiet and calm in the classroom, as the children began to develop inner controls that helped to inhibit their former aimless and purposeless activity.

3. *The C Groups* provided a warm climate for younger and more dependent children, who needed an emphasis on the preliminary steps necessary for developing good daily living habits. These children ranged in age from 20 to 34 months, with IQs from 40 to 72. They had already established good object relationships, were aware of changes in their environment, and were also able to manipulate the adult world to some extent in order to achieve their needs.

Although the children in the *C groups* were alert and active, their play was still on a parallel rather than a shared level, and sustained attention was difficult for them. The *C group* curriculum therefore emphasized the development of a longer attention span through the use of a variety of media. Since the receptive level in language areas in these children was higher than their expressive skills, many special activities were also organized to stimulate and encourage the development of additional means and higher levels of communication.

4. *The D Groups* were composed of children functioning on severely and profoundly retarded levels. Their ages ranged from 27 to 41 months, and their IQs from 20 to 41. Several of them had obvious orthopedic defects, and their gross motor coordination was at a low level of development. These children needed individual attention in almost all areas. Much emphasis was placed on stimulation and motivation, to help them develop greater control in the use of their bodies. Many of the *D group* children were quite content merely to sit passively, so that the teachers often had to provide special activities that encouraged movement.

Teaching the *D group* children to walk was a major training goal, and several pieces of special equipment were utilized to teach the related skills of climbing and balancing. Most of the children had no speech, and either babbled or made undifferentiated sounds. Many did not recognize their own names, and those who could respond to simple commands did so only if gestures were also used. The children in the *D groups* were obviously not ready for training in self-care, since they were not even aware of many parts of their bodies as yet. Their rate of development was extremely slow, and their educational potential quite limited.

Additional selection criteria. In addition to the more obvious selection criteria for school groups, the choice of a suitable group placement for a specific child may often be influenced by extraeducational factors, such as physical appearance and personality characteristics. The case histories that follow illustrate two such situations:

> John H. was a 38-month-old child with gross physical anomalies such as six fingers on each hand, a short neck with gill slits from his ears to his shoulders, webbed fingers, bulging eyeballs, a grossly misshapen jaw, and erratically placed teeth. Mrs. H., ashamed of her son's appearance, pathetically attempted to hide some of his disfigurements by dressing him in gloves and a hat and covering his neck with a scarf.
>
> The possibility of plastic surgery to correct some of John's anomalies had been investigated but was not considered feasible on a large scale. However, some improvement in the child's appearance was achieved during the period of his home training by surgical removal of the sixth finger on each of his hands and of most of the webbing between his fingers. Several protruding teeth were also extracted, and eyeglasses were prescribed, which corrected a visual defect and improved his appearance as well.
>
> Evaluated as a borderline-to-mild retarded child, John was extremely reticent to demonstrate his abilities. Hidden at home and avoided or teased in public, he entered social situations with obvious fear, although his exceptional manners and actual sweetness were evident. The educational director decided to counter John's anxiety by placing him in a small class of children who functioned well below his own level. In this group, it was felt that John's acute sensitivity might be assuaged in two ways. The other children, who were severely retarded, would be largely unaware of

his physical anomalies. Further, the setting provided him with the opportunity to excel, and, in fact, to assist others for the first time in his life.

Extreme self-consciousness characterized John's initial behavior in the class to which he was assigned. He refused to remove his hat, gloves, and scarf. He peeked out through the door to make sure that no one was in the hall when he ran to the bathroom. He refused to eat in the classroom, perhaps because he felt that chewing would make his facial distortions even more apparent. Gradually, however, because of his comparatively superior abilities and amiability, John became the teacher's "special helper" and a patient assistant to the other children, who greeted him with hugs and shrieks of welcome. Eventually, as his self-confidence increased, John began to remove the clothing that hid his disfigurements. At the same time, he started to draw normal human figures with hands and fingers, rather than the monsters with cloven hooves he originally produced.

After about a year in the low-functioning class, John was promoted to a class of mildly retarded children. Here, he met with the anticipated taunts and temporarily regressed. For a time he visited his former class frequently, although he always returned voluntarily to his new class. Within two months, he had established firm friendships with several of his new classmates, who no longer seemed to notice his appearance. He began to function at a much higher level and was shortly placed in a reading readiness group in preparation for special classes in public school. John will have a difficult future, for his appearance is still quite startling, even shocking. However, his self-esteem had greatly increased, he was developing his abilities, and he could at least tolerate exposure to other people.

Terry P. was a very dependent, pretty child, very spoiled and accustomed to having his own way. The youngest of four children, he was 30 months old when he was first brought to the center, and 36 months when he was considered for a group experience. His parents had treated him like a baby, indulging and overprotecting him. Though he was only moderately retarded and had the potentiality for even higher functioning, he had been encouraged to remain almost completely dependent. Whatever he wanted or needed was brought to him.

Terry had never lacked for toys, instructions, and verbal and sensory stimulation. He was able to associate sounds and objects and could even perform some simple categorization tasks with colors and shapes. His frustration tolerance, however, was extremely low. He was virtually unable to initiate activities and had minimal self-care skills. He was extremely passive and had only a minimal concept of himself as an individual. The educational program that was set up for him was planned to foster this essential sense of self as a major goal.

Terry was placed in a group of more or less withdrawn children, so that he would have to assert himself if he wanted to receive attention from them. He needed to learn that he could alter his environment by his own efforts and did not have to depend on adults to bring the world to him. Terry initially sat passively and merely waited for people to come to him and bring things to him. When it was apparent that this would not happen, he slowly began to make a few tentative efforts to engage the other children. As his efforts increased he began to meet with success, and he was simultaneously encouraged by the teacher to go out into his surroundings more actively.

Terry was very fond of music and loved to listen to records. He was permitted to play them in the classroom, provided he selected the records and turned the phonograph on himself. When he first discovered that he could handle the phonograph by himself, he turned it on and off continually for fifteen minutes, in obvious delight at his ability to control it. These and similar experiences helped Terry to gain feelings of control and purpose, and permitted a much greater range of expression for his abilities. His skill level improved quickly as his confidence in himself increased, and he was moved shortly afterwards to a class of active children whose potentialities were about on the level of his own.

The curriculum. Educators sometimes classify special curricula as designed for the profoundly, severely, moderately, or mildly retarded child. Such an approach, however, deliberately limits the uses of a particular curriculum. More recent thinking tends to favor a total program that incorporates a wide range of possible levels of development within a sequential continuum. The differences that make up the individualized program for each child are essentially in the emphases and intensity of repetition used in his training.

A practical curriculum for very young retarded children includes specific training techniques for achieving limited but realistic goals. The curriculum is designed to meet the goals of facilitating maximum cognitive development, developing wholesome attitudes toward the self, fostering coordination skills, increasing social adaptation, acquiring adequate and efficient communication skills, and developing realistic habits for recreation and future vocation. The curriculum starts at the very simplest level of average infantile functioning, wherever possible, and moves sequentially to levels of performance that occur at about 5 years of age in the normal child. A curriculum suitable for a small class of young retarded children is outlined below, with specific examples of selected activities grouped under the major training areas to which they are applicable. Training for the younger and more retarded children begins at the simplest developmental levels. Greater complexity and range are introduced as the development of their skills permits.

1. Sensory and motor development: Training in the development of motor skills and movement can range from very elementary activities such as holding the head erect in mid-position, grasping for an object, creeping, squatting, and sitting, to more complicated activities involving finger dexterity and coordination, rolling and tumbling, throwing, lifting, marching, and dancing.

Neurological disorders can impair the retarded child's sensory and motor abilities, so that the pathways to learning are deficient and the child requires intensive sensory-motor training in specific areas. Stimulating the senses of touch, vision, and hearing helps the child to develop simple motor skills. Different surfaces such as a hard floor, carpeting, mats, and other tactile stimuli are introduced to the child, perhaps by rolling him along the floor or holding up his feet while he tries to balance on his hands. A flashlight lit in a dark room can help him learn to judge distances; he can be encouraged to try to touch the light as it moves about the wall, or attempt to step on it when it appears on the floor.

The child's arm movements may be gross and random. Instead of frustrating him by trying to make him draw within narrow boundaries, it is more helpful to encourage him to finger-paint on a washable tabletop or use poster paints on large sheets of newspaper. As his motor control increases, more intricate tasks to improve coordination can be attempted, such as making stencils. This can be done by placing a sheet of paper in the bottom of a shallow box with a shape cut out of the box top. The box is then closed, and the child is shown how to use thick crayons to trace the shape onto the paper. Using boxes of different depths helps the child to improve hand and finger coordination. Etching designs with pointed sticks in cookie tins filled with wet sand reinforces the child's sense of direction and also strengthens his finger muscles. Whenever possible, motor tasks in the curriculum should be related to activities in daily living, such as brushing teeth, serving food, or setting the table.

Plastic arts and crafts media are particularly helpful in developing kinetic, visual, and tactile discrimination. The child can be taught to feel the difference between plasticene and clay, and realize the effects of mixing water with the clay. Simple toys made of vinyl, rubber, foam, and metal can be profitably used to develop tactile perception and discrimination. A variety of attractive pull toys, many of which make sounds, are useful for developing visual-motor skills. Air mattresses, rocking chairs, small trampolines, swings, and other equipment help to develop body movements and control. Balance beams of different widths help to develop coordination and equilibrium in a series of gradual steps. As the child's balance becomes more secure, small obstacles can be placed in his path, while the teacher encourages him to practice stepping around them. Movable wooden stairs are a particularly versatile piece of training equipment. They can be used to practice crawling, walking up and down, skipping, and jumping from various heights.

Many movements that are acquired naturally by a normal child may need to be carefully taught to a retarded one. Playing ball is an example. While the average child usually learns to play ball with little or no formal training, the retarded child may need considerable help. The teacher might introduce the class to ball play by seating the children around a table and encouraging them to roll the ball around. Then, as the teacher calls out the name of one of the children in the group, the child who has the ball at the moment is instructed to roll it to the child she has named. In another version of this technique, pairs of children sit across from each other on the floor with legs outstretched and roll the ball back and forth from one to another. To improve accuracy, the ball may be rolled along a path mapped out on the floor with tape. The teacher can also show the children how to hold the ball, drop it, and catch it.

Teaching the child to drop the ball (or, at first, a beanbag) into a bucket helps to increase his accuracy. As the bucket is moved farther away, the teacher shows the child how to use both hands to toss the ball "underhand" into the bucket, and as this skill is mastered, to throw the ball to her. Learning how to catch the ball requires another whole series of lessons. Sitting or standing with backs against the wall, the children can be shown how to hold out their arms with elbows bent and hands slightly cupped up. The teacher then puts the ball in their arms and moves back gradually, slowly increasing the distance between her and the child. Initially a large ball is preferable, but as the children become more proficient, balls of decreasing sizes should be used. The teacher can also ask the children to throw the ball back to her from increasing distances, combining throwing and catching practice. The children can also practice the throwing and catching sequence with each other from increasing distances. Some children may begin their throw by holding the ball over their heads. Others may be more proficient with a scooping action. It is best to teach the child to throw in several ways.

2. Self-care and health: The curriculum area of self-care and health includes such basic activities as washing, toilet training, eating, dressing, and acquiring general health habits. Within each of these categories a wide range of sequential activities can be planned in order of increasing complexity. At the youngest infant age levels, the child can experience activities related to care and health only in a passive way. However, by the age of 18 months, some retarded children can begin to participate more actively, although on a limited basis. For example, while the child may not be able to understand why cleanliness is important, he can nevertheless learn to wash himself, especially if he is rewarded for his efforts.

A set routine for washing before eating and after toileting can easily be established by the teacher. Children readily learn to associate water with fun as they play with floating toys in a tub or sink, splash about, or dip their hands into a sink filled with water and soap bubbles. Playing with washcloths, wetting them, squeezing out the water, and putting them to their faces are activities that acquaint the children with the equipment and procedures for washing. A film presentation of children washing their faces, with the class returning to the sink and, using a mirror, practicing what they saw on their own faces with damp cloths, has proved to be highly successful. Showing the children how to clean dolls and other play material, and wash one another's hands and faces, provides further practice they enjoy.

Dressing and undressing involves many finely coordinated movements, such as those that are used in opening and closing buttons, operating a zipper, fastening snaps, and closing a belt. The teacher needs to employ specific techniques in teaching these skills. A good first step, after the children have removed their shoes, is to help the boys open and slip down their trousers, and the girls to take off their dresses or pants. Preliminary help may also be necessary with the untying or unbuttoning of the shoes. If the pants do not have an elastic waistband, the teacher may also have to open the fastener and zipper, hooking the child's thumbs in the waistband and showing him how to "pull down." Practice in front of a full-length mirror is helpful here and may improve coordination. When the pants are lowered, the child can sit on the floor and pull them off, one leg at a time. Depending on the level of skill he has already reached, the teacher may perhaps pull off one pants leg for the child, encouraging him to remove the other one by himself. Some children will, however, need assistance throughout.

Before beginning to teach the child to put the pants on, it is helpful to mark the back with a label or a laundry marker until the child learns to distinguish the back from the front. After pointing out this mark to the child, the pants are laid on the floor in front of him, and he is helped to insert one leg at a time. If the girls are wearing dresses, they insert their arms into the sleeves in much the same way. Using the mirror while the pants are pulled up or the dress is pulled over the head will facilitate the process. The teacher will help the process by beginning each step with the children, gradually allowing them to perform the entire activity unassisted. Next, the child can work with a coat, slipping one arm out of the sleeve and then pulling off the coat with the teacher's assistance. To teach the child how to put the coat on, it can be laid on the floor or a table with the coat inverted, the back down, and the neck toward the child. Hooded coats can be positioned with the hood hang-ing over the edge of a table. The child, with his front to the coat, slips his arms into the sleeves and swings the coat over his head, a sweeping movement that most children enjoy, and one that is often quickly learned.

Shirts and sweaters come next. Short sleeves are easiest for begin-ners to handle. For sweaters and blouses that button down the front the coat method may be used. With pullovers the children may need help to find the neck opening and to pull the sweater over their heads. Many children initially dislike to have clothing pulled over their heads. How-ever, if the action is demonstrated first by the teacher, and particularly if the children are then allowed to pull the sweater over her head, their objections are usually overcome. When the children's sweaters have been pulled down to the neck, standing in front of a mirror to find the sleeves and put their hands through the armholes helps them complete the action. Encouraging them to help one another dress and undress, and to practice with dolls, are useful aids in teaching them how to handle clothing. To teach the child how to operate a zipper, large "practice" zippers can be stapled to pieces of cardboard, and the chil-dren shown how to zip and unzip them. The final step involves transfer-ring the skill to real clothing.

To introduce the children to buttoning, the teacher can accustom them to the necessary motions by teaching them to put flat, round objects through a slot. The children can, for example, put pennies in a piggy bank or drop buttons through a hole in an inverted paper cup. Other practice equipment might consist of button frames or oversize buttons and buttonholes attached to pieces of heavy cloth that are draped over the child's shoulders. The teacher can also sew a large button on one side of a necktie and cut a buttonhole on the other, asking the children to practice with the ties first on the table and then around their necks. Large dolls with oversize buttons and buttonholes on their clothing can also be used, the teacher guiding the children's hands and fingers at first. When the children have gained some dexter-ity, their coats can be laid on a table so they can work with their own buttons. If necessary, the teacher can push the button halfway through the buttonhole, encouraging the child to complete the task. The class can also practice buttoning and unbuttoning the teacher's coat and then their own, first in front of and then away from the mirror.

Developing good eating habits is a major part of the self-care curriculum area. It is good practice to plan a quiet period just before lunch or snack time, to induce a relaxed atmosphere. Tasks such as setting up trays, putting down place mats, folding napkins, and perhaps placing flowers on the tables can be assigned to children who can handle them. However, for a child who finds such tasks too difficult or anxiety-producing, it is wiser for the teacher to perform them herself. Untouched food, vomiting, wet and soiled clothing are frequent results of fear, tension, and anger during eating. On the other hand, soft music played during the meal will help the children relax and foster an atmosphere that they enjoy.

A nurse can be particularly helpful in the classroom with the child who has serious difficulty eating and who may need a great deal of expert attention. Some children may need to be fed several bites in between their own desultory attempts. Others may require finger foods, such as carrots and celery. By helping a particular child the teacher can also involve the other children, who may compete for praise and attention by chewing more thoroughly and trying more new foods. In fact, classroom snack and meal times provide excellent opportunities for specific training in chewing and swallowing and for introducing the children to new foods. The names of different eating utensils and dishes can be taught. Each child can be assigned a particular place mat and his own storage section for his utensils. He can also learn how to set his own place at the table by copying the teacher's sample setting, at first with her help and afterwards by himself.

When a child has learned to use a spoon he can be introduced to a fork and practice scooping up and piercing soft foods such as small potatoes and fish sticks. Using a kinfe can be taught by letting the child first practice holding the utensil comfortably, then cutting, say, coils of soft clay. Later he begins slicing soft foods such as frankfurters and bologna. Teaching the children how to serve themselves starts with using large spoons and easily handled foods such as applesauce or pudding, and going on to hamburgers and vegetables. The teacher can also devise many aids for teaching eating skills. There are game techniques such as holding up a utensil and asking the children to demonstrate its use. The class can practice table manners with dolls and toy dishes. Collecting pictures of tableware and foods from magazines and making scrapbooks or posters will involve the children and stimulate their interest. Playing with a large wooden spoon in a sandbox can help them develop the visual-motor coordination needed for eating. Every activity related to eating skills can be made into a source of enjoyment and pride to the children, so that good habits are associated with acceptance and fun.

3. Social adjustment and adaptation: The activities in the curriculum area of social adjustment and adaptation have a very wide range. They extend from developing basic perceptual awareness of the environment, which includes watching, listening, differentiating self from others, recognizing one's name, and identifying body parts, to more active participation in the environment, such as cooperating and sharing with others and accepting limits and responsibility. More sophisticated activities in this area would include the development of adequate work habits and skills, such as sweeping, watering plants, picking up toys, and observing rules for good interpersonal behavior, such as courtesy and cooperative work. Every child needs human contact and interaction, and even a severely retarded child can at least be introduced to a social atmosphere and learn to tolerate the behavior and activity of others.

The classroom situation is necessarily social. The child is a member of a group, and the setting itself demands that he learn to function and interact appropriately with the others. At first, he may be only vaguely aware of their presence, but he gradually discovers that temper tantrums and other devices he may have employed in dealing with his parents are not effective means for obtaining gratification in the classroom. Here he must learn to postpone immediate needs and to relate to his peers through more positive expression. Increasing self-awareness results in a reaching out to other children and finding new types of experiences in social play. The child's first social experiences may be quite limited, such as holding hands, throwing a ball to his neighbor, exchanging a bead for a doll, or helping another child handle his coat. Later the child may become more emotionally involved. He may, for example, miss a favorite playmate who is absent and even attempt to communicate his feelings, using gestures, facial expressions, sounds, and perhaps a few isolated words.

As his social skills increase, the child may begin to recognize the emotions of other children, sympathizing with them and devising ways to console a friend who is crying. He gains a growing awareness of differences in the other children, reacting to them selectively. He may, for example, avoid a child who frightens him and befriend one who is himself afraid and timid. He begins to recognize the child who will help him pull off his coat and turn to him for assistance. He also learns when to stop grabbing another child's cookie and when he is going too far in pushing him about.

Organization and set routines during the school day give the child a sense of security, as well as opportunities to learn what to expect and what is expected. Children who can learn to give up infantile egotism for enjoyable group cooperation and sharing of experiences do so readily enough. However, to make such social adjustments easily transferable to the home, it is helpful to emphasize a series of practical group living experiences of a kind that the home situation includes. The snack or lunch period, for example, can be used to teach not only specific eating skills, but also social amenities. At such times, the children have a chance to learn to communicate more effectively, to listen while others are talking, to pass food to one another, to take appropriately sized servings, to use a napkin, not to talk with food in their mouths, and other society-approved behaviors. Some children can be taught other aspects of cooperative behavior, such as using a two-way telephone or doing simple housekeeping chores. How to use appropriate greetings, to listen while others are talking, to address people by their right names, to share, and to take turns to help others complete tasks, are all appropriate inclusions in the curriculum.

Sometimes a teacher may want to plan an activity for one group of children while leaving another group free to organize its own play, the children in each group learning to control their voices and movements so that they do not interfere with each other. The classroom also provides a range of materials such as simple ring games, blocks, and triangles to help the children develop meaningful and purposeful recreational interests. Over a period of time, the child may learn to make intelligent choices and select the equipment he is competent to handle. On a group level, too, children can learn to use their particular skills in a combined manner; playing tag and relay games, engaging in simple folk dancing, and playing ball may eventually become activities organized by the children themselves and conducted with minimal supervision. The more proficient child can learn to follow rules and take turns in activities such as simple board games. Younger and more severely retarded children may acquire the same concepts through less complicated play, such as waiting in line to use a slide. Only gradually do children learn that cooperation brings a happy feeling of belonging. The retarded child needs help every step of the way.

4. Language and communication: The earliest levels of the child's language and communication program are best conducted at home, following much the same general procedures as have already been described in the section on home training. The later curriculum area of language and communication includes activities that develop auditory awareness and discrimination, basic listening habits, and the recognition that sounds have meaning and can be used for purposes of communication. The more highly specialized aspects of the program in speech and language to be carried out at the school level should be conducted by a speech therapist in individual and group sessions. These phases of the speech and language program are described below, in the section titled "The Communication Program." The teacher, however, can reinforce the program in the classroom, and working with the language specialists, can initiate a variety of activities designed to accelerate the child's progress in communication. Noise boxes, rhythm instruments, phonograph records, and games such as musical chairs help to develop auditory discrimination and retention. Simple techniques with a clear auditory focus will hold the children's interest. However, attempts to deal with multiple sound stimuli may discourage the class and should generally be avoided.

To help to develop the child's awareness of the direction of sound, the teacher might blindfold him, ring a bell or beat a drum at different points in the room, and ask him to walk toward the source of the sound. Rhythmic sense, important for both speech and body movement, can be taught through the use of a musical instrument, or more simply by merely knocking wooden blocks together. The teacher can also play or tap out different rhythmic patterns for the children to imitate by clapping or stamping their feet. The sound patterns can be made increasingly complicated as the child becomes more adept.

5. Perceptual and conceptual training: In training the younger retarded infant, the emphasis in perceptual and conceptual training is essentially on developing a sound basis for subsequent learning in these areas. The roots for this foundation are laid in many of the activities already described in connection with the home training program, such as offering the child a variety of brightly colored objects, moving him about physically, and introducing various sounds into his environment. The later activities in the perceptual and conceptual curriculum area begin with the basic concepts of time, space, direction, color, size, form, and number. Concepts such as "in and out," "front and back," "top and bottom," "many and few," "some and none," and "empty and full" depend on a complicated process of perceptual training for which many innovative play techniques can be used. Visual retention, for example, is improved through games like hide-and-seek or by showing a series of pictures with missing parts for the children to identify, such as a face without a nose or a house without windows.

Simple sorting and copying games are easily invented. For example, to develop the children's ability to differentiate between patterns, large swatches of wallpaper with different designs can be cut up and pasted individually on squares of cardboard, the child being asked to sort out the different designs in the pack. Empty egg cartons can be used for color sorting by painting the bottom of the carton's indentations with different colors. The child is then given a collection of large, colored beads and instructed to place each one in the section of the carton that is painted the same color. The child can also be taught to copy the colors and shapes of a simple chain of large beads, perhaps using a pipecleaner instead of a string. Flannel and magnetic boards, with large, clear, movable pictures, are also good material for training in visual perception. Many toy stores carry both the boards and special picture packets, and a kit can easily be made with cardboard and magazine pictures. Materials of this kind can help the children to recognize different categories, such as people, animals, foods, and toys. After placing pictures of, say, a dog, a mouse, and a cat on the flannel board, the teacher might ask the more advanced children to select from pictures of a man, a car, a glass of milk, and a horse, the one that belongs to the original group. Inventing new games with the pictures will further challenge the class.

Colors are often best taught through repetitive, concrete demonstrations, with each color introduced individually. Yellow is perhaps one of the best colors to teach first. Many children are already familiar with storybook pictures with a yellow sun, so that the teacher can begin by showing pictures of the sun and then pointing to the sun through the classroom window. Next, she can match a yellow crayon with a picture of the sun, and let each child color part of the picture. A bulletin board may be reserved for display pictures of yellow objects which the children have collected. It may be necessary for the teacher to emphasize only the color yellow for a week or more, drawing the children's attention to as many yellow objects as possible, pointing out yellow articles of clothing, for example, and helping the children to dress dolls and stuffed animals in yellow. A can or box covered with bright yellow paper can be filled with yellow objects collected by the class. The children can make special scrapbooks of their own yellow drawings and magazine pictures they have found, and they can pick out yellow buttons and beads from a collection and put them in a yellow box. It is best to introduce other colors gradually, with the same intensive technique.

Many of the procedures used to teach the children colors are also suitable for teaching shape concepts. A circle, the most basic shape, is best introduced first, followed by a square and a triangle. In teaching the concept of a circle, the teacher can begin by pointing out familiar circular objects such as plates, balls, the sun, and balloons, and asking the children for additional suggestions. The children can trace circles on form boards, in sand trays, and on the blackboard, make circles out of yarn, construct circle collages, color circles drawn by the teacher, pick out circles from pictures in books and magazines, identify circular objects in the classroom, cut out circles for a mobile, and keep a circle bulletin board and scrapbook. The teacher can make sketches or collect pictures and ask the children to pick out the circular elements, or the children can suggest circle pictures for the teacher to draw. Other shapes can then be taught one at a time, using the same matching and sorting techniques as are described above. After the children have learned to recognize several colors and shapes, they can be given cards with a few colored shapes pasted on them and asked to match other cards with them.

In addition to planning actual curricular content in perceptual and conceptual training, the teacher should plan special ways of approaching and introducing the material to the children. She needs to create a stimulating environment to motivate the children to learn as active participants, rather than passive receptors. Suitable instructional materials for retarded children are based on the current understanding of how all children develop, change, think, and learn. In the early stages, the child's responses are essentially reactions to internal stimuli. Later, he learns to manipulate concrete objects and is primarily interested in testing the effectiveness of his actions in controlling the immediate environment. Still later, he begins to internalize images and symbols from his experience, to think in terms of past, present, and future, to communicate with others, and to test his social surroundings.

Perceptual training as described here is concerned chiefly with providing a variety of stimuli and experiences to children at early levels of development. At these levels the child is basically egocentric, and his actions are determined almost entirely by his personal needs and wants. His attention focusses on whatever aspects of a given situation interest him most. He is distractible and unable to understand and integrate the separate segments of the situation into a meaningful whole. To engage the child at this level of development, the teacher must break down each learning experience into its simplest units and introduce them one at a time, in a direct and concrete way. "This is a plate," the teacher might say, very clearly, holding up a single large plate and adding, "Show me how we use a plate." Complicated instructions may well evoke confused responses. The simpler and more direct the instruction, the quicker and more appropriate the child's response is likely to be.

In view of the retarded child's limitations, it is more productive in general to emphasize concrete tasks rather than conceptual skills as such, minimizing the child's need to transfer training from one situation to another. It is best, for example, to use real washstands instead of models when the children are learning to brush their teeth. In addition to the content taught, it should always be remembered that overt expressions of encouragement, approval, and praise by the teacher are excellent reinforcers of appropriate learning responses on the part of the child. With continued exposure to rewarding social and interpersonal situations, the children gain in motivation to communicate, as their enjoyment, self-respect, and confidence in dealing with and contributing to the world around them increase. Such gratifications, however, develop slowly. The progression begins with the very basic skills and continues from routine abilities through social experience to self-confidence. This progression forms the essential foundation for the whole educational curriculum, as these early group experiences, achievements, and awareness provide in their turn the basis for the child's later training.

Individualizing the curriculum: Although the curriculum is developed as a sequential continuum, the programming for each child must still be largely individual in emphasis, as must the intensity of the repetition used for his particular training in the various curricular areas. On-going evaluation and observation of his progress, combined with continuing interdisciplinary planning, are essential to facilitate the child's movement from one level of training to the next. Since the total program is geared to meet the needs of all of the children, a wide variety of classroom experiences is necessary to permit every child to fit into each training area at the level of his own readiness.

For children who will probably be placed in a state residential school eventually, it is essential to include classroom activities that provide for maximum stimulation and growth in physical skills, sensory discrimination, communication, self-care habits, self-control, and group adjustment. For the child who may eventually participate in limited community programs, such as public school classes or sheltered vocational workshop, the curriculum needs to include more direct training for the development of specific skills. Experiences in family living, knowledge of the community, practical application of fine muscle skills, recognition of common signs and symbols, development of recreational interests, and the acquisition of organized, satisfactory work habits and attitudes can be included at appropriate levels for such children even at a very early age.

The goal of an individualized program should extend to the parents as well as the child. Parent-teacher conferences on an individual basis should be planned throughout the school year and should also be available if special problems arise. The teacher can do much to involve the parents in the child's growth. Informal contacts with a parent who brings the child to school can be a valuable supplement to more formal meetings. Free communication between teacher and parents helps to maintain the cooperation and interest of the family. The teacher can also learn about the child's behavior outside the classroom in this way, discovering how well he transferred his school experiences to the home situation. Further, these meetings enable the teacher to help the parent with training techniques to be continued at home. Home visits, too, may be planned, so that the teacher can actually observe the child in his daily environment, meet the members of his family, and prescribe more appropriate classroom activities for him. A truly individualized training program for the child requires an appreciation of as many of the unique factors in his life situation as possible. Involving the family in the training of the child is a major step toward accomplishing this objective.

THE COMMUNICATION PROGRAM

The program for the development of meaningful verbal and non-verbal communication is best conducted as a cooperative effort between the family and the professional staff. The communication specialist is needed to assist the family in utilizing the child's daily living activities to help provide him with the sensory and participatory activities that are necessary ingredients for cognitive and communicative growth. A close, warm family atmosphere is vital to all aspects of the child's progress. In the interdisciplinary center, the pediatrician, the social worker, the nurse, the teacher, and the speech therapist also work closely together and with the family to mobilize the positive strengths of all of its members as a group and as individuals. The family is increasingly motivated to foster, develop, and modify communication behavior as wholesome relationships are established, enabling the members of the family to share their thoughts, needs, and feelings.

Often the major barrier to genuine affection between parents and their retarded child is largely a lack of adequate communication, an inability to understand each other's ways of trying to establish contact. Progress in communication may bring quite dramatic improvement in other areas of living. This fact is illustrated by the following case history, which is only one of many others like it:

> When Mr. and Mrs. S. and their retarded daughter C. came for their first speech therapy session, it was clear that "duty" was the parents' major motivation in coming to the center. The parents' behavior throughout the diagnostic process and earlier treatment was never spontaneous. Their actions toward C. seemed planned, deliberate, detached, even stoic. "What should we do next?" Mrs. S. would ask the nurse on her arrival for a home visit. The mother followed through on the nurse's suggestions but seldom volunteered ideas of her own.
>
> Home training had resulted in unremarkable progress in C.'s abilities and the family's attitudes. The parents had told the speech therapist that they were participating in treatment for C. because "parents are responsible for their children." They seemed to expect little progress, but they promised and gave their cooperation dutifully. C.'s body movements were often merely random. She could, however, point to objects she wanted.

Her "speech" consisted of whines, cries, cooing, and vowel sounds. Use of consonant sounds was extremely rare.

The speech therapist had designed a program of stimulation for developing differentiated sounds. When C. pointed, the parents were asked to verbalize the name of the object she had indicated and then to encourage C. to imitate the sound. Mr. and Mrs. S. gradually became quite adept at describing C.'s communication achievements to the speech therapist in great detail. They began to notice differences in tone and vowel quality. C.'s initial attempts at using word partials were unexpected to them, and they were further encouraged. The child's verbalization of "Ma" and "Da" gave special impetus to their efforts.

As C.'s speech developed, even though progress was very slow, the parent-child relationship gained a new depth. Mrs. S. said she was "beginning to understand what she's saying," and her realization that the sounds, fragmented words, and a few complete words that C. was using had meaning encouraged the mother to invent new games and play routines. The parents became increasingly involved and interested as C.'s communication skills improved. They began to cooperate much more actively in the different areas of help that the training program offered, since the "communication breakthrough" had provided the basis for a closer parent-child relationship.

The case of Mr. and Mrs. S. and their daughter is but one of many instances in which more wholesome parent-child relationships, so frequently absent between parents and retarded children, may develop as the child learns even minimal communication skills. The characteristic lack of verbal skills of the retarded child can be particularly disturbing to parents whose other children learned to talk early and easily. The average home environment provides most children with sufficient stimuli for relatively easy language development. However, the process is delayed in retarded children, and the speech and language abilities that do develop may be so deviant that they are virtually useless for purposes of communication. These children need help to acquire a level of speech and language development that others reach earlier without special help. A program instituted in the early life of the child, and carried out by the parents at home with the guidance of a speech therapist, helps to foster maturational readiness, avoid later frustrations and failures, and enable the child to become a functioning member of the family.

Levels of language therapy. The level of language therapy to be undertaken with a particular child depends on many factors, including his chronological and mental age, his present communication ability, and those areas of function and dysfunction that are related to the overall process of communication. The very young child or the more severely retarded child is most likely to profit from maximum, daily living training on a prelanguage level in the home setting. The chief function of the language therapist in such cases is to assist the parents by demonstrations with the child and by prescriptive instruction to the parents in carrying on the training program in the home. Gains for these children will probably be achieved very slowly. Periodic visits to the language therapist's office, say once every two months or so, are usually sufficient for an evaluation of progress and instruction to the parents for continuing the program.

For children who have attained a level of function where increased services by the trained language therapist are indicated, more frequent visits to the center become profitable. Visits every few weeks allow better follow-up and closer supervision of the activities in the home language-training program. If the child's initial evaluation or his rate of progress indicates the need for more intensive work with the language therapist, weekly meetings become advisable. The kind of program that is best for each child involves the joint decision of the language therapist and the director of the language program, a decision made by weighing all the available information about the child and his family. Each program needs to be individualized to the needs and functioning of the child and his family and is reviewed as changes may indicate.

The setting for sessions at the center. Language therapy sessions at the center need a light, airy room, large enough to permit the child's physical movement and motor activities and small enough to foster a sense of security and intimacy. The room should be situated where outside noises do not produce a distracting background. On the other hand, it is not wise to eliminate "quiet" sounds, since a totally sound-free room is likely to be experienced as unfamiliar and strange. The room should be furnished with the child's physical and psychological needs in mind, using child's size chairs, tables, and cabinets at his eye level. Cheerful but subdued colors are suggested. The full-length mirror, which is valuable for body image and imitation activities, should be covered with a screen or curtain when it is not in use, since it is likely to distract the child's attention.

The language therapy room must provide a benign environment for children with varying needs. The setting should therefore have equipment that enables the therapist to change its character according to the needs of the particular child. The child who is in the treatment room at a given time determines the therapist's choice of materials and procedures. Some children need exciting and stimulating visual materials to arouse their attention and hold their interest. For more hyperactive children, simpler and subdued materials and more structured procedures are necessary to keep their attention on relevant activities. The sensitive and experienced therapist manipulates the environment so that it offers the best learning situation possible for each child.

Although the language therapist may work part of a session with only the child in the room, it is generally helpful to allow some time at each session for the parent to see what the therapist is doing and to be shown what should be done at home. Having the parent, equipped with earphones, observe the session through one-way-vision windows is a good supplementary means for helping the parent in his training function. It is important that the parent and therapist develop the kind of relationship in which the therapist understands the parent's problems, and the parent has confidence in the therapist's ability to help. At the practical level, programs for the parent's activities may need to be written out, stated very specifically, and carefully explained in terms of relevance to the special problems of communication that face the child and his family.

The communication curriculum for the young retarded child. A communication program suitable for the young trainable child requires special aims and related special activities. The following areas and procedures have been found to be appropriate for their training in communication:

1. *Developing awareness of and responsiveness to sounds in the environment.* Responsiveness to sound is an essential early step in the development of communication. It is also a stage that can be stimulated in the home by members of the family during the child's early years of life. Presentation of material during this period is best done casually, often, and without pressure or undue eagerness for a response from the child. His interest and reactions will be inconsistent at first, and progress will probably be quite slow. When a particular sound-producing object does attract the child's interest, it is a wise procedure to present it frequently over some period of time, with other objects slowly added. This kind of activity can be carried on throughout the day, while the child is in a crib, a baby tender, a playpen, a bath, and so on.

It is a good general rule to involve some sound-producing activity in as many person-to-person contacts with the child as possible. Any object that is part of the child's usual sound environment, such as rattles, rubber squeeze toys, or a cup and a spoon, may be used. The human voice is still one of the best sources of stimulation. Whenever a member of the family approaches the child while he is awake, it is helpful for him to make some sort of friendly sound of recognition and greeting. Cooing, clucking, or kissing sounds are useful and appealing, as well as simple words such as "hi" or "hello." It is best if the adult stands where the child can easily see him. If the child indicates awareness of the sound, the adult can repeat it, perhaps with a smile, which acknowledges the achievement.

A warm attitude and friendly sounds are great helps in the daily activities involved in caring for the child. During feeding, diapering, bathing, dressing, and other routines, the feeling of a close and warm relationship is enhanced by simple sounds and easy words with which the mother can accompany these activities. Using similar sounds in similar activities will encourage the child to develop associations between them, and the number of sounds or words can be increased as the child gains in ability to respond. The child's name may be profitably introduced at this time and used consistently whenever he is spoken to.

There are many different ways in which the child may respond to sound. He may look, smile, stop what he is doing, become more active, or even produce a sound himself. The first clear-cut sign that the child is aware of sound may be his reaction to a door slamming, a telephone ringing, or an object dropping. The child may be startled and even begin to cry. If this occurs, it is particularly helpful to hold and comfort him, repeating the sound, if possible, while the child is being held. This serves both to diminish his fear and reinforce his response.

Toys that produce sounds may be introduced early into the crib as play activities and demonstrated for the child, the adult showing him the toy while the sound is made. The toy may then be offered so that the child can make the sound himself. If he cannot hold the toy or exert enough force to produce the sound, the mother can hold the child's hand on the toy and produce the sound for him. If the child shows preference for a particular toy, especially if he seems to enjoy the sound the toy produces, it should be used as frequently as possible in playing with the child in this way. The preferred toy should also be given to the child to play with when he is alone. These activities are best undertaken when the child is relaxed and comfortable. There is little value in attempting them when the child is upset, unless the parent has found that the introduction of a particular sound or sounds serves to quiet and relax the child. Under such circumstances, repeated presentation of those sounds can be very useful.

2. *Developing the ability to localize sound.* Another important early training goal is to develop the child's ability to localize sound. Special exercises need to be undertaken to help him determine the direction from which sound is coming when its source is beyond his range of vision. After the child is aware of a sound, the mother can begin to introduce it at the side of the child as a beginning step in developing sound localization. The child's response may be a movement of the eyes or perhaps of the head in the general direction of the source of the sound. If there is no response, the concept of localizing the sound may

be facilitated by showing him the source of the sound and then moving the sound maker to the side beyond his range of vision, thus using visual ability to help establish the auditory skill. As the child progresses, it is very helpful to take him to and show him the sources of various sounds that occur regularly in his environment, such as running water, a record player, a radio or television set. A passing car or airplane outside can also be pointed out to him.

3. *Developing the ability to discriminate among sounds.* For effective sound discrimination, the child must learn to differentiate sounds produced by people and objects, and later, by different people and different objects. For reasons of safety, he must learn to recognize the sounds, and later the words, that are danger signals. In brief, he must learn to associate sounds with the objects producing them as a beginning step in developing the ability to recognize relationships between auditory and visual stimuli. The development of this ability starts with the awareness that different sounds come from different things.

More complex activities can be introduced as the child's responses indicate that he is ready. When he has learned the sound of a rattle and a bell, for example, specific training in distinguishing one from the other can be instituted. With both placed in front of him, the adult can pick up one of them and produce its sound from a position where the child cannot see it. The object can then be replaced within his range of vision, and through the use of pantomime and gesture the child can be asked to produce the sound. When he has been consistently successful with the bell and rattle, other sound makers can be used in the same way. At first, it may be necessary to assist the child in giving the correct response, gradually helping him to react on his own initiative.

It is possible to progress from the more simple achievements to more complicated training goals. Play records that ask the child to bang a drum, blow a whistle, ring a bell, clap his hands, and the like are particularly helpful and can usually be obtained fairly readily. Some of the objects referred to in the records can be provided and actually used in demonstrations of the sounds they make. In other cases, the sounds can be demonstrated vocally, a drum goes "boom-boom," a whistle goes "tweet-tweet," hands go "clap-clap," and so forth. Successes should be rewarded with a smile and some sort of verbal reinforcement such as "good baby!" or "nice!" to convey a feeling of success and approval to the child. In all of these activities, the adult can expect to give active physical participation initially, reducing the level gradually as the successful achievements of the child increase.

Training outside the home is as important as training conducted inside. When the child is outside the home, the sounds of the external world begin to be part of his experience. The source of these sounds also should be pointed out at each opportunity. The child should be shown a dog, a fire engine, a police car, and other sound-making objects, with appropriate verbal reinforcement such as "Hear the dog, look!" while the adult directs the child's attention to the source of the sound. It may even be necessary to grasp the child's head gently and turn it in the right direction. Such procedures, if followed repeatedly, will help to develop the child's self-directed looking and pointing, as the sound and its source become associated in the child's mind. Only when this level of meaning has been reached has another step toward the goal of verbal communication been achieved.

4. *Developing the ability to reproduce nonverbal sounds.* The ability to reproduce sound sequences is facilitated by encouraging the child's listening to and reproducing mechanical, nonverbal sequential sounds such as banging, clapping, horn blowing, bell ringing, and the like. This is best done as a game for which the adult picks up cues from the child. When he is using a noise-making article, perhaps banging a spoon in a cup, he may do so in a simple sequence such as banging twice. Following his lead, the adult can take his spoon and bang twice in imitation of his own behavior, or bang twice with other objects that make a similar sound. The child's timing should be followed, with subsequent encouragement for him to continue the game. Later, the adult may initiate the activity by banging the spoon in a cup, transferring the object to the child's hand, and repeating the demonstration with his hand holding the object. Increasing the complexity of the game by adding sound-making activities such as hand clapping and bell ringing can begin as the child becomes more adept.

5. *Developing the ability to produce simple sound sequences.* The ability

to produce simple sound sequences is a natural outgrowth of the development of nonverbal sound reproduction. Here again, activities are best chosen by taking cues from the child and allowing him to initiate the performance. When the child begins to make his first baby sounds, the adult can imitate them and stimulate their use. Any sound that the child produces can be used repetitively by the adult, along with encouragement to the child to continue. As with the other practice areas, the repetition of sounds in sequence can be easily increased in complexity as the child becomes more adept in vocal productions.

6. *Developing habits of listening and attending.* The activities described thus far are basic to developing good listening habits. The ability to attend to sounds develops as they become meaningful to the child. Sounds that mean nothing to the hearer are easily ignored. Even adults find it difficult to listen consistently to sounds they do not understand. However, it takes time and patience to teach a retarded child to listen. He will not really listen unless he understands. The adults who participate in training him must be prepared for slow progress and must not allow themselves to become discouraged. They may have to direct the child at very elementary levels at first. For example, it may be helpful and even necessary for the adult to cup his hand under the child's chin and turn the child's face toward him as he talks. Accompanying this with verbal instructions such as "look at me" and "listen!" will serve as reinforcement. The use of colorful, stimulating material will also help to arouse the child's attention and interest.

7. *Developing primary modes of communication.* Achieving meaningful nonverbal communication is an important step toward the ultimate goal of spontaneous verbal communication accompanied by minimal gesture, body activity, and facial expression. All children go through a stage of development in which there is much nonverbal and little verbal communication activity. The child pushes the spoon away. He closes his mouth tightly. He points to the refrigerator. He jumps up and down. He smiles. He wrinkles his nose. He is clearly trying to communicate something in all this behavior. The message is readily understood if the cues are present, the gestures clear, and the activity common to others. Sounds may accompany the gestures, but these may be largely random.

The retarded child uses gestures, body activity, and facial grimaces as his major means of communication for much longer than normal children do. It is therefore important that the child's gestures become clearer and more direct. The adult might tell the child, for example, to stop shouting and point to what he wants. The adult can also point to what the child wants and tell him to get it for himself. He can be taught that shaking his head from side to side means "No," while nodding his head up and down means "Yes." He can be trained to choose. For example, if two bottles are in the refrigerator, the mother can ask him, "Do you want the milk or the soda?" and accept his pointing as a substitute for the word partial or word which may not yet be available to him.

It is helpful to try to coax the child to use verbal responses, but it serves no purpose in the learning process, and may, in fact, be actually detrimental, to pressure him with, "You won't get anything unless you ask for it." Nor is it wise to insist that, when a word partial is finally used, the child omit the accompanying gesture. Even in highly verbal adults all manner of hand, body, and facial gestures still accompany speech. Many children will continue to use gesture activity as their basic mode of communication for a long time, and some will do so for life. Those with serious oral language deficiency may, however, learn to use pantomime and facial expressions so skillfully that they can communicate surprisingly well. If a child fails to use words as his major communication medium, nonverbal means may enable him to function with minimal vocal skill, placing him in a position where he can at least respond meaningfully to those around him, as they can respond to him. Such interaction is essential for the whole process of socialization. For the young retarded child, the ability to make some contact with others and to make his wants known, however imperfectly, are major steps in enabling him to become a functioning member of the family.

8. *Developing awareness that sound combinations have special meaning.* Awareness of the special meaning of specific sound groups includes learning the names of people and things and achieving some degree of conceptualizations. A program of verbalizing by the family during the child's daily activities is of major help in developing his ability to

recognize that people and things have names. The retarded child's conceptual skills are usually limited and slow in developing, so that the naming of objects used in dressing, eating, playing, and in other daily activities must be limited in number and repeated as frequently as possible. It is good practice to name each object when it is clearly visible, preferably as it is being used for the purpose for which it is intended. Similarly, the names of actions should be verbalized often and while the activities are being performed by the adult within the child's range of vision.

The child's recognition of the association between the object or action and its name is reinforced by manipulation of the object or the performance of the action, and the establishment of sensory or motor relationships. Responses to simple verbal requests such as "Give me_____." or "Please, get _____." add another facet to recognition and increase the child's use of communication behavior as an aid to daily living. Activities like the matching of similar objects, recognizing differences, categorizing things by use or by properties of size, shape, color, touch, taste, and smell are all stages in increasing the usefulness of his communication. All such abilities make his communication more exact and add modifying concepts that broaden its range and applicability. In the process of gaining increased understanding, the child may begin to carry out simple, single-element requests, which become more complex with training and experience.

9. *Developing sounds and words as meaningful communication.* Many children will begin spontaneously to produce sounds in the course of receiving sounds and learning their meaning. Some of the sounds the child makes may not be easily related to words, while others may be quite recognizable parts of words that have been used in the parent-child communication. The production of such recognizable sounds in particular should be rewarded and encouraged. However, it is unwise at this point to urge the child to say more of the word, or to say it more clearly. Acceptance of and reward for successive levels of performance are major helps in further stimulation and growth. On the other hand, progress can easily be halted by demands that the child cannot meet.

The use of praise and reward has long been recognized as an

important reinforcer of learning and a modifier of behavior, regardless of the philosophy of education espoused by the teacher and the parent. In recent years, however, behavior modification and reinforcement have emerged in a more clearly defined form, with an accepted nomenclature and processes. Operant conditioning has been used more and more frequently in the language development areas, especially with nonverbal or minimally verbal children. Programmed instruction in a variety of forms has already been reported in language training for young retarded children. The literature includes a number of promising studies which will hopefully stimulate further work in this area and lead to more definitive evaluation of the use of these techniques in development for the young retarded child.

10. *Developing intelligibility and clarity in verbal communication.* Developing clear verbal communication wherever possible is the ultimate goal of the child's communication training. However, while an attempt is made throughout to secure the production of clear and meaningful sounds, this activity is carried out largely by indirect means. The focus is largely on meaningful growth in quantity and extent of communication usage. However, when the child produces a meaningful verbal communication marred by unintelligibility, a more concerted effort can then be made to train for greater clarity. This process is multifaceted and involves auditory, visual, tactile, and kinesthetic techniques. Fostering growth in communication must be an open-ended process, with content sufficiently broad to permit the child to grow in whatever areas his potentialities lie. The extent to which the total environment provides him with the necessary emotional and intellectual material for fostering growth will determine to a large degree his ability to achieve his own potentialities.

CHAPTER 4

Family Treatment

A truly comprehensive treatment program for the retarded infant offers psychotherapeutic assistance for the child's family and for any others who come into intimate contact with him. Some severely or profoundly retarded infants may derive little benefit from direct services. A more effective contribution can be made by improving the mental health of the family. In helping them to make a more realistic adjustment to the many problems which the presence of the child induces, significant gains may be made to the welfare of both. The parents are of chief importance in the life of the infant. The siblings, too, sometimes assume vital roles as well. In the sections that follow, the major emphasis is on treatment services for the parents, those for the siblings being largely reserved for later discussion.

An adequate program for parents at a multidisciplinary center needs to offer services at many levels and to be kept sufficiently flexible to adapt readily to changing parental needs. Educational guidance and individual and group psychotherapy should be available. Treatment may be conducted by psychiatrists, psychologists, or social workers under psychiatric supervision. The more educationally-slanted levels may be led by a teacher, with supervision and consultation in other areas provided at need. Severely disturbed parents may require more intensive treatment than many centers provide, and referral to services elsewhere may be needed for them. For the parents who can profit from less extensive services, however, therapy can be offered at many centers, both on an individual basis and in a group.

It is often difficult to predict the level and form of therapy that will be most helpful for a particular parent. Sometimes it is necessary to shift a parent from primarily educational guidance to psychotherapy, or from a child-oriented approach to one that aims at a deeper understanding of the self on conscious and unconscious levels. It is difficult even to isolate criteria for the most appropriate form of therapy with which to start. Among the factors that are probably relevant are the socioeconomic, educational, and ethnic background of the family, the age and level of retardation of the child, and the psychodynamics of the family. Even a casual consideration of some of these factors makes it apparent that the parents of retarded children are anything but a homogeneous group. Further, while many observable changes do occur during and after psychotherapy it is difficult to identify their causes, and scientific precision in establishing therapeutic procedures and evaluating their results is virtually impossible. Nevertheless, some broad generalizations can be made.

PARENTAL PSYCHODYNAMICS

The range of the possible emotional reactions of parents to the arrival of a retarded child is very wide. In fact, these reactions closely resemble those that might occur in response to any catastrophe in a family. There are, however, several trends that seem to appear more frequently than others in families of retarded children and that often emerge in the course of their treatment (193).

Perhaps the most common defense utilized by parents in trying to cope with the fact of retardation is denial. Initial use of denial may spare the parents from profound and too sudden shock at a time when they are still unprepared to cope realistically with their situation. The real danger occurs when denial becomes a habitual problem-solving approach. For example, parents may realize that their child is retarded, and yet verbalize and function as if it were not true. This internal contradiction, if prolonged and extreme, can lead to quite serious emotional difficulties. As one mother put it, "I must believe that my son will be normal even though I know it's impossible. If I didn't believe it, I would go crazy." This mother was quite aware on the intellectual level of the conflicting attitudes that her statement involved. Yet at a deeper level she could not relinquish her false hopes. Living with such contradictory beliefs can engender great internal conflict and carries a risk of inducing a dissociative process. In the instance mentioned above, however, the denial acted primarily as a support for the maintenance of the mother's psychological equilibrium until she was ready for a more realistic acceptance.

Denial is also implied by the fact that many parents come to a special treatment center with, say, a 4-year-old child already diagnosed as retarded and insist that his real problem is lack of speech. Such parents are often clinging to the unrealistic belief that if the child could be taught to talk, he would not be retarded. There is little doubt that increased ability to communicate will help the child to make a better adjustment. However, it is apparent that learning a language will not increase the child's actual intellectual potentiality.

Parental guilt at having borne a defective child is a very common reaction. In the course of treatment, it is often found that the global term "guilt" has many roots. For example, guilt may arise as a reaction to repressed anger at the child, to self-recriminations about unsuccessful abortion attempts, or to fears that the child's condition is a punishment for parental sins, among many other possibilities. A major goal of the treatment process is to free the parents from irrational guilt feelings, release them from unconsciously dictated rigid or stereotyped behavior, and permit freedom of choice about their own future and that of the child. Depression is an understandable parental reaction to the child's condition, particularly in the early stages of the identification process, and a period of sorrow afterwards is natural enough. Many parents emerge successfully from these difficult phases in adjustment without external help. However, should grief continue and become a chronic condition, therapeutic intervention is indicated.

There are also a number of neurotic tendencies that may make parental recovery difficult without professional help. A retarded child is a tremendous blow to the self-esteem of many parents. This can be best understood perhaps in the context of the pride of accomplishment and the feelings of fulfilling societal expectations with which many pregnancies are invested. In an already self-deprecating individual, the feelings of worthlessness that may accompany the birth of a defective child can be truly monumental. The child becomes the externalized symbol of the parent's own perception of basic inferiority. As one mother reported during a therapy session, "I always thought of myself as a failure until I got pregnant, and then I felt as good as anyone else. But after my retarded child came, I realized how little hope there really was for me."

Feelings of martyrdom, with neurotic expectations of reward, may undermine the husband-and-wife relationship, with hitherto repressed hostility breaking through and often supported by indignant rationalizations. As one angry mother put it, "I sacrifice myself for this child all day. Let my husband sacrifice himself for me in the evening!" Hostility may also develop on a more indiscriminate basis, sometimes directed toward other children in the family in addition to the marital partner. Thus, another mother said flatly, "I have always spared my family from the burden of taking care of my retarded child. I shouldn't have to be burdened with them, too." This mother had become totally unaware of her obvious neglect of the family. Indeed, such considerations had become relatively meaningless to her in the presence of her intense drive toward self-glorification through martyrdom.

Sometimes the parent's repressed hostility toward the child is masked by overprotectiveness and overconcern. This often presents a very difficult barrier to effective treatment for both the parent and the child. Such a tendency is illustrated by the following dream, which was reported in a group therapy session by an intensely overprotective mother: "I dreamed that my child was cuddling lovingly in my arms, and a hand came through the window and pulled my poor dear little baby away from me and hurled him out of the window. I tried to save him, but it was no use. I could hear him screaming as he fell." The hostility in this dream was easily recognized by the other group members, who in later sessions helped this mother to express her underlying resentment toward the child more openly. This, in turn, enabled her to deal with her anger on a much more realistic basis.

Feelings of shame, embarrassment, and frustration are also common parental reactions to their retarded child. Many parents may even respond with feelings of depersonalization, detachment, and withdrawal. A mother may feel, for example, as if "it's all happening to somebody else." A strong symbiotic relationship may also develop between mother and child, which, in extreme situations, may be experienced by the mother as her only real relationship. One mother who was withdrawing more and more said quite openly, "I love this child and this child loves me. Nothing else in the world really seems to exist." It is just such highly complicated defensive structures that require detailed and careful therapeutic assistance, instituted as early as possible in order to minimize their destructive implications.

Influence of the age and level of retardation of the child. Other things being equal, therapeutic intervention for parents of retarded infants seems to be more quickly effective than it is for parents of older retarded children. At this early point, the parents' defenses are not yet tightly organized and their reactions are more apt to be acute than chronic. This permits the parents to have a more flexible and accepting attitude toward help. They are not yet embittered by a long series of disappointing experiences in a desperate search for assistance. They have not as yet acquired a large body of myth and misinformation about retardation, and they are more available for a realistic orientation toward themselves and their child.

The level of the child's retardation also seems to be a significant factor in determining the course of parental treatment, particularly in the case of the profoundly retarded infant. Such parents often want and need intensive, individual help that focuses on their attitudes toward the child and on long-range plans for him and for the family. On the other hand, parents of less severely retarded children may prefer and actually do better in educational guidance and group counseling than in an intensive therapeutic relationship. Nevertheless, it should be possible for them to have more intensive individual sessions in times of crises, when, for example, reactive depressions might otherwise result in an inability to behave constructively, or perhaps in impulsive decisions to withdraw themselves and the child from treatment.

Ethnic considerations. The cultural and ethnic background of the parents sometimes exerts an effect on the course of their treatment. There are, in fact, some obvious advantages in having therapist and patient from the same ethnic background, particularly for patients who are recent immigrants. For example, families from Puerto Rico, Cuba, and other Latin-American cultures may have entirely different values and attitudes toward retardation than do American-born parents. These problems are sometimes due in part to language and cultural differences, and sometimes also partly attributable to the inferior living conditions that exist in ghettos in our large cities.

INDIVIDUAL PSYCHOTHERAPY

Individual psychotherapy that focuses on the parent's emotional reactions to the retarded child is an important part of an adequate parent treatment program. This aspect of the program can be conducted by a psychiatrist, a psychologist, or a social worker. Many—probably most—family agencies use social workers for this purpose. If a social worker is to conduct the parent treatment at the center, there are many advantages if the same worker remains with the family from the time of their entrance into the training program. The initial interview serves as their introduction to the center and the professional staff, while the informing interview becomes a kind of natural bridge from the diagnostic to the treatment phase. After giving the diagnostic information to the parents, the social worker may offer them a variety of services ranging from minimal to intensive treatment, depending on their particular needs. The extent of their ability to deal with their problems, their attitudes toward professional help, and the degree of their involvement in the treatment program are among the factors to be considered in connection with determining the most suitable level of treatment at which a parent can best begin. Parents given minimal services might be seen chiefly at times of change in the child's program, and perhaps also at his periodic reevaluations, which are likely to be somewhat anxiety-provoking for them. Limited treatment services of this kind are sufficient for some parents. Others may not require even this much. However, still others may need more intensive treatment, with sessions scheduled once a week or more, and extra meetings made available during periods of stress.

Approaches to treatment. Once treatment is undertaken, many approaches can be used, based on individual needs. Treatment can be environmentally oriented, supportive, dynamically oriented, parent or child focused, and should be shifted as the needs of parents change.

While it is difficult to generalize, many agencies have found that environmental therapy is likely to be most effective with low-income families with limited education. Their most compelling problem is usually lack of sufficient financial and social resources to maintain adequate nutrition, housing, and medical care for the entire family. The first step in helping them, therefore, is to mobilize the available resources in the community to improve the family's basic living conditions. With the cooperation and support of other social agencies or public health and welfare departments, it is often possible to raise the family's standard of living dramatically by obtaining a new apartment, arranging for increased public assistance, and establishing a source of medical care for them. Only when at least the basic living requirements of the family are met can the parents be expected to undertake the additional tasks involved in the training of a retarded child and in coping with their feelings about him.

Supportive therapy may be child or parent focused, and offered on a sustained or an at-need basis. Most families can probably derive some benefit from occasional meetings, even those who have adapted to their child's retardation with minimal emotional distress. With such parents, a helpful and sufficient therapeutic relationship may not require more than, say, three or four sessions a year. Even such limited contact may also provide the parents with a meaningful resource person to whom they can turn in times of crisis.

One basic purpose of more intensive parent therapy is uncovering and working through their emotional problems associated with the child. As with Mrs. X., some of these problems can be open to constructive change fairly quickly:

> Mrs. X. discussed all the difficulties she experienced in teaching her retarded child to feed himself, dwelling on them at great length and with much anger, before she realized that she was bitterly resentful of her own mother's interference in the process. She recognized that her anger was due to her belief that her mother was trying to infantalize and overprotect the child much as she had herself been infantalized and overprotected by her. Having seen this parallel, Mrs. X. was also able to perceive her own resistance to the child's independence and her own tendency to make him overdependent. Recognizing this, she was able to ease her overcontrolling behavior toward him. Since the child had sufficient ability to do so, he began to feed himself shortly after the mother began to encourage him to do so. He also began other independent activities with minimal direction on his mother's part. Having relinquished her need to infantalize the child, Mrs. X. began to take pleasure in his accomplishments and to enjoy helping him to add to them.

Frequently, the conflicts raised in the therapy sessions are initiated by but are nevertheless largely independent of the child's retardation, as was the case with Mrs. Y.:

> Mrs. Y.'s childhood had been marked by many rejecting experiences with her own mother, who had strongly favored an older sister. As Mrs. Y. grew up, her feelings toward her mother were highly conflicted, as were her mother's toward her. Her mother's ambivalence later turned toward her daughter's retarded infant, to whom she expressed affection while at the same time insisting that he should be institutionalized. Mrs. Y. could recognize her mother's conflicting emotions, a pattern that still characterized their own relationship and was now extended to the retarded child. After a number of sessions in which Mrs. Y. expressed her own conflicted feelings toward her mother, she began to experience less anger and less dependence on her. Gains in her composure resulted in lessened

depression, increased self-confidence and initiative, and greater ability to handle the child herself.

In treatment, parents handle their problems about retardation in different ways. For example, some will not discuss the retarded child directly, dwelling more on their concerns about his effect on their other children or perhaps on the family's position in the community. Others will openly discuss their hesitation in exposing the child and themselves to the community. Still others express fears about the child's emotional impact on themselves or frankly state their reluctance to rearrange their lives to suit their retarded child's disabilities. The content of the therapy varies greatly, as does the particular therapeutic approach, both depending on the parent's tolerance and the therapist's understanding of the family and of the child.

Impact of the training program. Regardless of the form that parent treatment takes, it is likely to be most effective if it is integrated with the child's training program. The therapist must be particularly sensitive to periods in the child's training that are likely to arouse apprehension in the parent. One of the more difficult periods for the parents generally occurs immediately after the diagnostic informing interview. However, there may well be other times during the child's training that are equally or even more difficult, perhaps raising profound uncertainties for the parents. Such periods of stress may include the child's initial participation in training, the periodic reevaluations of his progress, and any major changes in the child's program.

The initial period of the child's training program can be quite upsetting to the parents for several reasons. While they may feel relief and even optimism because the child is to be helped, they may also perceive the training as the first concrete proof of his actual disabilities. Conflicting reactions of this kind are illustrated by the case of Mr. and Mrs. T.:

Mr. and Mrs. T. had calmly accepted the confirmation of the diagnosis of mongolism for their 15-month-old son, Richard. They had asked few questions in the informing interview, and Mrs. T. was apparently eager to participate in the training program. She did not feel that she needed or wanted regular therapeutic sessions and requested that future meetings be on an "as needed" basis.

When the nurse arrived for Richard's first home training session, Mrs. T. proudly "demonstrated" that he was already learning to walk. She grasped the boy firmly under his arms and guided his legs by shifting the upper part of his body from side to side. It was apparent to the nurse that Mrs. T. was in fact carrying Richard, whose feet were barely touching the ground. However, she made no comment to Mrs. T. at that session, since she was already aware that Richard had been severely overprotected and had not yet been encouraged to develop even basic skill in crawling.

During the next few home training sessions, the nurse showed Richard's levels of development to Mrs. T. through concrete demonstrations of his abilities. As it become apparent that he could not even crawl or creep and was not even close to taking his first step, Mrs. T. became increasingly apprehensive. She could no longer hide the fact of his limited development behind a screen of defenses. After several months in the training program, Mrs. T. asked to see a therapist to help her with her feelings about Richard's progress. The initial discussions led to an intensive therapeutic situation that centered on Mrs. T.'s difficulty in accepting her son's retarded status.

The physical and psychological burdens involved in participating in the training program, combined with the lack of immediately visible results, may engender considerable parental frustration, anger, and guilt. If the mother has already established a sound relationship with a therapist, there will be someone available with whom she can openly discuss these feelings. Sometimes a mother's initial reaction may be "train my child but leave me alone." However, as she discovers that she herself is the child's most effective teacher, emotional reactions that she previously handled maladaptively, perhaps by limiting her contact with the child or remaining emotionally aloof from him, may now become highly threatening to her. She may then ask for and require frequent and regular contacts with the therapist to help her deal with her actual feelings. During the initial stages of treatment, hidden fears, misconceptions, and self-deceptions can be dealt with most effectively.

As the treatment process continues, it develops a special quality of intensity and importance that may heighten at times when the child's progress is being reevaluated. Although there is continual informal assessment of the child's achievements between parent and staff at the center, a formal evaluation, particularly of the intellectual aspect, may assume an importance far beyond its objective value. Parents will often reveal still hidden unrealistic hopes about the child's achievements and potentialities. Frequently, parental anxiety focuses less on the child's present level of achievement than on what the tests may indicate about his future. It is at such times that the therapist can be particularly effective in uncovering and helping the parents to handle their covert hopes and expectations.

Often, a frank discussion of their real expectations is more helpful to them than the actual discussion of the results of the child's reevaluation. In fact, the reevaluation itself rarely reveals the unexpected and is usually more or less consistent with the original diagnostic and prognostic findings. It may, however, be at this time that the parents actually realize that retardation is chronic and not amenable to sudden, dramatic, or even surprising improvement. Given this realization, however painful it may be, the parents can perhaps be guided from unrealistic hopes to realistic adaptation and constructive planning for the future.

Changes in the child's program that his reevaluation may suggest sometimes have serious implications for the family as well as for his own future. For example, the child's promotion from a home training status to a small school group, or from a part-time to a full-time class, may involve a great change for the parents. On the other hand, continuation in home training rather than advancement to the next step can seriously influence a parent's feelings about the child's future possibilities. Any major change in the child's program can precipitate the need for a full discussion of his future in the family and the community. A basic and often recurrent consideration is whether the child is to remain in the family or whether residential placement in a state or private facility is a possibility for consideration now or in the future.

The question of residential placement. The issue of whether or not to maintain the child in the family is influenced by many factors, including the functioning level, age, maturational and developmental progress of the child, the availability of community facilities, and a vast complex of personal, social, attitudinal, emotional, and religious features of the family.

The whole question of institutionalization is so complex that it is frequently impossible to isolate the relative weight of any single factor in deciding on a course of action. It can be said, however, that level of retardation is often one of the more important variables that influence the decision. While there are many exceptions, generally the more profoundly retarded a child is, the more likely the parents are to consider residential placement as a viable solution. Much depends, however, on their individual perception of the problem. For example, in one group session the mother of a profoundly retarded child stated, "I could consider placement for my child if he wasn't so dependent on me, and could take care of himself," while the parent of a moderately retarded child responded, "I would consider placement if my child were more retarded, but he knows me and would miss me, so I can't really think of it." The availability of community facilities and the child's ability to participate in them is also likely to be a determinant of the decision about institutionalizing. For example, if a review of the child's progress suggests that he can probably participate in an available special public school class in the future, the likelihood of his remaining in the family increases. In fact, the more community facilities that are set up, the less pressure many parents are likely to feel to plan for residential placement.

The reasons parents give for or against residential placement are extremely complex and often accompanied by intense emotion. Some perceive it as a rejection of the child that is akin to killing him. "To put a child away" is seen as a sinful, frightening, and brutal thing to do. It should also be remembered that the parents' decision in this matter is often based upon unconscious factors not available to simple introspection and reporting. It is therefore of paramount importance that the therapist have the highest respect for and sensitivity to parents who are faced with this agonizing decision. This concern is perhaps best demonstrated by helping them to explore their feelings openly and freely in a therapeutic setting, with no restrictions or preconceived notions about what action the parent should take. The importance of such an accepting role is highlighted by actual cases in which the outcomes were quite unexpected, and authoritarian attitudes on the therapist's part might well have been detrimental. The following case histories are illustrative:

Carl B. was 16 months old when he was first brought to the center. Mrs. B., 37, born in Cleveland, Ohio, was the youngest of five daughters in a poor Irish family. She had supported herself while attending Ohio State University, and after graduation she came to New York City to teach in a public elementary school. At the beginning of her second year of teaching she suffered an acute depression and sought psychiatric help. She married Mr. B., a wealthy investment broker eleven years older than she, when she was 28.

Mr. B., now 48, was associated with a prominent investment firm. He was an only child, whose previous marriage to a college sweetheart ended in divorce after two years. He had graduated from an Eastern preparatory school and an Ivy League college and had a Master's degree in business administration. Neither parent reported anything unusual in their family medical histories. Carl, a planned baby, was a second child. Mrs. B. had had two miscarriages between the birth of her older son, Ernest, then 6, and the birth of Carl. Both parents suspected that something was wrong with Carl immediately after he was born. His head appeared to be disproportionately small, and when he cried one side of his face seemed to be paralyzed.

Mr. and Mrs. B. were both quite anxious about Carl, but they tried to reassure each other, especially as the obstetrician had not found anything definitively wrong. However, during Carl's first year at home, Mrs. B.'s fears grew daily. She consulted her family physician who, in turn, referred her to a specialist who admitted the child to a hospital for a complete neurological examination. After all the tests were completed, the parents were given a diagnosis of "cerebral agenesis" for Carl and were then referred to the center.

The diagnostic staff at the center confirmed the previous medical findings and arrived at a diagnosis of mental retardation, cerebral dysplasia, and cerebral atrophy on X-ray, etiology undetermined. The staff noted that Carl's developmental defects appeared to have occurred prior to birth, and that, at best, he could probably function at a moderately to mildly retarded level. It was also agreed that the parents should be offered immediate treatment to keep them from "shopping" further for more acceptable diagnoses and cures. Mrs. B.'s attempts to assuage her own guilt feelings by blaming unusual labor contractions and neglect by physicians for Carl's condition suggested that she would probably require more intensive therapy than Mr. B., in order to help her build up her threatened self-esteem.

Both parents attended the informing interview, at which they were told of the results of the diagnostic process. In sessions prior to this interview, Mrs. B. had appeared to be an intelligent, critical, and demanding woman. She had already solicited a great deal of advice from friends and had begun an intensive reading program on retardation on her own. She had decided that she should not allow herself to devote her life to Carl at the expense of her normal son, Ernest, yet she continued to be unsure of what she "owed" to Carl in view of his damaged condition. The parents offered no objections to the staff's diagnosis. In fact, as the projected training program for the child was being outlined to them, Mrs. B. broke in rather abruptly to say that, after much soul searching, she had concluded that Carl would have to be institutionalized, since his presence at home would embarrass and, she thought, harm the development of her other son.

Mr. B. was visibly upset by his wife's pronouncement and hastened to state that no definite decision had been made as yet. His wife replied that she was willing to wait several years before placing Carl but wanted to use the intervening time to visit the best institutions and "study Carl's case." She expressed obvious irritation at the idea of a home training program for him and specifically asked that visits be scheduled once a month, at most. She felt that since she already had an older child she knew how to take care of a baby and resented being unnecessarily "told what to do." Mr. B. remained aloof from his wife's opinions. He apparently had little to do with the day-to-day running of the household, and his professional commitments, he explained, kept him away from his family a great deal. While he seemed to have sincere involvement in Carl's problem, his home and children were apparently his wife's domain, and he seemed reluctant to encroach upon it.

When the nurse visited the home, it became quickly apparent that Mrs. B. left most of the responsibility of running the household to her housekeeper. Her own life style had shifted hardly at all to accommodate to Carl's needs. She spent a great deal of time away from the home in club and volunteer activities, and most of her evenings were filled with social engagements. She refused to participate in the parent group at the center, stating that her family's higher socio-economic status would make her and her husband "outsiders" to the other group members. Later, she admitted that she was afraid to face the emotions that these sessions might arouse. Mr. B. participated in none of the activities of the program, but his wife seemed to find this natural. Their marriage had been built around his long work hours, and the family had always been wealthy enough to leave housekeeping and child care largely to domestic help.

Very early in the training program, Mrs. B stated that "we aren't the kind of family who can keep Carl with us." The child made only negligible progress. He was cared for by a housekeeper and a maid, who were quite overprotective of him. Mrs. B. was therefore encouraged to bring Carl to the center as frequently as possible, so that he could be exposed to a freer environment and particularly to other children his age, with whom he had had no previous contact. Carl entered a small group school program when he was 24 months old and made very substantial gains. His teachers described him as a sweet, pleasant child, who was eager to learn. He responded well to individual adults, showed an awareness of toileting needs, was curious about words and objects, and showed rapid improvement in gross motor performance. By the time he was 3½, he was completely toilet trained, could communicate with single words and follow simple directions, and was socially responsive to his classmates.

Carl's rapid progress clearly indicated that he would be an excellent candidate for public school classes for "educable" or higher-functioning retarded children when he reached the appropriate age. However, Mrs. B. was becoming increasingly upset and requested therapeutic help in dealing with the situation. Her conversations with the therapist centered around plans to institutionalize Carl. She still felt that keeping him at home would be detrimental to her older son and also to her husband's position, and she interpreted Mr. B.'s silence in the matter as an indication that he agreed with her. She was particularly concerned that her own social contacts would be jeopardized by the stigma of having a retarded child in the family, and that Ernest would be excluded from "the right social groups" because of it. She remarked that Ernest had begun to hit his brother and throw things at him. On one occasion, he had asked her to kill him. Mrs. B. regarded all this as clear evidence that keeping Carl at home would totally disrupt the whole family, a process that she saw as already well under way.

The underlying conflicts in Mrs. B.'s disturbance took some time to uncover because of her facade of indifference and hardness. Despite her apparent surface rejection of Carl, she felt an underlying affection and responsibility for him that she could not afford to admit. Nevertheless, although she turned him over to someone else's care whenever possible, when she did handle him her unexpectedly gentle and caring behavior was quite convincing. Mrs. B. was a dominating and often manipulative woman, but she was also very honest and sincerely wanted to do what was best for her family. Her own insecurity and the extent of her actual conflict began to emerge as treatment continued.

During the initial treatment phases the therapist did not question or challenge Mrs. B.'s defenses, allowing Mrs. B. to argue continually in an attempt to prove that her plans for Carl were "right." She would point out that Carl would be happier living with children like himself and that it would be unfair to "impose" him on her own or her husband's family. Mrs. B. often became angry when the therapist would not accept the challenge to debate her position, for it was obvious that she was debating it herself. It became increasingly obvious that the problems involved in Carl's retardation had been superimposed on Mrs. B.'s preexistent neurotic tendencies and insecurities. As Carl's achievements continued Mrs. B. experienced increasing conflict. On the one hand, she mentioned some of the child's recent accomplishments to the therapist and also spoke with pleasure of her husband's pride in his son's gains in verbal and social skills. On the other hand, she still emphatically added that she was proceeding with her plan to place Carl in a residential school shortly.

Gradually, Mrs. B. grew willing to look at her conflicting feelings. As she did so, it slowly became evident to her that she identified closely with the child and that many of her descriptions of his feelings really reflected her own. This became particularly apparent when she remarked on the irony of his retardation, in view of the eminence of her husband's family, while she herself "came from nowhere, really." Still later she remarked that she and Carl were in a sense "both outsiders," and perhaps neither of them would ever really feel comfortable in the world. For several months afterwards, she spoke almost exclusively about her own family, from which she was estranged. She talked about how poor the family was, how hard she had worked to put herself through college, and how successful she had felt when she married Mr. B.

Mrs. B. began to realize that Carl's arrival had somehow seemed to threaten everything she had worked for. She concluded, however, that "it really isn't Carl's fault." Then, for the first time, she began to question her long-held determination that Carl could not remain in the family. She also began to express increasing approval and acceptance of Carl as his gains increased and his behavior became more socially acceptable. She even remarked that the slight flattening on one side of his head was barely noticeable and that he was really quite good looking. Since he was doing so well in the training program, she decided to postpone placing him in the private residential school she had already selected. Mr. B., who seemed to be quite neutral in the matter, was clearly pleased at this decision. He had, in fact, grown quite fond of Carl and was also glad about the changes in his wife.

Carl continued his training at the center for two years more, after which he was enrolled in a suitable class in the local public school. Meanwhile, Mrs. B. continued in therapy and slowly grew stronger in her conviction that Carl belonged with the family, at least for the foreseeable future. In one of her last sessions she recognized that in rejecting Carl she had been in fact rejecting herself. Simultaneously, she also understood that her acceptance of her son reflected her own increased self-acceptance. In the occasional sessions she requested thereafter, she expressed no doubt that she had made the best decision for the whole family.

Marie C. was 11 months old when she was referred to the center by the neurological clinic at a city hospital. She was Mrs. C.'s fifth child, with four living brothers. Mrs. C., 42, was born in Canada and immigrated to the United States at the age of 26. She was the fourth in a family of nine children. All of the others were married and had normal offspring. Mrs. C. attended school through the sixth grade and then withdrew because of financial difficulties. She had taken odd jobs until her arrival in New York, where she had held a series of unskilled positions. She was quite obese, stating that when she felt overwhelmed by family problems she could not help overeating. She also reported several episodes of depression during the previous two years.

Mr. C., 42, was the sixth in a family of seven, all of whom were living. He was brought up in Canada, completed elementary school, worked as a shopkeeper, and came to the United States at the age of 24. The C.'s were married when they were both 27. When they came to the center Mr. C. was working as a waiter, earning comparatively little. His wife, who came to the initial interview without him, reported that he was an alcoholic and said that his drinking problem had become more severe after Marie's birth.

Marie's diagnosis, agreed on at the staff conference, was of severe mental retardation, chronic brain syndrome, right hemiplegia, spasticity, cerebral dysgenesis, convulsive disorder (mixed type), and microcephaly, etiology undetermined. The staff was unable to trace Marie's basic pathology. Both the microcephaly and cerebral dysrhythmia were considered secondary. However, whether her defects were due to a possible intrauterine disorder or perhaps to postnatal cerebral maldevelopment remained undecided. The staff was particularly concerned about Mrs. C.'s emotional status. It was not clear whether or not her reported depression was actually chronic, and it was also feared that the marked feelings of helplessness and self-deprecation she expressed could lead to a martyr-like aloofness that might further complicate the situation. Although Marie's prognosis for development was obviously poor, it was felt that a home training program might bring some limited gains for the child but would be especially helpful for the mother.

During the informing interview, which both parents attended, Mrs. C. stated that, although she knew Marie was retarded, she could not believe there were such serious limitations on the child's future development. She said that doctors who had seen Marie earlier had been more optimistic, and she expressed hope that eventually Marie's condition would improve and perhaps even be "cured." She was not considering placement because she felt that "God had a reason for giving me this child and expects me to take care of her." Mr. C. stated flatly that his wife should care for Marie, since the older children did not need much attention, and she could manage with little difficulty. Questioned about his own relationship with Marie, Mr. C. said that because of his fatigue in the evenings his involvement was limited, but he had great confidence in his wife's ability to cope with the situation.

When Mrs. C. was asked if she felt physically and emotionally prepared to care for Marie indefinitely, she replied that though her health was not good and running the house was hard for her, she could not bring herself to "give the child away." Mr. C. interrupted to say that, according to newspaper reports he had read, most institutions were understaffed and poorly equipped, and that the children deteriorated rapidly. Mrs. C. added tearfully that Marie would die in such a place and that the child seemed to respond a little to the family's attention and affection. The parents were told that the center would accept Marie for a home training program, but they were cautioned to expect limited, even minimal, gains on the part of the child.

The poor prognosis made for Marie never underwent significant change. She did not advance beyond a limited home training program, and her improvements were very slight. Even when she made a few marginal gains, she often regressed to her former level of functioning after a series of convulsive episodes. Throughout the training Mrs. C.'s enthusiastic reports of Marie's accomplishments were not usually substantiated by the staff's observations. It was true that Marie's seizures decreased in frequency over the next year, and at one point disappeared entirely for about two months. She also tried to crawl, dragging her right leg. In time she sat unsupported, and at the age of 3 she could take a few steps if held firmly. Otherwise, there was little or no improvement.

The attitudes of both parents during the first six months of therapy at the center were characterized by exaggerated hopefulness. During one joint session, Mr. C. mentioned that he knew of a child in the neighborhood who had begun to walk spontaneously at the age of six, and he continued to state that Marie was "getting better." Mrs. C., although she verbalized recognition of the extent of Marie's impairments, also harbored unrealistic hope at this time. During the second six months, she vacillated between pride in the care she was giving Marie and complaints about how difficult it was to give the amount of attention the child required. Mrs. C. also began to express disappointment in Marie's slow progress but remained hopeful that there would be improvement as she got older.

At this point Mrs. C. came close to seeing herself as a martyr. She complained increasingly about her burdens, her fatigue, and her many tribulations but still concluded that this was her lot in life, and she "would manage somehow." She continued to participate actively in Marie's training program, although she was becoming more and more aware of Marie's lack of progress and the relatively small impact the training program had upon her level of performance. Only very gradually did Mrs. C. cease to report unsubstantiated improvement for Marie. However, Mr. C., who had little direct contact with the child, continued to insist that Marie was doing well. He also began to drop out of the joint therapy sessions, saying that it was too hard for him to attend.

During the second year of the training program Mrs. C. became increasingly depressed. The "satisfaction" she had previously found in being a devoted mother and a martyr to her family no longer sustained her, and she talked more and more openly about her resentment about the burdens she was carrying. She admitted that she was glad to be so needed, but also said that the situation was not sufficiently rewarding to offset the strain. Her own moodiness frightened her, and she was finding it increasingly difficult to take care of the family. Finally, she "confessed" that it had crossed her mind how much easier her life would be without Marie. She also began to speak angrily of her husband's insistence that the child was improving so much, which she now regarded as quite unrealistic.

At Mrs. C.'s request, her husband was urged to attend several sessions with her to discuss Marie's present level of functioning, and, for the first time, to consider possible alternate plans for her future. Mr. C. was surprised to hear his wife express doubts that Marie would ever really improve. Mrs. C. then gave a description of Marie's performance over the past two years in terms of the child's realistic gains and limitations. Mrs. C. also spoke quite openly about her own depression, and her constant need for the medication prescribed by the hospital clinic to help her through these periods of stress. Mr. C. was visibly shaken by the confrontation with the reality of Marie's status and requested a meeting with the nurse and the other professionals who were participating in the training program.

A meeting was subsequently held with Mr. and Mrs. C., the nurse, the speech therapist, and the therapist who was working with the parents. Marie's probable future was frankly discussed, in terms of what she could realistically be expected to achieve in the next five years. The professional consensus was that, unfortunately, the child would very probably not be substantially different by that time. She might learn to walk unsupported and could perhaps be toilet conditioned eventually, but it was most unlikely that she would feed herself and dress herself or speak coherently. This meeting was very difficult for both parents, as were the next few joint sessions. However, Mr. C. did begin to question his beliefs about Marie's improvement and hopeful future.

Mrs. C. continued with weekly sessions for the next four months. Her mood had brightened somewhat after the joint sessions with her husband, and she felt more hopeful that she might gain his support and understanding. She began to take more care with her appearance and even started to diet successfully. At the same time, the nurse reported that Mrs. C.'s interest in the training program had diminished, and while she kept all appointments, she was no longer so intense and anxious about the child's performance. When Marie was 40 months old, Mrs. C. announced that she and her husband had decided to apply for residential placement for her. Mrs. C. said that in being such a "good mother" to Marie, she had probably been a "bad mother" to her other children and had not given them enough of her time and energy. Her husband agreed with her decision, having become concerned with the welfare of the family as a whole.

Application to a residential institution was made, and Marie entered when she was a little over 4 years old. Mrs. C. continued in therapy for several months afterward. She found visiting the institution where Marie was placed very difficult at first and needed help in dealing with the intensified guilt and depression she experienced initially. She was, however, finally able to accept the constructive aspects of the solution, recognizing that Marie's physical needs were not being neglected at the institution and that the family as a whole was benefiting from the decision to place her there.

The preceding case histories illustrate some of the unexpected developments encountered in parent treatment, particularly in regard to institutional placement. This is a question which, in one way or another, probably confronts the parents of every retarded child. In fact, when parents of retarded infants come to a diagnostic and treatment center, many have already been advised to institutionalize their child or at least to apply for institutionalization immediately, since by the time the child's place on the waiting list is reached the parents may have decided on placement. Most parents of retarded children have been given abundant guidelines, suggestions, and even orders about the wisest path to follow. Such advice may be based on moral attitudes about parental duties, religious convictions, financial considerations, mental health principles, or social philosophy. Such considerations often establish the course that the parents "should" follow. Parents are often more likely to be dictated to than counseled.

It is perhaps true that decisions based on authoritarian directives sometimes seem to have advantages, particularly for more dependent parents. For example, being told what to do permits them to project their guilt and disavow responsibility. Too frequently, however, these advantages are short lived, and the parents are left in a state of continuing conflict, perhaps with regret for a too-hasty decision that was based on someone else's beliefs. A truly therapeutic process, while time-consuming, difficult, and often painful and frustrating, has the major advantage of permitting freedom of choice based upon the unique personalities of the parents themselves. Perhaps the ideal therapeutic situation is a structured interpersonal relationship in which the parent is encouraged to give free expression of emotion, while the therapist, though warm and interested, retains a basic objectivity without preconceived ideas. It is the therapist's responsibility to support the healthy, adaptive core of the parents. For Mrs. B., in the first of the two cases described above, this meant supporting a perception of herself as a valuable person, able to accept her child realistically. For Mrs. C., in the second case, it meant supporting her basic need to maintain herself as an intact, functioning individual, without succumbing to either martyrdom or depression. In both of these situations, as in therapy in general, the therapeutic process involved consideration of the pathognomonic features of the parents as they related to the additional burdens the child's condition imposed. In neither instance could a satisfactory resolution have been reached by authoritarian suggestion on the part of the therapist.

The case histories also illustrate the necessity for taking into account the many factors that are involved in what may seem to be a fairly simple problem. Perhaps, had Carl been profoundly retarded and Marie only moderately so, the impact upon their respective families would have been altered—possibly even reversed. It may be that Mrs. B. could not have accepted a profoundly retarded child, while Mrs. C. could have devoted herself genuinely to a moderately retarded one. Nevertheless, even under such reversed circumstances, it would still be possible for both to have gained enough from the therapeutic situation to prevent lasting depression and serious loss of self-respect.

Therapy programs for both parents. The chief participants in treatment programs for parents of retarded infants are usually the mothers. This is understandable, since the care of the infant is essentially her responsibility, and the participation of the father and other members of the family is usually limited by practical considerations and less direct and intense personal involvement. Typically, the mother assumes maximal responsibility in a training program for the child, with the occasional participation of the father, usually at more or less critical periods. The pattern that a particular family follows usually involves its particular economic needs and is consistent with its individual views on child-rearing practices. However, it is often advisable to promote treatment involving fathers as well as mothers in a planned program of therapy.

It is impossible to generalize about differences in the dynamic reactions of fathers and mothers to the presence of a retarded child. It does seem, however, particularly with a retarded infant, that fathers are often less emotional and less threatened than the mother. This is perhaps more closely related to the greater intensity of contact the mother has with the child than it is to basic role or sexual differences. In any case, at least in the typical American family, the mother is usually more influential than the father in making decisions about the child's future. Nevertheless, when the mother is in intensive treatment it is often indicated and sometimes imperative that the father be involved in a therapeutic situation as well. A successful treatment outcome entails significant attitudinal and behavioral changes which, whether subtle or obvious, are often highly threatening to the marital partner. Without appropriate involvement of both parents, such changes can seriously interfere with previously established patterns of relationships. A therapy program for fathers may involve individual or family treatment, or perhaps most successfully, group therapy.

Individual treatment for siblings. The siblings of the retarded child usually have to face a special set of problems in addition to those encountered by children in general. Many hypotheses about the effects of a retarded brother or sister on the siblings have been advanced. Problems of embarrassment and shame are frequently discussed. There may be envy at the special treatment and care the retarded child requires, and perhaps fear of becoming similarly afflicted. Anger at responsibilities expected of the normal child on behalf of the handicapped one is often coupled with fear of expressing the anger openly, for fear of parental disapproval, a conflict that can become quite intense. Many of these problems emerge more clearly as the retarded child matures and becomes more obviously demanding. While he is still an infant, he is generally resented no more than a normal infant is apt to be.

A major influence of the retarded infant on the siblings is his effect on his parents. The sibling reacts to his parents' anxieties and fears and often mirrors their reactions in his own. Otherwise, the initial effects of the retarded infant on the other children in the family is usually minimal. However, as the retarded child matures and needs increasing attention, the siblings sometimes become emotionally upset and insecure, so that it is often helpful and even necessary to offer treatment services specifically to them. The nature of the service necessarily depends on their age, the adjustment of their parents, and the nature of the whole family constellation. Group sessions are often preferable to

152 Family Treatment

individual treatment, although the latter may be needed for emergency or special situations such as the following:

Philip F., an 11-year-old normal boy, was seen in individual treatment after the death of Saul, his 30-month-old mongoloid brother. Mrs. F. had conscientiously participated in Saul's training program since he was a year old. She was divorced, and though somewhat bitter about being burdened with a profoundly retarded child without the help of a husband, she cooperated extremely well in the program. She was a strong, pragmatic woman, well organized and able to manage her family efficiently, although sometimes with a certain lack of warmth. Saul was particularly difficult to care for. He was a sickly infant, continually beset by severe bronchial difficulties. Philip shared the only bedroom in the small apartment with him, while the mother slept in the living room.

On awakening one morning, Philip discovered that Saul had died during the night, apparently of a bronchial attack. Mrs. F. was calm and even fatalistic about Saul's death, but Philip reacted very badly, entering into a prolonged period during which he was noncommunicative and obviously depressed. Mrs. F. described his behavior to a therapist at the center and asked for help for the boy.

Philip was referred to the center's psychiatrist, who described the boy at the first meeting as a timid, confused youngster, who appeared to be extremely tense and depressed. He was willing enough to see the therapist and agreed to come once a week for individual sessions, even accepting the suggestion that he talk about Saul. During the next few sessions, he repeatedly described the experience of finding Saul dead. After several weeks of this, he ended his usual description of the event by adding, "It was my fault that he died." When the therapist questioned this, Philip said, hesitatingly, that if he had heard Saul cough, or if he had awakened in time, he could have saved his brother's life.

After his "confession" and subsequent discussions in which the therapist pointed out that there was no reason to believe Philip could have saved Saul's life, Philip's mood lightened somewhat and he became more verbal and communicative. Nevertheless, the therapist realized a deeper and more disturbing implication in Philip's admission of guilt. Philip was secretly afraid that in some way he had really killed Saul. He had harbored considerable hostility toward his brother and had often wished the child were removed from the family—in fact, were dead. Now he felt the guilt for the wished for event. The therapist did not approach this aspect of Philip's difficulty directly but spoke to him about how annoying a retarded brother can be, and how often one gets angry at him and actually hates him. Philip listened with great interest, implicitly receiving the therapist's permission to hate his brother, which fostered the ability to recognize and accept these feelings in himself.

As Philip identified with the accepting attitudes of the therapist, he began to emerge from his depressive reaction. However, at the conclusion of the short-term therapy for Philip's specific symptoms, Mrs. F. accepted the therapist's recommendation that Philip be seen in more intensive psychotherapy, to help him resolve some of the more basic personality problems that allowed him to assume such a massive and unrealistic burden of guilt for the death of his brother. For Philip and other children who, like him, may experience intensely ambivalent feelings toward their retarded siblings and considerable associated guilt, it is wise to provide at least short-term treatment, with more intensive help available if it is needed.

GROUP PSYCHOTHERAPY

Group therapy on a regularly scheduled basis is often a particularly effective service for the parents of retarded infants. The overall aims of these groups include creating a positive environment in which the parents can assess their attitudes to the child and others, providing reinforcement for their attempts to change them, and offering them an opportunity to examine their problems related to retardation and other areas of difficulty. In such groups, parents can learn to understand their roles more fully by exploring the psychodynamics of the parent-child relationship in a living, concrete, shared problem-solving situation. This situation has the added advantage of decreasing the parents' sense of social isolation by providing association with others who share many of their own goals and problems. Various kinds of groups for parent treatment may be established, differing in initial goals, selection of group members, frequency of meeting, duration of sessions, and the training and discipline of the therapist. Perhaps the most usual kinds are group educational guidance and group psychotherapy on varying levels.

Educational guidance. Informal educational guidance for the parents at some level is an integral function of every staff member at the center who works with the child. Independent home training activities for the parents to conduct are suggested and encouraged. Appropriate play materials are supplied, with instructions as to their purpose and use. The child's progress is continually related to the parents through regular conferences with the teacher, speech therapist, psychologist, physician, and nurse. All these activities are part of the overall educational guidance program. However, more formal, planned sessions constitute the main body of this phase of assistance for the parents.

Planned discussion groups are probably most effective for parents who are just entering the program, particularly if the child is an infant. The groups may consist of a lecture series, or perhaps, structured discussion groups held for a limited number of sessions, involving both parents, if possible. Various formats may be used for the lectures. For example, a question-and-answer period may be included, during which parents can be encouraged to raise issues of their own specific concern. For this purpose, small groups can be established after a lecture, with the discussion led by a staff member, or only small discussion groups can be planned without a formal lecture, with the staff member serving primarily as a leader and resource person.

Topics covered by the planned lectures or discussions might include subjects such as the overall training program at the center, a survey of out-patient and residential community facilities for retarded children, relevant medical information, and the special emotional difficulties both child and parents are likely to encounter. This kind of information is particularly important for parents of retarded infants, many of whom have only recently learned of their child's status. Not only are they still likely to be in a period of emotional shock, but they usually lack the kinds of factual information they need to deal more constructively with the difficulties confronting them. It can be particularly helpful to plan the topics to be dealt with so that the earlier ones emphasize more factual information, and emotional problems, as such, are reserved until the later sessions. A series of lectures for parents of retarded infants might, for example, be planned in the following way:

The first lecture or two might deal with definitions and descriptions of mental retardation. Questions of etiology could be included, and the distinction between mental retardation and mental illness clarified. The next lecture could be profitably devoted to the meaning of the IQ—how it is obtained, what it measures, and what it can and cannot predict. This session might include a discussion of intelligence in general, the different emphases placed on it at various periods in history, and its present place in the cultural values. Logically, this topic could be followed with an account of what constitutes a more inclusive and useful psychological evaluation for a retarded child. This session would provide a good opportunity for stressing the necessity of identifying the child's individual strengths as well as uncovering his particular weaknesses. The speech and language development of retarded children might be a helpful topic to be discussed next. Emphasis could be given to the special problems that often arise because of the child's difficulties in communicating, as well as the difficulties others have in communicating with him.

The special education and training needs of the retarded child might follow next. Included here might be descriptions of the kinds of special schools available in the community, the types of children they service, and the educational programs they provide. In view of the type of parents for whom these discussions are planned, emphasis should be placed on services for the younger retarded child and the special goals of programs geared to his special needs. Perhaps the next session or two might be devoted to special training materials suitable for the infant retardate, concentrating on how the parents can construct and utilize suitable materials with the child in the home. At least one session needs to be devoted to community resources available for various special services for retarded children and their families. Hospitals, clinics, special schools, nursery classes, recreation facilities, and social agencies are relevant.

Toward the end of the series "specifically" emotional problems can be introduced. A good beginning might be an overview of the special emotional difficulties that so often confront families of retarded children both within the family itself and in the larger community, emphasizing constructive methods of dealing with these problem areas. The next session or so might then concentrate on the special emotional difficulties that may be encountered by the child himself. Here, the child's emotional needs might be reviewed, followed by a discussion of the ways in which they can best be met in order to facilitate a constructive later adjustment. Following this, factual and emotional issues related to the siblings in the home, the attitudes of other children in the community to the retarded child, and the many related problems that often arise might be introduced. An important emphasis for these topics is on ways in which such problems can be minimized by constructive parental direction. A concluding session might be devoted to providing the parents with an opportunity to raise whatever additional questions they may have with the staff. The number and sequence of sessions and topics in such a series can be easily changed, depending on the needs of the particular parents involved and also those of the center itself. It is advisable to limit attendance to no more than fifteen or twenty parents. Further, since it is best to plan the topics sequentially, late admissions to the educational sessions should be avoided.

An educational counseling program can serve a number of purposes simultaneously. It can provide much necessary information, bring the parents out of isolation and into a group that shares their problems, and in many cases it can also lay the groundwork for subsequent participation in psychotherapy or counseling.

Group considerations. One of the more useful levels of group therapy for the parents of retarded infants can be best described as content-oriented, child-centered guidance, in which efforts at basic personality changes are minimized and process material and dynamic interaction are de-emphasized. Nevertheless, these groups require the same careful attention to selection of members, size of the group, preparation for participation, initial instructions and goals, and frequency and setting of meetings, as do more intensive psychiatric groups.

Selection of group members. The usual guidelines in the literature for the selection of members of therapy groups are often not applicable to the somewhat special needs of parents of retarded infants. Nevertheless, mistakes in group selection can be disastrous. For example, one therapist included a mother who was later found to be schizophrenic, with marked paranoid tendencies. The group disintegrated rapidly because of her excessive hostility and irrational suspicion and was able to continue only after she was removed and referred for individual psychiatric treatment.

Good procedures for group selection are very difficult to set up, especially since some of the factors that make for highly successful groups may not be immediately apparent. For example, one group at a center where selection was usually very careful was formed primarily on the basis of expedience. In the carefully chosen groups, members were chosen on the basis of similar educational background, socioeconomic level, and presenting psychological problems, while the "expedient" group consisted simply of mothers who remained at the center while their children attended the school. Surprisingly enough, this group was unusually successful. It was later found that these group members had crucial variables in common that the other groups lacked: their children were all moderately retarded and six of the seven were mongoloid. While many other factors in the more carefully selected groups had been considered, these two had not been taken into account. Although generalizations from a single experience are hardly warranted, it may be that the degree of the child's handicap and his diagnostic category are important in selecting candidates for this level of group work. It can be anticipated that such considerations will be less relevant in selection of members for more intensive group psychotherapy.

Initial issues. The size of the group is an important factor in determining the nature of the relationships the group members will have. It is probably best to hold the number to no more than twelve or thirteen for a primarily child-centered group. As a rule of thumb, it can be said that the larger the group the less intense the interpersonal relationships among the members. Thus, for a more intensive group experience, the number should be much smaller. Six or eight members are better for such groups, since they must be small enough to permit extensive participation of all members in the group interaction.

Adequate preparation for intensive group experience includes at least one individual session with the therapist prior to the first group session. However, for more problem-centered groups, which focus at least initially on issues directly related to the child, it may be enough to introduce the parents more informally to the process. Sometimes, the simple statement that the sessions will include discussions about the problems encountered by families of retarded children is enough. The frequency of meetings and the expected course of the sessions might also be briefly reviewed.

Initial introductions and the clearcut establishing of goals in the first session of the group meetings are extremely important and often tax the skill of the most experienced therapist. In general, it can be said that the more active and directive the therapist is at the initial session, the more passive, dependent, and silent the group members tend to become. Since the basic philosophy of group work is that its members can help each other through participation and sharing, it is incumbent upon the therapist to establish this process from the beginning. This can usually be done most effectively by a well-organized but relatively inactive therapist.

Parents of retarded children have generally been talked to, talked down to, and talked at too much already, and the group situation is often their first real opportunity to make themselves heard. The therapist must therefore establish the appropriate climate to help them do so. The basic technique for accomplishing this is deceptively simple. The therapist permits the members to determine the directions of the sessions and their content within the realistic limits of the center and its goals. If the purpose of the group is, at least to some extent, to help in decision-making about the child, then this process must become part of the group itself. It is the therapist's task to establish the initial goals of the group. However, the parents may have implicit goals of their own and pressure the sessions to move strongly in these directions. Thus, an educational discussion group may move to the counseling level within several sessions, while an intensive psychotherapy group may shift in the direction of educational discussion in a similar period of time. Basically, it is the motivation and needs of the particular parents that must remain the major factor in determining the nature and conduct of the group.

Frequency and duration. The frequency and duration of the group sessions must be suited to the goals of the members and their availability. Generally, the more frequently a group meets the more intense the interpersonal experience becomes. If meetings are less frequent, defenses are more easily reconstituted between sessions, and the therapeutic impact is apt to be diminished. For an intensive experience, groups should generally meet at least once a week, for no less than two hours. More infrequent meetings may be planned for educationally-oriented groups and also for a less intense counseling experience. However, it is important that the duration and frequency of the sessions be discussed and at least tentatively established at the first meeting, since these considerations are relevant to the kind of experience the group will provide. It is unwise, for example, to permit the development of intense interaction in a group planned for a fairly limited period, since time would not allow for the resolution and consolidation of the resulting feelings.

While intensive group work may require at least twice as many sessions, those with more restricted goals can perhaps be limited initially to twenty to forty meetings. The parents may afterwards ask to extend the sessions beyond the stated limit, which may be done provided the therapist and the other group members are available and the center can accommodate the extension. Meanwhile, a clearly stated timetable for the frequency and duration of the meetings, even if it is later changed, will permit the group members and the therapist to plan for and participate in a meaningful sequence of the group process.

Additional issues. Among other relevant issues are considerations of confidentiality and the nature of continuing group enrollment. These questions should be discussed at the early meetings of the group. The importance of confidentiality is likely to depend at least partly on the nature of the group. In general, the more intense and personal the group the more importance confidentiality assumes. In some intensive therapy groups, members are specifically requested not to discuss the session with nonmembers to protect privacy and to foster a greater sense of group cohesiveness. If this rule is established, infractions should be handled by the group, and more often than not, a member who has broken the rule will want to bring the matter up himself. It is not generally necessary, however, to establish such requirements for groups limited to the counseling level, and the issue rarely arises in connection with primarily educational groups.

In deciding the question of continuing enrollment, the goals of the group and the needs of the center often determine whether new members may be admitted later, or whether admission should be closed after the first few sessions. In either case, the decision should be stated openly at the outset, as part of the required structure. With this issue, as with many others that affect the group, a democratic choice can be honestly offered only if the members are really in a position to make the decision. Deception is destructive to the group and therapeutic process. On the other hand, self-regulation can be of great therapeutic value when and where it is feasible.

Mothers' groups. Group participation may be offered to the retarded infant's mother, his father, his siblings, and also to anyone who comes into regular close contact with him. Probably the most frequent groups consist of mothers, since they are most closely involved in the child's care and are often most receptive to and available for treatment services. Major themes in mothers' groups are usually the care, training, and anticipated future of the child, a child-centered level being often most helpful for them. This emphasis is subject to the influence of the therapist and the needs of the group. Given freedom of movement, however, many mothers' groups prefer to remain fairly close to specific problems related to retardation. Yet even here, the themes that are raised are likely to be strongly influenced by the proposed duration and frequency of the sessions. A long-term therapy group often moves through successive stages, focusing on problems related to the child chiefly in the earlier sessions. The next stage will often emphasize marital difficulties, followed, perhaps, by discussions of problems with the sibling, and then more intimate considerations of personal issues with little or no direct connection with retardation. The focus sometimes returns to problems related to retardation prior to the termination of the group. The actual sequence of group content does, of course, vary greatly from session to session, and its direction, in actuality, is neither consistent nor predictable.

Groups for both parents. There are many advantages to providing group sessions in the evening, so that both parents can attend. In such joint sessions, the mothers are likely to express anger and despair at being compelled to carry so much of the burden of the child's training themselves. The husbands, on the other hand, may openly resent their wives' demands or perhaps express guilt about not having been more available to help them with the child. Many of these evening sessions can be profitably devoted to resolving these feelings and working out constructive future plans. These joint meetings are also valuable as opportunities for discussing possible disagreements between husband and wife about the diagnosis, treatment, and prognosis of the retarded infant. The importance of this aspect of the joint group process is illustrated by the case history of Mr. and Mrs. E.:

> Mr. and Mrs. E., a young couple married about three years, had brought their 18-month-old son, Jim, to the center some four months prior to their enrollment in group treatment. They had consulted several clinics and a few private pediatricians in the hope of refuting the diagnosis of microcephaly, which had been reached when Jim was 6 months old. Each subsequent confirmation seemed at first only to provide the parents with the motivation to seek still another opinion. However, with the repeated confirmation of the diagnosis and a prognosis of probably moderate retardation for Jim, Mrs. E. had eventually accepted the reality of the child's status. It was, in fact, at her insistence that Jim was enrolled in the infant training program at the center.
>
> Mr. E., on the other hand, did not accept a realistic position. At the first group session, he stated that his son was "only temporarily microcephalic," and would be cured by surgery. He then went on to describe his talks with several physicians that had convinced him that Jim would "soon be cured." Mrs. E.'s obvious failure to support her husband's optimism

made it apparent to the other group members, even at this first session, that Mr. E.'s position was actually based on wishful thinking. However, neither Mrs. E. nor the other members of the group openly challenged his statements at that time.

In sessions during the next few months, Mr. E. reported on his progress in finding a brain surgeon who would perform the operation and would "make Jim normal." Mr. E. had contacted many hospitals, clinics, and medical specialists and had finally managed to locate a neurosurgeon in a nearby city who was willing to evaluate Jim as a candidate for possible brain surgery. Mrs. E. turned to Mr. G., whose daughter was also microcephalic, and asked him to relate his own experiences. Mr. G. said that he knew of no corrective surgery for microcephaly, and Mrs. E. reminded her husband that the doctor had said only that he was willing to examine Jim. She was certain, she added, that he would tell them exactly what they had always been told: that there is no cure.

During the next several sessions, Mrs. E. subtly began to ask for help from the group members in convincing her husband that he was being unrealistic, and some of them told of their own earlier search for a magic cure. Mr. E., however, responded angrily that he could not understand how they could abandon hope, since it was "the duty and obligation of a parent to do everything possible for his child." This led into a discussion of the goals of the training program and the obligations and expectations of the parents, topics that continued for several sessions. As other parents spoke of their own more or less limited expectations, Mr. E. was obviously astounded that they could live with the idea of having a child who would never be normal.

It took a while before Mr. E. was willing to say that he, too, might finally have to accept the idea that Jim would always be retarded. He still felt, however, that he had to make very certain that there was no cure before he could consider doing so. He was obviously still unable to accept the whole reality of Jim's status, but interaction with the group members had begun the process. He made the trip with Jim to the neurosurgeon, who evaluated the child's condition and reinforced the opinions of the previous physicians. When Mr. E. reported this to the group, he stated with obvious sincerity that he was not really so disappointed and depressed as he had been on similar previous occasions because he expected this result. Remaining in the group for the next eight months or so, he was finally able to give up his frustrating search for a "cure" for Jim and began, instead, to invest his energy in cooperating actively in the child's training program.

Fathers' groups. Groups designed specifically for the fathers of retarded infants can make a valuable contribution in their own right. Such meetings are, however, usually difficult to set up, since most fathers are available only in the evening and may be reluctant to come. It is often necessary to schedule relatively infrequent meetings for them, and perhaps to enlist a larger group than usual, since absenteeism is apt to be high. However, once the group is established attendance will often improve, particularly if the therapist permits the group the freedom to develop its own directions and standards. These are often quite different from those evolved in a mothers' group. As one member of a fathers' group said, "These are really good meetings, and they're different from the other meetings we have, which always end up talking about toilet training and diapers and speech." Even in groups for both parents, there are characteristic differences in emphasis and timing between the fathers' and mothers' expressed concerns. Fathers tend to spend less time talking about the retarded child and concentrate more on marital problems, particularly on difficulties in communicating with their wives. When they do discuss the children, the fathers may stress the child's appearance or perhaps his future, rarely dwelling on his training program and his current level of functioning. The following remarks, taken from a transcript of a group session with fathers, most of whom had mongoloid children, illustrate the self-consciousness that the child's appearance may arouse:

Mr. H.: My wife is always accusing me of being ashamed of Alice when she dresses her up to take her out with us. But she does look funny all dressed up.

Mr. J.: I know what you mean. Some clothes make them look more retarded. Sometimes you can tell a mongoloid child from the back, just by the way his clothes fit.

Mr. A.: Yeah, I know what you mean. I got very angry at my wife for cutting Janet's hair so short, because it really does make her look retarded.

Mr. J.: There's a certain thing my wife puts on Johnny that makes him look just terrible. It covers up his head almost down to his eyebrows and goes from his chest up to his chin. All you see is his nose and his eyes, and boy, he looks awful!

Mr. H.:   Well, you know, there's a hat I always hated to see Alice in, but my wife keeps telling me I used to love it on our older daughter. I guess it's really Alice, not the hat.

Mr. J.:   Maybe deep inside we're ashamed that our kids look so funny. I bet most parents of mongoloid children feel this way.

Mr. A.:   I remember when we were in a store a while back, and someone made a remark about the way Janet looked. I didn't say anything, because I didn't want my wife to hear it.

Therapist: Were you trying to protect her?

Mr. A.:   I guess so, or maybe you think maybe if you don't talk about it, it doesn't hurt so much.

A frequent topic in fathers' groups is how the retarded child has affected their marriages. Some fathers feel that the child's handicap has made the marriage stronger, while others are afraid that the marriage will be wrecked by it. Either extreme is generally modified and made more realistic by the group process. Many fathers prefer group to individual treatment, finding the group less intimidating, more supportive, and more meaningful. Since contact among the fathers is generally quite limited in their usual life situation, the group also offers a viable means of sharing experiences and feelings and identifying and resolving common problems.

Siblings' groups. Sibling groups present a unique opportunity for the brothers and sisters of retarded children to discuss their special experiences, obtain some factual information, and speak openly about their feelings. In the group setting they can also develop meaningful interpersonal relationships that can be used as a laboratory for further self-understanding and growth. It is interesting that in some sibling groups the common ground of having a retarded brother or sister is discussed largely in the first few sessions, after which the group will, of its own accord, take a more psychotherapeutic direction. Obviously, when the siblings make few subsequent references to the problem, it is not the central difficulty in their lives. More important may be questions related to their own parent-child relationships, to school, friends, and to planning their own present and future activities. The early emphasis on retardation may be followed by or tied in with whatever concerns are of primary importance to the children. The following excerpts are taken from the first meeting of a group conducted with six siblings, ages 12 to 14, each of whom had a younger retarded brother or sister. This was a group which, in addition to formal sessions, took trips into the community and engaged in various activities together. The conversation took place shortly after they had met:

Steven: My brother loves to bang things like pots and pans.

Sandra: My brother likes to tear things apart, especially books and magazines. It's his favorite thing.

Richard: So does my brother. Boy, can he make a mess! Then I go over to him and pick him up and talk to him very slowly. I tell him not to do it anymore, and sometimes he listens.

Laura: My brother's favorite thing is to throw food around. There are seven of us, and we all sit at one end of the table, and Mom sits at the other end with Dick. He likes to spit his food out all over the place. That's why she keeps him by himself. We try to tell him not to act like that, but all he does is laugh. That's all he ever does.

Bob: Boy, I bet that can drive you crazy!

Laura: Yes, it sure can! Even if you spank him, he just laughs.

Richard: Freddie likes to throw things, too. When we eat, he sits between my mother and my older sister. They try to keep an eye on him, but he still manages to throw his food around anyway. He has the most fun throwing spaghetti on the wall. That's what he likes best.

Therapist: Steve, your brother is older than the others. What's it like with him at the table?

Steven: Well, he still likes to throw things sometimes, but he's usually too busy talking. He talks all the time, and he won't let anybody else get a word in.

The group, much surprised: *He talks?*

Steven: Sure! He doesn't say whole sentences or anything like that, but you can understand what he's saying most of the time.

Sandra: They really learn to talk? Janet can't even say "ma-ma." All she does is scream when I'm taking care of her.

Therapist: How do you feel about taking care of her?

Sandra: Well, I don't like it. We sometimes have fights about it at home. She's so dumb, and there are lots of other things I'd rather do.

Steven: I take care of Greg sometimes, but most of the time I like it. He likes to wrestle, and I do, too. We have a good time wrestling on the bed. And we play catch with a great big ball. He really gets a kick out of that. I kind of look after him, and he likes me a lot. He's all right.

Bob: But what do you do when they grow up?

Therapist: Steve, what do you think about that?

Steven: Well, I know a grown-up retarded man who lives in our neighborhood. He gets along all right.

Therapist: How does he act?

Steven: Well, he keeps to himself and doesn't talk to people much. Kids sometimes tease him, but they don't mean any harm. He doesn't seem to mind. He's grown up but he wears overalls, the kind with the straps that little kids wear. And he talks to himself a lot and waves his hands around.

Bob: Yeah, but some are just vegetables. They have to go to institutions, don't they?

Steven: I guess some of them do, but not all of them. My brother's getting smarter. He'll be able to go to public school, at least that's what my Mom says.

Richard: We have a big family, and Freddie can stay with us. We'll all take care of him when Mom and Dad can't do it any more.

Sandra: But what about our lives? I wouldn't want to be a nursemaid to Janet the rest of my life. I wouldn't be able to do what I want ever!

Steven: My mother wants us to promise to take care of Greg after she's gone. I get worried when she talks like that, but she doesn't want him put away.

Therapist: How do you feel about that, Steve?

Steven: I don't know. I don't think I feel so good about it, but he's a good kid. I don't know, really. I don't think I want to think about it.

Bob: Hey, why are we talking about them so much? I thought we were going to have a club and do things together.

Therapist: That sounds like a fine idea. Why don't we discuss it?

This session represented the first opportunity these children had had to talk about their retarded siblings outside of the family group. In this and subsequent meetings they continued to refer to their retarded siblings, particularly in connection with their own roles and the demands of their parents in this respect. Nevertheless, the importance of themes related to retardation diminished, and many sessions put major attention on other issues. This shift is illustrated by the following conversation, taken from a later session of the same group:

Laura: I'm on time for a change. Where is everybody?

Therapist: I'm really proud of you. Richard is ill today but I expect Bob will get here soon.

Sandra: Does he have to come? It's so nice and peaceful when he's not here cracking jokes and not letting anybody else talk.

Laura: I really don't like him either, and I'm glad I told him that last time.

Sandra: What bothers me most about him is that he doesn't really care about anybody else's feelings but his own.

Therapist: Maybe we could help him see what he does and how it makes people feel. I don't think he means to act like that. It might help if we talked to him about it.

Sandra: Maybe that's a good idea.

Steven: I think Bob really likes you, Laura. That's why he kids you all the time.

Laura: You think so? He has a funny way of showing it. Well, I don't like him anyway.

Deena: Well, I think you were mean to him last time, and maybe that's why he might not come today. Besides, sometimes he's pretty funny, and I like to listen to him tell jokes.

Steven: I thought we were going to make things out of clay today, and not just sit around and talk. I want to make that horse we saw at the museum last week.

Bob (just arriving): Hi, everybody! Did you miss me? We can get started, now that I'm here.

Laura: Don't be so conceited! We were doing all right without you.

Sandra: I knew you'd make a wisecrack as soon as you came in. You always do it, and I may as well tell you that it really gets me angry.

Bob: OK, OK, next time maybe I won't do it.

The group members continued to react to each other, and the therapist permitted a limited amount of process material to emerge in future sessions. As the children grew more secure they became more open in their feelings toward each other and were increasingly able to examine their own contributions to the reactions of the others. Each of them also assumed a particular role in the group. Richard emerged early as a leader. Laura supported him for the most part and took over the role of leader when he was absent. Bob continued essentially as a provocateur, but largely with the therapist's influence and support he had gained much better judgment by the end of the sessions. Sandra acted primarily as an organizer of activities and a supporter of other people's ideas, while Steven consistently maintained his position as a logical, thoughtful, but somewhat detached decision-maker for the group.

Around Christmastime, Steven suggested that the group make Christmas presents for some of the children in the center's training school. This gave the group an opportunity to be exposed to older retarded children, which led to much subsequent discussion and an increased understanding of the nature of retardation. As time went on, the group took responsibility for planning their own discussions and activities, sometimes bringing in material about retardation, but also actively arranging to obtain supplies for anticipated projects or gathering information about trips they wished to take. Each of the children grew and developed during the group experience, not only in regard to their attitudes toward retardation, but also in their understanding of themselves and the effect of their own behavior on their interpersonal relationships.

Advantages of the group situation. There is little question that group situations have many advantages in helping the family of the retarded infant cope with the many problems that confront them. In particular, the group members can be mutually supportive and helpful in dealing with difficult and sensitive problems. For example, the question of institutional placement can often be raised in the group setting in a way that can help a passive, frightened mother who may simply need to listen for a while. Group discussions can promote greater insight in the overprotective and overpunitive parent alike. Open discussion and sharing of previously hidden fears and anxieties have a cathartic effect and also encourage realistic problem solving. Accepting the attitude of the therapist toward retarded children frequently occurs on an unconscious level, particularly with siblings. However, the unconscious and emotional components of problems under discussion are by no means the only factors that can be handled in a group with benefit. The most helpful therapist is also prepared to give concrete information about retardation and child-rearing when necessary, since the simple acquisition of necessary information will sometimes alter previously maladaptive patterns of thought and behavior.

Besides the goals that are common to psychotherapy in general, groups for the members of the families of young retarded children, and for the parents in particular, are designed to help them adapt to the child's condition as a basic reality of their lives. Joining with others who share this problem can be of major assistance in enabling them to confront the reality of the child's status, to work out their conflicts related to it, and to take constructive action in dealing with it.

CHAPTER 5 The Story of Frances L.

This chapter follows one little girl and her family through the various services and programs that can be provided by a large, multidisciplinary center for retarded children. The way this story begins, develops, and concludes is unique, as is the story of every child and family. There is no typical course, and no typical outcome. Even the ending of this story is tentative, since it is impossible to predict the unique future of any child.

BACKGROUND

Frances, a mongoloid child, was 28 months old when she was first brought to the center. The parents were referred by the hospital where the child was born. Mrs. L. was born in South America and came to the United States in her late teens. She was one of seven children. Her mother died when she was about 5 years old, and her father remarried some two years later. She initially reported that she had "married very young" and had not completed high school for that reason. It was, however, learned later that Mrs. L. was some ten years older than her husband, a fact she was initially unwilling to reveal. At the time of her marriage she had actually been employed as a sales clerk in a large department store. She was 35 years old when she first brought Frances to the center. Although she still retained traces of a Spanish accent, her English was quite fluent. Mr. L., the oldest of three children, was born in upstate New York. Both his parents were living. He did not complete high school, entering the Navy at the age of 17. At the time of his marriage he was still in the service, which he left shortly afterwards at his wife's insistence, taking a semiskilled position in the field of electronics, where he was still employed.

The parents reported nothing exceptional in their own family medical histories. They both stated that Frances was a "planned baby," and that they had been very pleased when they learned of the pregnancy. Although neither parent mentioned anything of major significance that took place during the pregnancy, Mrs. L. spoke of headaches, frequent urination, and periods of occasional dizziness toward the end. The gestation period was 37 weeks, and the birth was uneventful according to both the mother's report and the hospital records. The baby's one-minute Apgar rating was 10, and evidence of mongolism was noted in the birth record. The baby was premature, weighing 4 pounds and 5 ounces at birth. Mrs. L. had kept a careful record of Frances' progress almost since her birth, noting many developmental items in a "baby book," and comparing her child's responses to the developmental norms, which she wrote down beside her own entries. She had also brought these notations frequently to her husband's attention, emphasizing the child's retarded development. According to the mother's written observations, the baby held her head up at 5 weeks of age, rolled over at 5½ months, sat at 14 months, crawled at 17 months, and stood with support at 22 months. Vocalization appeared to have been quite retarded.

Mr. L. said that he had been informed that the child was mongoloid within a week after she was born, and Mrs. L. stated that, while still in the hospital, she had been advised to institutionalize the child immediately. She was willing to do this, since, as she put it, "in my country we hide mentally retarded children because they are shameful." She had not changed her mind in the interim. Mr. L., however, was strongly opposed to institutionalizing the child from the start. The issue was still a point of bitter parental contention when the family arrived at the center.

INTERVIEWS WITH THE PARENTS

During the initial interview, Mr. L. directed his conversation almost exclusively to the social worker, virtually ignoring his wife. Mrs. L. did not assert herself at that time and appeared to be quite willing to let her husband take the lead. It was noted, however, that Mr. L. apparently felt the need to be in control of the situation. He stated that his wife's knowledge of English was insufficient to allow her to answer the questions that were asked, so that he would do so for her. Mrs. L. seemed quite relaxed and was quite able to speak for herself when the occasion arose. She observed that she "gets upset about how Frances will make out when she grows up." She remarked that the child "is happy and generally easy to take care of," although she also referred to occasional temper tantrums. Mr. L. was considerably more tense than his wife and even seemed to resent her essentially placid attitude. He indicated, in fact, that he did not think she "really understands." She agreed that her husband was much more upset about the child's condition than she was.

At the informing interview, which took place some three months later, the parents were again seen jointly. A number of changes were noted this time in their behavior. Mrs. L. seemed much more self-assured and verbal than she had been at the previous interview and was reconciled to the child's status as it was presented to her. It also became apparent that Mr. L. had hoped that the diagnostic procedures would not support the information given him at the time of the child's birth. During the subsequent discussion, Mr. L. emphasized virtually every positive feature about the child, while Mrs. L. gave a consistently negative picture. It also became increasingly evident that the unassertive position that Mrs. L. had adopted at the first interview was by no means typical of her, nor did it represent her actual position in the husband-wife relationship. She was obviously the more dominant of the two. She was frankly neither interested in nor sympathetic to her husband's attitudes toward the child and had no intention of reconsidering the question of institutionalizing the child, which she was fully determined to do as soon as possible.

At the end of the interview, Mrs. L. did consent to enroll Frances in the center's home training program, although her reasons, which were quite explicit, remained consistent with her goal. She believed that if her husband became involved in a program in which his participation was required, he would realize that the child could not be kept at home. She also stated firmly that she would not have another child as long as Frances remained in the home. Since her husband was eager to have another child, she added that the sooner he "came round" to her viewpoint, the better off everyone concerned would be. Mr. L., on the other hand, wanted the child enrolled in the home training program for quite different reasons. He hoped that Frances' progress might induce his wife to want to keep the child at home and perhaps even demonstrate that the whole question of retardation was in reality "just a mistake of the doctor's."

DIAGNOSTIC EVALUATIONS OF THE CHILD

At Frances' first medical examination at the center, which took place about a week after the initial interview with the parents, she was found to have obvious mongoloid facies, a prognathic jaw, and a short neck. Her nutrition was good. She was 32 inches in height and weighed 23 pounds and 10 ounces. Her head measured 44½ centimeters and was described as "square shaped with frontal bossing." There was slight slanting of the eyes, with a left epicanthus. The intercanthal distance was 2½ centimeters. A slight horizontal nystagmus was noted in the left lateral gaze. She had 11 irregular teeth, and her oral hygiene was considered adequate. Her fingers were short, the fifth being turned inward. Simian lines were noted on both hands. Except for muscular hypotonia with hyperextensible joints and a "toddling gait" the neurological examination was essentially negative, and the electroencephalogram showed no abnormalities.

When Frances was seen for her first psychological examination shortly afterwards, she was noted to leave her mother with relative ease although she was initially somewhat tearful and whimpering. Nevertheless, she quieted down when the examiner held her and talked to her, and despite some early negativism she became increasingly willing to follow directions. She was interested and aware, exploring the environment in a purposeful way. She communicated primarily in gestures, although she used some sounds and jargon. Her fine finger coordination was very poor, and she used both hands with no indication of preference. Her mental age on the Cattell Infant Intelligence Scale was estimated at 16.4 months, and her Intelligence Quotient at approximately 53. Her social age was 18 months on the Vineland Social Maturity Scale, giving her a Social Quotient of 53.

At the speech and language examination a few days later, the communication specialist found that Frances was aware of sounds and could localize their origin reasonably well. She verbalized a few word partials, such as "si," "da," and "ma." Her comprehension level, however, was limited to grasping very simple requests such as "give me" and "don't" if they were accompanied by gestures. She did not identify simple objects by pointing and failed to match or name them when they were presented to her. She expressed her own needs primarily with gestures, also utilizing babbling, jargon, and a few unclear word partials. Since the child was considered ready for intensive work in the language of daily living, a speech therapist was assigned to the case, to visit the home at regular intervals and work directly with Frances and also with her mother. Mrs. L. was to be taught how to stimulate the child's speech to facilitate her progress, and both mother and child were to be seen periodically at the center for detailed evaluations to help in planning next steps. The prognosis for her future language development was considered good.

During the child developmentalist's classroom observation, which took place later in the same week, Frances had to be picked up and held many times to induce her to stop crying and remain attentive. It was quite apparent that her gross motor coordination was very immature. Although she tried to walk up the stairs with support, her movements were extremely insecure. She moved about a great deal but could not be described as hyperactive. She walked on a broad base with a toddling gait and was able to run without frequent stumbling. While she could climb onto a large chair fairly skillfully, she was unable to manage the smaller child-sized chairs, apparently failing to estimate the necessary positioning and turning of her body. It was also noted that she resorted to crawling when she was in a sitting position and wanted to reach an object quickly.

In the classroom, Frances was obviously aware of the presence of other children, following them with her eyes. She even made some overt attempts at socializing by handing blocks to a child sitting nearby. However, she did not maintain this interaction for more than a brief period and in general preferred to engage in parallel play activities. She spontaneously explored a number of the classroom materials and enjoyed pushing or pulling wheel toys. She could also be easily involved in ball playing, and she readily imitated the educator in strumming a toy banjo. She was apparently unaware of form and color differences except on a very gross basis and only vaguely imitated scribbling with a crayon. She was, however, extremely responsive to the sound of a phonograph, attempting to play with the dials and moving her body in response to the rhythm. Frances was obviously aware of sounds and responded quickly to her name. Although she generally required accompanying gestures, she could sometimes follow very simple verbal requests without them. She could, for example, respond appropriately to "sit down," "come here," and "give it to me." While she was unable to identify pictures she could point to her shoes, recognize a spoon and a doll, and turn her head to the light when it was named. Although she used a great deal of jargon, she seemed to appreciate sound as a means of communication.

Frances was not yet toilet trained and was wearing diapers. There were some indications that she could chew and could also recognize a few different foods. She sipped water from a cup when it was held in front of her. She frequently held her hand to her mouth and rubbed her gums, and there was some slight drooling. At times she became obstinate and willful and began to throw toys on the floor, stamp her foot, and bang her hands on the table. She was also observed to grind her teeth frequently. She held objects quite close to her face apparently in an attempt to see them better, raising the question of a visual problem. When she was returned to her mother, she immediately reached out her arms to be carried and waved "bye-bye." The child developmentalist concluded that Frances was functioning on a moderately retarded level in general and would benefit from a structured home program that emphasized the development of finger coordination and self-care training. The impression was that the child should be ready for a minimum group program in about ten months to a year.

The special dental examination showed that Frances' teeth had a number of caries, which were subsequently treated. The ophthalmological examination revealed a significant degree of myopia, for which corrective lenses were prescribed and provided. A number of special problems were encountered in finding suitable frames, since Frances had the depressed nasal bridge so often found in mongoloid children, which could not support an ordinary frame. Consultation with several optometrists resulted in a number of adaptations introduced into an existing frame, thus making it suitable for the child's nose structure. Shatterproof glass was considered to be both superior and less expensive than plastic lenses, the latter being too easily scratched. Although Mrs. L. predicted that Frances would never consent to wearing the glasses, when the child put them on she was obviously delighted with her greatly improved vision. In fact, she refused at first to take them off even when she went to bed and required considerable coaxing before she agreed to do so.

The public health nurse made her first home visit while Frances was still 28 months old. The nurse first obtained a family medical history and also a full account of the child's early developmental milestones. Mrs. L. described herself as in excellent health. Mr. L., on the other hand, reported many episodes of illness sufficiently severe to keep him from work for varying periods of time. He was considerably overweight and seemed to be very tense. In her observations of the child, the nurse noted that Frances became very resentful if she were asked to part with a chosen toy, reacting with loud cries of "no-no" and attempts to hit. When she was angry—for example, when she fell—she also hit herself and cried "no-no." She fed herself with her fingers, and although she drank from a cup if it was held for her, she was still being given a bottle. Mrs. L. described her as a "poor eater and a poor sleeper." She could turn on the television set, respond when called, and climb on large chairs and sofas without apparent difficulty. Overall, she seemed to be reasonably alert and responsive.

THE HOME TRAINING PROGRAM

The home nursing program, the first level of training to be provided for Frances, was planned to emphasize nutrition, muscle stimulation, self-care, and social behavior. During the eight months of Frances' home training there was little difficulty in inducing considerable progress in these areas. With regard to nutrition, additional dietary items were added to provide the child with a more balanced diet. Mrs. L. had fed Frances from the general family menu, allowing the child to select only the things she liked. Her eating habits also improved rapidly under a firmer approach that made less allowances for the child's whims and offered encouragement and rewards for greater cooperation. To help in the program of muscle stimulation, Mrs. L. was persuaded to accompany the nurse to the playground and to encourage Frances in a prescribed course of exercise games. The child showed evident enjoyment in using the special materials employed to increase fine muscle tone and obviously liked the playground exercises. Mrs. L. was willing to continue these procedures on her own, discussing the child's progress in some detail with the nurse at subsequent home visits. Additional materials and exercises were added as indicated.

In the area of self-care, Mrs. L. was urged to withdraw the night bottle immediately, which Frances accepted with little difficulty. The child's sleeping habits also improved fairly rapidly. Her exercise periods in the playground and at home seemed to help considerably in this respect, and she was generally ready to go to bed without resistance. She also began to sleep through the night within a matter of a week or so. Although it took some time before her earlier feeding patterns were entirely eliminated, Frances was encouraged to handle a fork and spoon, which she did in an awkward and infantile manner. She seemed to be quite proud of these accomplishments, and shortly thereafter she began to prefer using utensils rather than her fingers as tools for eating. Frances also responded well to encouragement in rudimentary dressing habits. While it was some time before real progress in dressing herself was made, she was soon able to associate various articles of clothing with the appropriate body areas. She was not toilet trained until later, but she was able, with encouragement, to become partially conditioned and to cooperate when she was placed on the toilet at regular intervals.

Frances' socialization had obviously been neglected. No attempt had been made to encourage self-initiated play activities, for example, or participation in play with other children. In both respects the nurse felt that Frances had achieved a greater readiness than was being utilized. Mrs. L. was therefore encouraged at the outset to give the child toys and play materials and to allow her to play with them by herself at various periods throughout the day. Frances adapted readily and soon began to entertain herself quietly and with evident enjoyment. At the playground, she also became gradually willing to leave her mother and go toward other children, although it was not until she entered school that she actually participated to any real extent in group activities. During this period, however, she did become increasingly aware of the presence of other children and gave some indication of a desire to interact with them.

THE EDUCATIONAL PROGRAM

Orientation. The child developmentalist reappraised Frances before her first direct participation in the orientation class. This was a small group nursery program that met regularly several times a week. Although Frances had already made many gains during her home training, the goals for this second phase of her education remained quite limited. She still preferred parallel or solitary play, her gait had improved but she still reverted at times to ambulating on her buttocks, and her attention span remained quite limited. In her first group experience, the primary goal was to develop an awareness of the needs of other children and to introduce the concepts of sharing and participating, since her major method of relating was still essentially one of disregard or dominance. Some of the significant factors that indicated Frances' readiness for participation in a group program had been slowly emerging while she was still being trained at home. She had become a well-motivated child, who wanted and needed physical and emotional contact and interaction with those around her. She had developed sufficient body motor control to be more exploratory and outgoing in the physical environment. She had also received sufficient individual attention and interest to be more trusting of new adults and more willing to separate from her mother. Frances entered the orientation group when she was three years old. The group consisted of five children working with two teachers. The nurse had occasionally brought the child to the orientation classroom during the latter part of her home training to familiarize her with the environment, the materials, the adults, and the other children. Consequently, when Frances was ready to enter the orientation class it was already a fairly familiar setting.

In the orientation class, Frances refused initially to leave her mother, partly, perhaps, in an attempt to maintain her dominant position with the mother and with the teachers as well. Almost immediately, the child "sized up" the situation and realized that she could be a forceful personality in the group. She could get by demanding, and demand she did, chiefly through recourse to persistent passive resistance. At the same time, she was quite observant and persevering, qualities that were socially endearing and educationally helpful. At first these traits led the teachers to overestimate the skills that Frances had achieved in the home training program; she appeared to be quite self-sufficient, and her strong personality tended to conceal the fact that she still needed a great deal of help and had not yet learned how to share attention. The value of the nonpunitive, planned organization became increasingly clear as Frances slowly began to develop into a less self-centered and more cooperative child. During the first few parent-teacher conferences, the teacher discussed with Mrs. L. some of the ways in which Frances tried to control adults and to dominate the situation when she and her mother arrived at school in the morning. Mrs. L. was encouraged to leave Frances in a firm and matter-of-fact way and to avoid expressing her own ambivalent attitudes about relinquishing control of the child. It was helpful to the mother to gain a clearer understanding of the child's aggressive maneuvers and helpful to the teachers to secure her cooperation in encouraging Frances to use more gentle approaches to the other children.

It was decided that for Frances herself the primary goals in the orientation program should emphasize corrective social techniques rather than the acquisition of additional skills. Because of Frances' aggressive and "bossy" approach, many of the children did not readily accept her, becoming quite resentful of her. In response, Frances became actually timid and afraid of the other children for a while, as they began to stand up to her assaults. Gradually, she recognized that her behavior was not "paying off." As she acquired and integrated more positive and cooperative approaches, the children began to acknowledge and even respect her abilities and leadership qualities. At the same time, Frances began to realize that the teacher could be an ally and a positive, helpful person, and she started to develop a fairly good relationship with her. However, she was not yet prepared to go directly to the teacher for help and support, apparently needing to retain a facade of independence and self-sufficiency.

In the classroom Frances developed her own ways of relating to the other children. Her communication skills and her high activity level were advantages in leadership. In the playroom she would go over to the other children and coax them to join in the activities, even trying to see that they were using the equipment correctly. When she saw a child being instructed by the teacher she would watch carefully and often continued the "lesson" when the teacher had finished, accompanying her demonstrations with single words or a stream of inflected jargon. The children responded favorably for the most part and often appealed to her for help. At the end of twelve months of regular attendance in the orientation program, Frances had gained in many areas of development. She was now completely toilet trained, going to the bathroom herself. She did not require adult help and was in fact likely to resent it, being quite proud that she could manage by herself. She also took pride in her personal appearance, having learned how to adjust her own clothing and primp in front of the mirror. Snacktime had become a social function she especially enjoyed. It was a period of some sharing, although she still insisted on a few special "rights" of her own. She insisted, for example, on having a particular chair, and most of the children were willing to tolerate being yanked off her self-chosen seat from time to time. They had come to like Frances enough to let her have her way in this, and they preferred getting on with the pleasures of cookies and juice to squabbling with her about the chair.

Frances had also made considerable progress in self-feeding skills, but her development in this respect was still quite uneven. Her earlier home training had led to rapidly maturing chewing ability. She could also hold a cup successfully with one hand now and drink from it without spilling. She had not yet learned, however, to pour liquids from a pitcher into a receptacle. Nevertheless, her gross coordination was rapidly improving as she was given freedom to explore the equipment in the playroom. She could now climb the parallel bars using both feet simultaneously, push herself across the bar with minimal assistance, and swing unaided. She had overcome her fear of climbing, and no longer clung to a side railing when she went up to the large slide. She had also learned to walk stairs, holding lightly onto the bannister. On the other hand, fine finger coordination was still relatively inferior. She now used a combined palmar and raking grasp, and handedness had not yet been fully established. She could handle large (3″ x ½″) and smaller (2″ x ¼″) pegs well and had begun to have some trial-and-error successes with the four-piece coordination form board, although she was unable to handle larger ones. Color differences still had little meaning for her. While she could complete a solid two-piece puzzle, she could not grasp the concept of a two-piece broken-line puzzle. She could, however, make a long string of beads, handling even quite small ones well, holding the string in one hand and the beads in the other, and making all of the necessary movements with no apparent difficulty. She had also begun to use building blocks appropriately, and carefully constructed buildings and towers with them.

During the year in the orientation class, a great deal of dramatic play was encouraged in the "housekeeping corner," laying the foundation for the development of specific skills like sweeping floors, dishwashing, and setting the table. Frances had begun to understand and follow simple verbal commands such as "come here," "sit down," "listen," "stop running," and even more complicated instructions such as "you can't go out of the room." However, although her attention span had increased, she often needed a great deal of verbal firmness to redirect and focus her activity. Otherwise she tended to give up easily, especially on difficult tasks, and would proceed to throw the materials onto the floor or disturb and disrupt the functioning of the group by taking other children's materials away from them. Because Frances really needed and wanted social approval, removing her briefly from the group at such times was usually sufficient to induce her to change her behavior. Having two teachers available was particularly helpful in the management of such behavior problems and in providing the quick and individualized treatment that Frances required in order to encourage rapid recovery.

The daily half-day program. After a year in the orientation class, Frances was considered ready to participate in daily half-day classes. In evaluating the gains she had made thus far, it was felt that she had made many improvements in the orientation class but still needed continued emphasis on corrective social techniques. There was a temporary period around this time in which Frances lost considerable ground, became angry and aggressive toward the other children, and grew quite difficult to control in the classroom. This was after the birth of her brother, when Mrs. L. became quite hostile toward her daughter for a time. This situation is discussed in some detail in the section devoted to the progress of the parents. As the mother's attitudes improved, however, Frances' behavior, too, began to show improvement. She made considerable gains in social behavior in this program, but she still found it difficult to share toys and to give up activities in which she was engrossed. While she learned to be much more helpful to the other children and had established generally friendly relationships with them, she remained quite "bossy" and obviously wanted to convince them as well as herself that "Frances knows best." At times she teased the other children but bitterly resented being teased in return. She also refused to follow the teacher's instructions from time to time, and unless she was handled with consistent firmness, she would literally attempt to take over the class.

There was little significant early change in Frances' use of manipulative play materials. For several months she chose to work only with familiar puzzles and stack rings, peg boards, and beads, hesitating to use the hammer and knockout bench, finger paint, or wet clay. During a staff case conference, it was learned that Mrs. L. was particularly proud of her ability to maintain a clean and orderly household and was quite meticulous about Frances, who was always brought to school neatly and fashionably dressed. It took much parent-teacher discussion to help the mother understand the advantages of dressing the child in denim dungarees or slacks so that she could enjoy crawling and rolling on the floor during music and physical recreation sessions. Within six months of the subsequent changes in her school clothing Frances had lost her fear of touching "messy" substances and had begun to enjoy participating in activities such as finger splatter painting. The daily school program also allowed Frances to participate in a more enriched and varied curriculum. The class was taken on special trips to local food and clothing stores, and these excursions became the basis for a series of lessons on planning which involved verbal discussions and story-telling. These activities introduced a number of new words into Frances' vocabulary and improved her ability in picture identification and recognition. She began to use language more freely and spontaneously, although her enunciation was often quite poor.

In this program Frances was also introduced to a variety of new foods as she participated in the more organized and structured snack periods. She was expected to pour from a pitcher, pass the cookie plate, and use a napkin appropriately. She learned to control her impulses to get up and play, remaining seated quietly until the other children had finished. She could be held responsible for throwing away her own paper cup and for cleaning up her section of the table. She learned to hold utensils properly, to differentiate one from another, and to use all of them appropriately. These gains made mealtimes much easier at home as well as in the classroom and also helped to prepare Frances more adequately for the full-day school program she would enter next.

The daily full-day program. Following a year in the half-day program Frances was enrolled in the full-day program. It was immediately apparent that she felt quite at home in the larger full-day classroom, where the class consisted of six other children who were supervised by one head teacher and a part-time assistant who was available for specific activities during the day. Frances quickly began to take command. Several of the children had been in the previous class with her, and she began to order them about, sometimes quite roughly. Her response to both familiar and unfamiliar adults was also very negative at times, particularly when the classroom routines were not geared to her whims. The teacher saw Mrs. L. frequently during the first two weeks following Frances' shift to the new class in order to elicit her help in instituting at home some of the responsibilities now placed on the child in school and in improving her tolerance level in the home situation generally. Mrs. L. was cooperative in reporting the daily activities and progress in the home when she brought Frances to school each day. Gradually, the child's behavior and play patterns began to indicate growth. She became less belligerent and self-concerned, while developing a more constructive sense of "me" and "mine."

Slowly, Frances began to develop a genuine group spirit and could cope more appropriately with give-and-take situations. She wanted the other children to play with her, and she would persuade them, often quite affectionately, to do so. She learned to wait her turn with reasonable patience, rather than shoving ahead and pushing the other children aside. It was more difficult for her to acknowledge the teacher's authority consistently. At times requests or requirements still brought on negativism, and her reaction to difficult materials was still apt to be merely to push them roughly away. When the teacher interfered with her own preferred plans, Frances often ignored the teacher entirely. She also became very jealous when the teacher's attention did not involve her. Meanwhile, gross motor coordination showed continued improvement. Frances learned to pedal a tricycle and began to balance herself successfully on learners' roller skates. Fine finger and visual-motor coordination developed more slowly. Although Frances was now entirely independent in self-care and grooming skills, it took another six months before she could refine her buttoning techniques. This was finally achieved through constant practice with real wearing apparel, rather than through the use of dressing frames. Mrs. L. was asked to cooperate in these attempts by not helping the child with the buttons even when Frances stamped her feet and insisted she needed help. This, plus the teacher's patience in dealing with Frances and her encouragement of the child to persevere, were major factors in helping Frances to improve.

Frances' dominant but outgoing personality was now a real asset in the group, especially during the music periods. She was eager to mimic the teachers and was genuinely helpful in maintaining order among the children as they participated in group circle games. She herself enjoyed performing in front of an audience and demanded silence and attention from the other children when she did so, but she also remained attentive when the others performed. Yet despite her many gains, Frances' conceptual and pre-academic abilities developed very slowly. Only after a full year was she beginning to match colors and pictures, and although she knew the names of colors she often used them incorrectly. She still consistently confused the names of circles, squares, and triangles, and the concepts such as "big" and "little," "in" and "out," and "up" and "down" were meaningful only when used with concrete, familiar objects and activities. In many ways, her most impressive gains were in social and interpersonal areas. Toward the end of the year, Mrs. L. reported that Frances had improved considerably in her behavior at home and had developed reasonably dependable control of her temper. She could now be taken to public playgrounds, since she no longer hit out at strange children. At school she was willing to try new materials and had become much more receptive to instruction, direction, and authority. This growing maturity helped to open up many areas for further work. For example, she could now be given the specific materials needed for perceptual training, which she needed because of her evident difficulties in foreground/background discrimination. Since she could now accept verbal reinforcement and remain seated until an activity was completed, it was much easier to teach her, and her learning was greatly facilitated.

Frances also developed pride in her work and often asked the teacher to exhibit her drawings on the classroom bulletin board. Her work was, in fact, showing much improvement in this area. Left-handedness had been established, and she was exhibiting more control in using a beginner's pencil. She progressed from outlining geometric shapes with a stencil to duplicating them with tracing paper. She acquired directional concepts through repeated practice in drawing vertical and horizontal lines with dots as starting and finishing points, and she could handle eight-piece broken-line puzzles with ease. She could now understand concepts such as "differences" and "similarities," and she had learned to categorize pictures of objects through their use, dividing them appropriately into "things to eat," "things that go," "things to wear," and so on. She could recognize and name many fruits, vegetables, breakfast foods, and articles of clothing and could even read a few short, simple sentences. Meanwhile, the need for constant supervision was reduced as she developed a realistic appraisal of hazards and danger. She also began to accept changes in her routine without reacting negatively and generally enjoyed cooperating with the other children, although she still lapsed into her former bossiness at times. Fine motor coordination improved considerably. She could now handle small buttons and close intricate fastenings. She could keep a crayon within prescribed lines and use a scissors well, cutting along outlines carefully. She had also learned to follow simple patterns on sewing cards, using a large needle and yarn.

Frances participated eagerly in the hot lunch program, frequently stimulating group conversation. She could sort and stack the trays, dishes, and utensils. Here, too, skills and behavior patterns acquired in earlier phases of her training held her in good stead. She waited her turn comfortably and quite pleasantly, followed moderately complex directions, tolerated movement easily, and communicated spontaneously and purposefully. Mrs. L. reported that mealtimes in the home had become pleasant and rewarding, and that Frances could safely be taken to restaurants. She knew how to behave in public places and enjoyed going out with the family. Knowing she could generally be depended on, her parents liked to take her along. Her greatly increased communication skills facilitated her social and formal training gains to an incalculable extent. The language training program in which she participated is described below.

THE LANGUAGE PROGRAM

Frances' language program more or less paralleled her classroom training. After her initial speech and language evaluation, it was recommended that a program of language stimulation be started, emphasizing intensive work in the language of daily living. Since Mrs. L. spoke English quite well, the speech therapist advised her to speak only English to Frances, as a bilingual environment at this time would create unnecessary problems. The language emphasis during the home training period, in which the nurse was working in the home with both mother and child, was placed on the comprehension of simple requests and the recognition of the names of common household objects. Mrs. L. was asked to use the objects' names in her daily activities around the home, repeating them aloud as frequently as possible so that Frances could become accustomed to the names of pieces of furniture, foods, and articles of clothing. At the end of the home training period, an evaluation of Frances' language level showed that she had developed the ability to respond appropriately to most simple requests without gesture and could now identify many common objects by pointing to them and using some word partials. At the interdepartmental conference where it was decided that Frances' progress was sufficient for her to be enrolled in the orientation class at school, a more inclusive language program was also planned for her.

The language program in the orientation class. When Frances moved from home training to the orientation class, the language development program continued to emphasize the cooperation of the mother and the use of the home environment in the development of Frances' language. Dolls, pictures of children and adults, and mannequins were introduced by the speech therapist, to develop Frances' awareness of self. Objects of different colors were used in various activities, such as sorting, matching, and naming colors. Meanwhile, training continued in developing a larger noun vocabulary, while the first simple action verbs were introduced through actual demonstration of the activity involved, as well as through the use of pictures and drawings. At the end of Frances' participation in the orientation class, a reevaluation of her language level showed that she had now learned to follow moderately complex requests and to recognize most common object nouns and some simple action verbs. Her expressive language had developed so that she was able to combine simple nouns and action verbs into phrases. She could name all the parts of the face and most gross body parts and was also aware of their functions. She could now name the primary colors in direct question-and-answer situations, although this did not yet carry over into her spontaneous speech.

The language program in the daily half-day class. When Frances was enrolled in the daily half-day school program the language program could be conducted on a more intensive basis, although it continued to stress language training for the activities of daily living. The primary goal during this period was to increase the length of utterance in her expressive language and to facilitate her comprehension of more complex requests. However, the temporary setback in Frances' progress after her brother was born, already noted in her educational training, also influenced her behavior adversely for a time in the language sessions. Mrs. L. indicated her own temporarily changed attitudes toward Frances' continuing in the program by questioning the value of "bothering" with the child's training. She spoke to the speech therapist about the attitudes toward women in her native country, where, she said, girls were generally regarded as having little need for education, and a handicapped girl as having even less. As Mrs. L.'s cooperation in the language program lessened and her attitudes became increasingly negative, Frances became difficult to handle and grew shy and fearful in the presence of strangers. When the speech therapist recommended that Frances be encouraged to speak to shopkeepers and other members of the community, Mrs. L. stated flatly that she could not manage this, as the child was rarely taken out now, and was "too much trouble" to be taken along on daily shopping trips.

In view of Mrs. L.'s resistance, attempts were made to continue with the language program for a time without involving the mother. However, Frances' resistance and tendency to withdraw became more and more pronounced, and it became apparent that she would not respond to efforts at establishing direct communication for the time being. In a series of interdisciplinary conferences at which Frances' behavior and the current home situation were discussed, it was agreed that a more indirect approach for the language program should be undertaken. This proved to be quite successful, and Frances soon began to respond actively. She could, for example, quickly become involved with a doll or other inanimate figures and would communicate with the therapist through the use of such toys, even though she would not do so directly. Role playing thus became a primary tool in this indirect method of communication. Frances obviously enjoyed participating in the role playing approach. She liked adopting the character and mannerisms of "the mother," and would "explain" to the doll her actions as she carried out the activities of cooking, cleaning, and caring for the "baby." At the therapist's suggestion, Frances would also become a "teacher" or a "speech therapist." At such times, she would learn by "instructing" the doll in the activities that the therapist was trying to teach her. As Mrs. L.'s attitudes toward Frances became more constructive, it was possible to return to a more direct method of treatment. Thereafter, Frances made steady progress in both receptive and expressive language.

Toward the end of this period in her educational training, Frances' language levels were sufficiently high to permit an emphasis on the acquisition of some of the more basic abstract concepts. Basic forms were taught through the use of tracing boards grooved to the shapes of the figures described, and various materials cut to the shapes of the basic forms were used for sorting, matching, and naming exercises. The concepts of "big" and "little" were taught with various-sized common objects such as shoes, boxes, telephones, and balls. The concepts of "up-down," "in-out," "over-under," "front-back," "open-shut," "hot-cold," and "stop-go" were taught in similar ways. Work was also done to improve Frances' functioning in the areas of auditory discrimination and auditory memory. Sounds common to Frances' environment, as well as nonsense syllables and actual words, were used for these purposes. Meanwhile, Frances' spontaneous speech showed growth in both quantity and quality. A greater proportion of her spontaneous utterances were now made in simple sentences, and progress in the quality of her responses to verbal requests was apparent. She could now follow two-part requests quickly and easily and could point to and name the three basic forms, although she could not yet identify them in everyday objects. She could approximate the shapes and positions of the face and body parts when drawing and respond appropriately to questions dealing with the various concepts to which she had been introduced, although she used them only rarely in her own spontaneous language. Auditory memory and discrimination also showed steady and continuing improvement.

The language program in the daily full-day class. When Frances entered the daily full-day class she maintained her gains in both receptive and expressive language and participated willingly in group language sessions in the classroom. At first, however, she objected strenuously to accompanying the therapist to the speech room for individual sessions. Her resistance to this lasted for about a month, at which time she informed the therapist verbally that she wanted to go to the speech room. Individual as well as group sessions were then undertaken. Now the emphasis shifted to much more complex material. Efforts were made to develop Frances' ability to make up simple stories and to recount her past experiences in meaningful sequences. Although she was not yet able to organize her thoughts sufficiently well to do so, she did develop the ability to repeat familiar stories and fairy tales with minimal prompting. She could also recount some of her own experiences if cues were provided when she became uncertain or confused.

At the end of a year in the full-day school program, combined with intensified language training on an individual and group basis, Frances was developing into a self-reliant child with a strong sense of self, tempered with a reasonable amount of consideration for others. She had made prominent social and classroom gains, and her language skills showed marked improvement. During the summer, the family moved to another state, and Frances was well prepared to enter a special class in a public school setting there. She made the change with fairly little difficulty. Mrs. L., who kept in touch with the center for some time afterwards, reported generally good progress. Even before she left the center, Frances had already succeeded in integrating many skills that can provide the basis for future prevocational training as she grows older.

THE PARENT TREATMENT PROGRAM

When Frances' home training program was initiated, a series of individual casework sessions were also arranged for Mr. and Mrs. L., some of which were attended by both parents and others by each of them separately. The chief purpose of these sessions was to develop an understanding of their marital situation and their relationship to Frances, in order to formulate a suitable treatment program for them. The parents themselves were eager to attend these sessions, although, it soon became apparent, for very different reasons. As had already been noted when the parents had originally agreed to enter Frances in the training program, Mrs. L. was interested primarily in having the caseworker convince her husband that caring for Frances was too great a burden for her to carry, so that institutionalization should be undertaken. Mr. L., on the other hand, hoped that the caseworker would be able to change his wife's mind about institutionalization and that she would cease to "badger" him about it. Thus, the parents regarded the sessions primarily as a means of obtaining gratification for their individual and conflicting needs, and the situation began in the spirit of destructive antagonism rather than one of constructive planning. The worker's impression was that the issue of institutionalizing had become the focus for underlying and long-standing marital problems to the point where plans for the child could no longer be constructively approached until considerable preliminary work had been done.

Mrs. L. was clearly more assertive than her husband. She was a determined and frequently rigid woman who, although she recognized Frances' limitations, was unaware of the actual extent of her anger and resentment toward the child. She was, however, quite conscious of her strong resentment toward her husband. She generally made the more important decisions for the family, and Mr. L. was usually passive and acquiescent, agreeing with her decisions. It was, in fact, on the question of institutionalizing Frances that he had taken his first firm stand. The worker felt that he may have become overidentified with the child, regarding her situation as much like his own: one in which a helpless, dependent "victim" was suffering from his wife's arbitrary and ruthless domination. His unyielding position on the question of institutionalization might thus represent primarily a stand against his wife's control of his own life. Despite his wife's insistence to the contrary, he did recognize that Frances was retarded, and did not expect a "miraculous cure" for her. His stated explanation for wanting to keep Frances at home was that she was "our child," and it was their duty to take care of her. He was unaware of the extent to which he was utilizing the child as a means of dealing with his own difficulties in self-assertion. Mrs. L. was similarly unaware that much of her resentment toward her husband was due to "being forced" to continue to care for the child toward whom she harbored intense but unrecognized anger.

Mrs. L.'s ambivalence toward the child rather clearly paralleled her ambivalence toward her husband. Even the way in which she handled the child was much the same as her method of dealing with her husband —a combination of infantalizing, controlling, and rejecting. Mr. L.'s insistence that his wife keep the child at home had given rise to a continuing sense of crisis in Mrs. L.'s emotional adjustment. She was constantly faced with her own need for punishment on the one hand

and with her rage at being punished on the other. She had also become very fearful of losing control of her unconscious anger under the pressure of continuous stress. Nor could she count on her former methods of controlling her husband, since he had openly defied her. Unable to face her own conflicts, Mrs. L. had a strong need to make her husband rather than herself responsible for her difficulties. She accused him of being irrational in insisting on maintaining the child at home and of being willing to sacrifice his wife's well-being for a futile and punitive whim. Her chief weapon in attempting to stabilize her own tenuous adjustment and regain control over her husband was an adamant refusal to have another child until Frances was removed from the home. Mr. L. regarded this as a form of personal blackmail, and his resistance and anger were greatly increased by her unyielding attitude. By the time they came to the center, the parents' mutual alienation had grown to the point where Mr. L. virtually disregarded his wife's feelings and Mrs. L. had become equally unconcerned about her husband's. When treatment began they were barely communicating and were diverting their energies largely toward using Frances as a means for acting out their hostility toward each other.

The worker's impressions of the parents' relationship suggested a suitable initial treatment program for them. In view of their evident hostility toward one another it was thought best to begin with separate counseling sessions, although joint meetings were to be conducted when indicated. In addition, Mrs. L. was to join a group of mothers that met weekly under the leadership of a clinical psychologist and emphasized a child-centered therapeutic approach. The major goal for the individual sessions was to offer each parent an opportunity to recognize and accept his own real feelings about the child, while the overall treatment goal was to help both parents arrive at a mutually acceptable agreement about a future plan for Frances. Neither "insight" therapy nor more intensive marital counseling was considered appropriate at this time, since both parents stated and apparently believed that, apart from their disagreement about the child's future, their marriage was "a happy one." It was only on this one problem that they agreed to accept help.

In the joint counseling sessions provided during this period, Mr. and Mrs. L. gradually began to listen to each other for the first time in many years, and each heard the other express his ideas, attitudes, and perceptions. For example, Mr. L. repeatedly spoke of the way he thought "a mother should behave," while Mrs. L. with equal frequency repeated "if my husband really loved me, he would not do this to me." They addressed their remarks primarily toward the therapist during this period, apparently not being ready to communicate directly with each other as yet. Initially each reacted to the other's statements with obvious antagonism, and their antagonisms were then dealt with in subsequent individual sessions, after which they were again brought together in a joint meeting. After a period of time, the joint sessions became less strained and hostile. Each parent became better able to tolerate, and even to sympathize with, the other's point of view.

Concurrently, Mrs. L. attended group sessions conducted with only mothers. She did not engage in active participation at first, remaining silent and not identifying with the other group members. However, she did listen intently to the other mothers' difficulties, particularly to their expressions of anger and resentment toward their own retarded children. Mrs. L.'s emergence as an active member of the group began with complaints abut her husband's uncompromising attitudes and his unwillingness to "do his part" in caring for the child. Since other mothers in the group had similar feelings, many lively and provocative sessions on the appropriate role of the father in the family, as the mothers perceived it, resulted. It was at this point that Mrs. L. requested that her husband attend some of the group sessions. He agreed, as did several other fathers at various points in the group sessions.

Mr. L.'s initial reaction to his exposure to the group sessions was that his wife had merely succeeded in gaining "allies" in her attempts to justify her own point of view. A similar initial reaction was expressed by most of the other fathers who attended. These reactions, too, were then discussed at subsequent individual sessions, where it was possible to work out some of these resentments; and in later group sessions both "sides" were able to modify their positions to some extent.

Simultaneously, Mrs. L. became increasingly more comfortable about expressing her antagonism toward Frances, particularly as she became more and more convinced that the other parents experienced similar feelings. She was also gradually able to take a more tolerant view of her husband's attitudes, a gain that was greatly facilitated by the interpretations the other mothers offered. Eventually she reached the point where she was willing to bring up her feelings about having another child. At first she discussed this question primarily in terms of the welfare of the family, rather than in relation to her own difficulties. She stated, for example, that she was afraid that another child would also be mongoloid and that even if he were not retarded himself, it would be a "terrible thing for him to have a retarded sister." Since several other mothers in the group had worked through similar situations, Mrs. L. found considerable reassurance in the fact that they had managed reasonably well, without serious family disruption. At about this time it was also arranged that Mr. and Mrs. L. should both participate in a genetic study to provide them with more factual information. The results indicated a very high probability that the next child would not be retarded, a form of reassurance that hastened the solution to this aspect of the problem.

About halfway through the period of treatment Mrs. L. announced that she was pregnant and admitted that although she was still somewhat fearful, she was also pleased and even proud of the new pregnancy. Mr. L. was obviously delighted by the prospect of another child. He also regarded it as an indication that his wife had modified her former attitudes. As a result, he became increasingly willing to retreat to some extent from his own. He even began to consider possible advantages of institutionalizing Frances at some future date. Mrs. L., on her part, no longer urged immediate institutionalization, although she reserved the right to take this step in the future, if she found caring for both Frances and the new baby too difficult. Both parents, then, had shifted their original irreconcilable positions at least to the extent to which a mutually acceptable solution was possible. By this time Frances herself was participating in the orientation program in school, and the parents, now more comfortable with each other, could see her many gains and were able to find considerable satisfaction and even pride in her beginning accomplishments in self-care. This reinforced their emerging confidence that she might become a "real" member of the family in her own right.

Frances was attending the daily half-day school program when her brother was born, which allowed the mother more time to care for the new baby. However, a number of unfortunate but temporary setbacks arose at this time. Mrs. L. developed unwarranted fears that Frances would hurt the infant and became harsh and punitive with her. Frances' behavior in the classroom became angry and difficult to control. In view of the situation that was developing, the caseworker suggested that therapy, which had been discontinued toward the end of Mrs. L.'s pregnancy, be resumed. Individual therapy was reinstituted for both parents, and the mother again participated in a group. As before, Mrs. L. was initially silent, although she became a participating member of the group within a short time. Now Mrs. L. was able to express intense anger toward Frances for her retardation and "stupidity," and also for the fact that she "looked different" from other children. The other members of the group had no difficulty in accepting these feelings and frankly admitted that they often experienced similar ones themselves. Mrs. L. continued to attack Frances for a number of sessions before she was finally willing to shift to a more positive emphasis on the child's progress. At length she began to tell the group of some of Frances' accomplishments in school and at home. While she continued to speak with enthusiasm of the baby, she did so decreasingly in terms of unfavorable comparisons with her daughter. Frances' behavior in school began to improve as her mother became more supportive and interested.

Mr. L. was proud of the new baby, although he also retained his affection for Frances. He did, however, transfer some of his intense identification with Frances to his son and became less defensive in regard to her. In the joint sessions, the changes in the relationship between Mr. and Mrs. L. were quite marked. They now spoke directly to one another, instead of addressing themselves almost exclusively to the therapist, as they had formerly done. It was also apparent that they were beginning to discuss their mutual problems together at home, making real attempts to resolve them. Toward the end of her second year of group participation, Mrs. L. had become one of the most candid and verbal group members and often proved of real assistance in helping other mothers resolve problems similar to her own. Shortly after Frances began attending the daily full-time school program, it was agreed that Mr. and Mrs. L. were ready for a less intensive treatment program. Their relationship to each other and to both of their children had become much less tense and more harmonious. Mrs. L. was now seen about once a month for individual treatment sessions, and Mr. L. participated on an "as needed" basis. Counseling continued while Frances was in the school program, with emphasis on realistic planning for Frances' future. Mr. L. attended occasionally, and it was evident that both parents were proud of Frances' increasing skills and accomplishments and of the fact that they were making a real contribution to the child's progress.

Toward the end of the school year, Mr. and Mrs. L. began preparations for their move to another state. They were both seen for counseling several times during this period and were advised that Frances was ready for special class placement in public school and that a suitable educational setting was available in the area to which they were moving. The parents had not yet come to any final decision about the possibility of ultimate institutionalization for Frances, but they both wanted to wait, certainly for the time being, in view of the progress Frances had already made. They had, however, arrived at a far more important decision: that they would work things out together, without recrimination and without involving the child in their own emotional difficulties, and would take whatever course would be most constructive for the whole family.

GENERAL CONSIDERATIONS

The case of Frances and her family illustrates a number of factors that influence the progress of many other children and families receiving special services geared to the problems of retardation. For example, as the child becomes more trusting and secure, he grows increasingly available for the more formal aspects of a training program. This availability, in its turn, will be greatly facilitated as the parents, particularly the mother, begin to relinquish excessive anxiety and overcontrol. Concerns about scrapes and bruises and paint and dust on clothing give way to parental satisfaction and pride in the child's improvement as realistic interest begins to replace overprotection.

As in the case of Frances, self-care is usually a major training emphasis for retarded children, and encouraging their physical development is closely related to this goal. The availability of special equipment specifically designed to foster motor coordination and perceptual skills, plus the calm, encouraging attitudes of the teachers, can do much to help the children participate in and ultimately succeed in mastering previously avoided and new activities. The cooperation of the parents in continuing the school training at home is a crucial factor in the child's improvements in these respects.

Like Frances, many of these children can be successfully toilet trained, and their eating habits and behavior improved. Children who had previously been kept on liquid diets or baby foods can often learn to chew and swallow solid food, drink from a cup, and feed themselves independently. As the added burdens of diapers and special foods are lifted, the parents can begin to enjoy taking their child with them to restaurants and picnics, as did Mr. and Mrs. L. Their increasing confidence and approval of the child typically meets with reactions like Frances': confidence and self-acceptance.

As the child begins to master the basic skills, his social and interpersonal awareness and interest also tends to increase. His inner need for relatedness impels him to use whatever means he can for communicating with the teacher and with the other children—whether through gestures, vocalizations, facial expressions, or words. As familiarity and communication skills increase, the child learns to anticipate the reactions of others, adapting his own social behavior accordingly. He learns, for example, which of the other children should be approached for help in fastening buttons and putting away play materials and which are more likely to reject his appeal. He also learns to go to the teacher with problems with which he really needed help and to complete unaided those tasks which he is expected to complete by himself.

The whole climate and organization of the child's school day should provide him with a sense of security, comfort, and consistency, enabling him to give up some of his more infantile needs in favor of the satisfactions of cooperation. As a result, decreasing amounts of time are needed for management problems and longer periods can be devoted to developing special activity programs. Gains in basic living skills allow the child to be better able to cope with areas of special difficulty, more comfortable in his relationships with his parents, and more adequately prepared for future training programs. Frances' gains in these respects represent similar gains made by many other retarded children in educational settings adapted in their special needs and appropriate to their limited abilities. The way in which Mr. and Mrs. L.'s changing relationships with Frances and with each other were reflected in the child's behavior is a typical example of the interdependence of the progress of the child and the family.

CHAPTER 6

Some Further
Considerations

Setting up and administering a multidisciplinary training program for retarded infants is a complex and difficult undertaking. In the course of its development, a miscellaneous store of information related to special problems, practical techniques, and theoretical considerations is naturally gathered. It is the purpose of this chapter to describe briefly a few of these considerations that have not been previously discussed.

THE PROBLEM OF DIAGNOSTIC DELAYS

The complete diagnostic process for a retarded infant may take between two and six months, and in some cases even more. This may seem excessively long, since theoretically, at least, it might be possible to complete the evaluation within a week. For a number of reasons, however, such speed is rarely feasible and in many instances would not even be desirable. For example, in assessing the developmental process, there may be definite advantages in allowing a period of months to go by in order to be better able to evaluate growth patterns before making the final diagnosis. The opportunity for periodic reassessments of particular functions over time may provide important clues as to rate and patterns of growth that would not be identifiable in a single examination. In addition to considerations of this kind, there are many practical difficulties that may greatly increase the waiting time. The need for obtaining prior diagnostic and treatment data, problems in scheduling necessary laboratory examinations, and cancellations of appointments by the parent are three common causes of delay.

A clearcut and well-documented diagnostic picture may involve accumulating a great deal of data, including time-consuming collection of all the records of the child's previous diagnoses and treatment experiences. It may take several months simply to obtain the child's birth record and even longer to secure reports from all of the private physicians who may have examined and treated him. If the child has a common surname, or if the family has recently moved, it may be hard even to identify the child promptly in agency records. Hospitals that assign clinic numbers to patients may require the child's number before they take care of requests for information, and if the parents have mislaid the number, a personal visit to the hospital may be necessary. It will often expedite information-gathering to some extent if the parents are asked to sign a release at the time of their application for services, giving the staff permission at least to begin the process of sending for the child's records as quickly as possible. The obvious value of establishing a central medical data bank for handicapped children to minimize delays in the information-gathering process has been discussed frequently but unfortunately has not yet been implemented. Such a service would do much to make the diagnostic process faster, more inclusive, and more accurate.

Additional delays in diagnostic procedures result from the current serious shortage of laboratory facilities. It is not unusual for a child to have to wait a month for an appointment for an electroencephalogram or skull X-rays and perhaps an additional month or two for a report to be sent out. Further, the first time the procedure is undertaken it may be invalid, resulting in still further delays. In addition, sufficient personnel are not available for many necessary special services. For example, staff and facilities for genetic analyses are so scarce that a three- or four-month wait is considered short. To some extent, an agency may be able to minimize long waiting periods by establishing an affiliation with a hospital laboratory, but here too there is strong competition for both personnel and equipment.

Cancellations of appointments by the mother of the retarded child are quite frequent, leading to still more delay. The mother's responsibilities to her other children and the retarded child's special vulnerability to certain illnesses often result in unavoidable cancellations and the need for rescheduling. If sufficient funds are available or enough volunteers can be recruited, it is possible to arrange housekeeping assistance and transportation services when necessary so as to decrease this cause of delay considerably.

Prolonged diagnostic procedures mean that parents must often wait a long time to learn the results of the child's evaluation, and still longer before a treatment program can be instituted. While this interim can be anxiety-provoking for the parents, the time can be spent constructively by setting up a limited treatment program for selected families and some types of problems during the waiting period. The social worker may, for example, help the family with a possible housing problem, or offer supportive counseling in connection with expressed interpersonal difficulties. The nurse may assist with family medical problems and make some tentative suggestions about a few training procedures for the infant. The speech therapist may explain language development and perhaps visit the home to give some preliminary lessons in speech stimulation, if the child is ready. The interim period can also serve to give some of the less realistic parents an opportunity to study their child, and perhaps later to be more prepared to accept his diagnosis without undue shock, as a corroboration of their own observations. It cannot be denied, however, that for many parents the usual diagnostic delay has largely negative results, including increasing uncertainty and exacerbating depression.

RESPITE CARE

Respite care is beginning to be available for the families of retarded infants in various communities in the United States. These programs provide care for the child for limited periods, in order to relieve the family temporarily of caring for him. These services may take the form of nursing help, baby sitting, or homemaker services in the home. It may also include temporary foster home or nursing home placement for the infant. At present these services are quite limited, but the great need that exists for them will hopefully foster their growth.

Meanwhile, state agencies are beginning to provide some levels of respite care for retarded children. Until recently, state facilities have offered only permanent placement for a retarded child, and in many cases services were limited to custodial care. Thus, parents were often faced with an inflexible and rigid policy of definite commitment of their child. Fortunately, this policy seems to be slowly changing as state facilities are instituting more progressive and flexible programs and are adapting to the immediate needs of parents who wish to keep their child at home but who may require temporary residential assistance. These new programs, many of which are still in the planning stage, include short-term admissions, trial separations from the family, resident care during a family emergency or perhaps for a family vacation, placement for a limited period for behavior modification, medical management, or some other form of training for the child. The development of these programs of respite care on a meaningful scale would be of great benefit to the child, the family, and the community.

PRACTICAL CONSIDERATIONS FOR PARENTS

There are a number of practical suggestions that can be made to help parents adapt more successfully to their new and difficult role as parents of a retarded child. Some of these are apt to be neglected by professional workers, who may feel that their simplicity implies that they are common knowledge. Others may be obtained by the parents only after specific questioning of other parents or professional personnel. Too often, the simple, pragmatic aspects of adjusting to the new status are overlooked by the professional worker or, perhaps even more frequently, are not communicated to the parents because of professional hesitation to give direct advice. The few simple suggestions mentioned here are offered with full appreciation of the dangers inherent in giving any general rules or guidelines. They are neither complete nor universally applicable and are actually nothing more than reflections on some practical steps that parents have found helpful in the past.

Most parents would probably benefit from joining a local chapter of an organization for parents of retarded children. The social and interpersonal advantages of such membership are obvious, and much factual information is made available through this means. Further, apart from the evident therapeutic effects of relating to others who share their own problems, the parents can meaningfully refer the educational and vocational needs of their children to the proper legislators through such an organization. Many of the legal gains that have been obtained for retarded children have, in fact, been brought about in response to pressure from these parent groups. Parents are also likely to gain a great deal by acquiring as much knowledge as possible about retardation through reading, asking questions of other parents, and consulting with professionals specializing in this area. The more knowledge a parent has about retardation, the more free and flexible he is likely to be in determining the future of the child. Lists of relevant reading material for parents are readily obtainable from the National Association for Retarded Children.

It is also helpful for the parents to visit special facilities that may be suitable for their own child. Usually, arrangements to visit these facilities are easily made. Actually seeing, say, a state school or a special public school class can provide some needed information and do much to dispel the many myths and misunderstandings that the parents are likely to gather as they go along. The parents should seek objective, factual material through every possible means. Knowledge of the facts can do much to avoid some of the pitfalls that have brought considerable emotional and financial tragedy to many parents. Retardation is a chronic condition, and whatever progress can be achieved will be slow. Parents should therefore be suspicious of any procedure that promises fast results or "cures." Too many parents have been tragically misled or actively deceived by fads or false claims that have served only to generate unrealistic hope while preventing the child from receiving sound professional treatment.

For many parents, it is both helpful and relieving to remember that there is rarely a need to make precipitous decisions or quick commitments to a specific course of treatment. There is almost always time to request an additional consultation, or further time in which to consider the wisest course to follow. And finally, it is very important for the parents to make every effort to learn about the legal, financial, and educational rights of their child. His future, and often theirs as well, can be greatly influenced by parental awareness of these areas. Many local libraries have reference materials on these subjects, and valuable seminars are often sponsored by parent and professional organizations dedicated to the needs of retarded children and their families.

MODELS FOR A DIAGNOSTIC AND TREATMENT CENTER

Most diagnostic and treatment programs for retarded infants are part of hospital settings or of specialized private or government supported facilities for the retarded. Both models have advantages. The hospital setting, even with its often intense internal competition for personnel and services, sometimes offers greater access to medical and laboratory facilities. Further, parents may have more confidence in a medical setting. They may also be more willing to have their child evaluated there, since a hospital examination does not necessarily imply that retardation is suspected. On the other hand, a specialized agency for the retarded offers a greater variety of specialized personnel, a more educationally-slanted orientation, which may foster a more inclusive prognostic evaluation, and, of even more importance, an integration of diagnosis and treatment services, which eliminates the need to locate a suitable treatment center afterwards.

Perhaps the most efficient arrangement, and one that would combine the best features of both types, would be for the hospital clinic to serve largely as a screening and identification center, making immediate referrals to the more specialized agency for more intensive diagnostic work-ups and for carrying out the treatment program. Such a cooperative effort might also serve to encourage screening for larger numbers of infants, resulting in earlier detection of defects and more efficient treatment for those who need them.

Regardless of the model, an important function of the specialized center is to undertake the training of suitable personnel. The growing movement for protecting the retarded child's right to education has led to a need for specialized personnel in all aspects of the programs. The multidisciplinary center for diagnosis and training can provide unequaled opportunities for preparing the future specialist for his chosen area of work. Physicians, psychologists, social workers, speech therapists, and educators can all gain the special experience and training they will need. Special programs for paraprofessionals can also be conducted at the center to help supplement the limited number of professional personnel available.

The center must also involve itself in the community it serves. It must reach out to encourage referrals for retarded infants and to orient other agencies to the problems of the retarded and encourage them to develop supportive programs for the children and their families. Staff members of the center must visit clinics, family social agencies, and parent groups, speak at various professional meetings, and distribute printed material for newsletters, bulletin boards, and training courses. Social services and health agencies in the community can often be utilized for ancillary services even if they lack specific programs for the retarded. Some family agencies may, for example, have available counseling and supportive services for multiproblem families. Visiting nurse associations and child health stations may be able to help supervise medical treatment and provide homemakers for home-care programs, supplying help that the center itself may not be able to provide.

What would constitute an ideal diagnostic and treatment center for retarded infants and their families is not yet even known. The model described in this book is not necessarily either the perfect or even the preferred one. In fact, there are some obvious extensions that would make it far more inclusive and long-range in its goals. With only a few additions to the services described here, it would be possible to envision a day training center for retarded infants that would combine diagnosis and treatment with personnel training and research and offer services on a more intensive basis for both child and parent. Such a program would, in effect, be a day school for retarded children from birth to about three years of age, providing daily attendance for four-hour sessions, part of which would directly involve the parents. The remaining part of their participation in the program would include various therapeutic, educational, and social activities that the center would plan and organize for them.

The availablility of the infant for such prolonged and consistent periods of time would permit more intensive training and stimulation than are possible even in a combined training and clinic visit program such as is presented here. Further, in such a setting it might be possible to control the infant's whole environment for considerable time periods, perhaps accelerating his adaptation and his learning. Under such controlled conditions, it might be possible to alter the presentation of stimuli systematically, so as to facilitate his sensory and perceptual responsiveness. A day training center of this kind would also provide an excellent setting for research into the basic parameters of the retarded infant's development and permit specific study of the actual conditions that facilitate his learning. Hopefully, the recent impetus for the establishment of day-care programs for normal infants will stimulate increasing interest in and pressure for equally needed programs for the retarded. Many of these infants will need lifelong help if they are to be anything but burdens to their community and drains on society. They will be handicapped throughout their lives. Many of them are nevertheless capable of becoming at least semi-independent, but none of them can afford the added handicap of a bad start.

Glossary

Adenoma sebaceum. A neoplasm occurring on the face, composed of a mass of sebaceous glands and appearing as an aggregation of red, red-yellow and yellow papules. The patients are sometimes mentally defective.

Amniocentesis. Aspiration of amniotic fluid usually for genetic studies.

Angioma. A swelling or tumor due to dilation of the blood vessels (hemangioma) or lymphatics (lymphangioma).

Anoxia. A deficient amount of oxygen in the tissues of any part of the body or in the bloodstream supplying such a part. When this deficiency occurs at birth, damage to the brain may result in mental retardation.

Apgar rating. Evaluation of a newborn infant's physical status by assigning numerical values to heart rate, respiratory effort, muscle tone, reflex irritability, and skin color.

Asphyxia. A coma due to a deficiency of oxygen causing anoxia.

Ataxia. A loss of the power of muscular coordination.

Audiometry. The measurement of hearing sensitivity and acuity; generally classified into pure tone audiometry and speech audiometry.

Cataracts. A loss of transparency of the crystalline lens of the eye or of its capsule.

Cerebral palsy. Paralysis or muscular incoordination due to intracranial lesion: the term is applied to a group of cerebral afflictions in children.

Cleft palate. A congenital fissure of the soft and/or hard palate, sometimes extending through the premaxilla and the upper lip, which is further described as a cleft lip.

Cognition. The set of mental processes by which knowledge is gained or integrated or problems are solved; such processes are based on sensory perception and include discrimination, judgment, memory, conception, and reason.

Congenital. Existing at birth, including either of two conditions: (1) that of heredity or (2) that of pathology following conception of the embryo. Congenital is always limited in use to describing a disease, deformity or deficiency.

Cretinism. A congenital condition due to thyroid deficiency and characterized by physical and mental retardation.

Down's Syndrome. See Mongolism.

Echolalia. Automatic reiteration of words or phrases, usually those that have just been heard.

Edema. An abnormal amount of fluid in the lymph interspaces of the tissues under the skin.

Educable mentally retarded. Term used to refer to mentally retarded persons who are capable of some degree of achievement in academic subjects such as reading and arithmetic. Also used to refer to those mentally retarded children who may be expected to maintain themselves independently in the community as adults.

Encephalitis. An inflammation of the brain resulting from an infection.

Epicanthus. An anomaly in which the inner junction of the eyelids is covered by a fold of skin. One of the stigmata of mongolism.

Epilepsy. A chronic disease characterized by the appearance of convulsions or their equivalents.

> *Grand mal.* Major form of the disease in which the convulsions are generalized over the body with accompanying alterations of consciousness.
>
> *Petit mal.* A milder form of epilepsy characterized by a momentary loss of consciousness.
>
> *Psychomotor epilepsy.* A type of epilepsy in which irrational reactions, such as temper tantrums, serve as substitutes for, or equivalents of, convulsions.

Etiology. The cause of an abnormal condition or disease.

Fontanel. An opening between the cranial bone covered by a membranous structure. There are normally six such intervals in the newborn and infant.

Galactosemia. A congenital disorder of carbohydrate metabolism resulting in an accumulation of galactose in the bloodstream. It is characterized by nutritional defects, enlargement of the liver and spleen, cataracts, and mental and physical retardation.

Hydrocephaly. Commonly called "water on the brain." A condition of increased secretion of serum into the cranial spaces with a possible consequent of pressure to such a point that the cranial organs may be damaged.

Hypertelorism. A congenital craniofacial deformity in which the distance between the eye sockets is abnormally great. Frequently associated manifestations are cleft lip and palate, malocclusion, congenital abnormalities of the fingers, hands, and heart, and mental retardation.

Hypoglycemia. An abnormally small concentration of glucose (sugar) in the circulating blood.

Jargon. Inflected but unintelligible utterances combined with a mini
mal number of words forming part of the transition from the earlier
babbling stage to the final acquisition of overall use of speech. Nor
mally occurring around the age of eighteen months.

Meningocele. A protrusion of the membranes of the brain or spinal cord
through a defect in the skull or spinal column.

Mental retardation. Subaverage general intellectual functioning that
originates during the developmental period and is associated with
impairment in adaptive behavior.

> *Borderline retardation.* Intellectual functioning ranging from 70 to
> 84 IQ as measured by standardized testing materials.

> *Mild retardation.* Intellectual functioning ranging from 55 to 69 IQ
> as measured by standardized testing materials.

> *Moderate retardation.* Intellectual functioning ranging from 40 to
> 54 IQ as measured by standardized testing materials.

> *Severe retardation.* Intellectual functioning ranging from 25 to 39
> IQ as measured by standardized testing materials.

> *Profound retardation.* Intellectually below 25 IQ as measured by
> standardized testing materials.

Mongolism. Mongolism is a syndrome in mental retardation characterized by such physical stigmata as epicanthic folds, webbed neck, short
fingers, inturned fifth finger. It is essentially based upon a chromosomal defect.

Negativism. Perverse opposition and resistance to suggestions or advice. Often observed in people who subjectively feel "pushed
around."

Nystagmus. A rapid involuntary fluctuation of the eyeballs.

Occiput. The protruding back part of the head at the base of the skull.

Paranatal. Pertaining to the period immediately following birth and to pathological conditions of the newborn related to the events of birth.

Phenylketonuria. A rare inherited metabolic dysfunction whose destructive effects (including mental retardation) can now usually be circumvented through special diet during the early years of life.

Pneumoencephalogram. X-ray picture of the brain under conditions where the cerebrospinal fluid has been replaced with air or gas for study purposes.

Refractive errors. Errors in the deflection of a ray of light when it passes from one medium into another of a different optical density. Eye examination determines the nature and degree of the refractive errors in the eye and the correction of the same by lenses.

Rigidity. Refers to muscular immobility. Also used as a psychological term to refer to inflexibility or lack of adaptability of behavior.

Rubella. Commonly called German measles. Congenital anomalies including deafness, cataracts, cardiac malformations, and mental retardation may result in offspring from mothers contracting rubella in the first trimester of pregnancy.

Spasticity. Increased muscular tension associated with exaggeration of deep reflexes, involuntary muscle contractions, and a partial loss of voluntary movement.

Strabismus. A visual defect due to inability to direct the eyes to the same point as a result of incoordination of the ocular muscles.

Esotropia. Internal strabismus. A deviation inward of the eye.

Exotropia. External strabismus. A deviation outward of the eye.

Toxemia. A condition in which the blood contains toxic or poisonous substances.

Toxoplasmosis. An infectious condition contracted in utero from the mother. Convulsions, spasticity, hydrocephalus, or microcephaly may be evident at or shortly after birth.

Trainable mentally retarded. A term used to refer to mentally retarded persons whose disabilities are such that they are incapable of meaningful achievement in academic subjects but who, nevertheless, are capable of profiting from programs of training in self-care, social, and simple vocational skills.

Tremors. Rhythmic, involuntary muscle movements.

Vineland Social Maturity Scale. An inventory designed to evaluate an individual's level of social adaptation in which information is usually supplied by the parents.

GLOSSARY REFERENCES

Bensberg, G. J., Jr., ed. *Teaching the Mentally Retarded: A Handbook for Ward Personnel.* Atlanta, Ga.: Southern Regional Education Board, 1965.

Heber, R. *Manual on Terminology and Classification in Mental Retardation.* Ohio: American Association on Mental Deficiency, 1961.

Robinson, H. B., and Robinson, N. M. *The Mentally Retarded Child: A Psychological Approach.* New York: McGraw-Hill, 1965.

Stedman's Medical Dictionary. 21st ed. Baltimore: Williams and Wilkins, 1966.

Travis, L., ed. *Handbook of Speech Pathology.* New York: Appleton-Century-Crofts, 1956.

West, Robert W., and Ansberry, Merle, *The Rehabilitation of Speech.* 4th ed. New York: Harper and Row, 1968.

References

1. Adams, Margaret, ed. *The Mentally Subnormal: The Social Case-work Approach.* London: Heineman Medical Books Ltd., 1960.

2. "A Handbook for the Primary Physician," *Journal of the American Medical Association,* CXCI (1965), 183–232.

3. Akins, Keith. "A Psychotherapeutic Approach to Reading Retardation," *Canadian Psychiatric Association Journal,* XII, v (1967), 497–503.

4. Albini, Joseph L., and Dinitz, Simon. "Psychotherapy with Disturbed and Defective Children: An Evaluation of Changes in Behavior and Attitudes." *American Journal of Mental Deficiency,* LXIX, iv (1965), 560–567.

5. Alexandru, Sen. "Citena Aspecte ala Atentiei la Copii Oligo Freni (Some Aspects of Attention Among Oligophrenic Children)," *Revista de Pschologie,* VII, iv (1961), 619–641.

6. Allen, Mary, Shannon, Gizella, and Rose, D. "Thioridazine Hydrochloride in the Behavior Disturbance of Retarded Children," *American Journal of Mental Deficiency,* LXVII, i (1963), 63–68.

215

7. Allen, Robert M. "Factor Analysis of the Developmental Test of Visual Perception Performance of Educable Mental Retardates," *Perceptual and Motor Skills,* XXVI, i (1968), 257–258.

8. Ambrose, A., ed. *Stimulation in Early Infancy.* London: Academic Press, 1969.

9. Ambrosino, Salvatore. *A Project in Group Education with Parents of Retarded Children. Casework Papers 1960.* New York: Family Service Association of America, 1960.

10. Anderson, Alice V. "Orienting Parents to a Clinic for the Retarded," *Children,* IX (1962), 178–182.

11. Anderson, F. P. "Evaluation of the Routine Physical Examination of Infants in the First Year of Life," *Pediatrics*, VL (1970), 950–962.

12. Anderson, J. E. "The Limitations of Infant and Pre-School Tests in the Measurement of Intelligence," *Psychology*, VIII (1939), 351–379.

13. Anderson, L. D. "The Predictive Efficiency of Infancy Tests in Relation to Intelligence at 5 Years," *Child Development*, X (1939), 203.

14. André-Thomas, Chesni Y., and Sainte-Marie, Dargssies S. *The Neurological Examination of the Infant.* London: National Spastics Society, 1960.

15. Andrey, B. "Recherches sur la Débilité Mentale (Research on Mental Retardation)," *Bulletin de Psychologie,* XX (1967), 870–873.

16. Auerback, Aline B. "Group Education for Parents of the Handicapped," *Children*, VIII (1961), 135–140.

17. Baer, Donald M., Peterson, Robert J., and Sherman, James H. "The Development of Imitation by Reinforcing Behavioral

Similarity to a Model," *Journal of the Experimental Analysis of Behavior*, X, v (1967), 405–416.

18. Balla, David A. "The Verbal Action of the Environment on Institutionalized and Noninstitutionalized Retardates and Normal Children of Two Social Classes," *Dissertation Abstracts*, XXVII, xiib (1967), 4547.

19. Bangs, Tina E. *Language and Learning Disorders of the Pre-Academic Child: with Curriculum Guide.* New York: Appleton-Century-Crofts, 1968.

20. Barr, B. "Pure Tone Audiometry for Pre-School Children," *Acta Otolaryngologica* Supplement, CXXI (1955), 5–82.

21. Barry, H. *The Young Aphasic Child.* Washington, D.C.: Volta Bureau, 1960.

22. Barsch, Ray H. "Explanations Offered by Parents and Siblings of Brain-damaged Children," *Exceptional Children*, XXVII (1961), 286–291.

23. Barsch, Ray H. "The Infant Curriculum—A Concept for Tomorrow." *Exceptional Infant*, Vol. I. Ed. Jerome Hellmuth. Seattle, Washington: Special Child Publications of the Seattle Seguin School, 1967.

24. Bateman, Barbara. "A Pilot Study of Mentally Retarded Children Attending Summer Day Camp," *Mental Retardation*, VI, i (1968), 39–44.

25. Bayley, Nancy. "Mental Growth During the First Three Years," *Genetic Psychology Monograph*, 1933.

26. Bayley, Nancy. "On the Growth of Intelligence," *American Psychologists*, X (1955), 805–818.

27. Bayley, Nancy. "Value and Limitations of Infant Testing," *Children*, V (1958), 129.

28. Bayley, Nancy. "Behavioral Criteria for Diagnosing Mental

Retardation in the First Two Years of Life," *California Mental Health Digest,* III, i (1965), 31.

29. Bayley, Nancy. "Research in Child Development: A Longitudinal Perspective," *Merrill-Palmer Quarterly*, II, iii (July 1965).

30. Beck, Helen L. "Counseling Parents of Retarded Children," *Children*, VI (1959), 225–230.

31. Beck, Helen L. "Casework with Parents of Mentally Retarded Children," *American Journal of Orthopsychiatry*, XXXII (1962), 5.

32. Begab, Michael J. "Precommitment Services in a Training School for Mental Defectives," *American Journal of Mental Deficiency*, LIX (1955), 690–697.

33. Begab, Michael J. "Child Welfare Service for the Mentally Retarded," *Children*, V (1958), 3.

34. Begab, Michael J. *The Mentally Retarded Child: A Guide to Services of Social Agencies.* Washington, D.C.: U.S. Government Printing Office, 1963.

35. Begab, Michael J. "Mental Retardation: The Role of the Voluntary Social Agency," *Social Casework*, XL (1964), 8.

36. Bella, Concepcion D. "Education of the Retarded in Manila Public Schools," *Mental Retardation*, V, vi (1967), 34–36.

37. Benda, C. E. *Mongolism and Cretinism*. New York: Grune and Stratton, 1949.

38. Benda, C. E. *Developmental Disorders of Mentation and Cerebral Palsies*. New York: Grune and Stratton, 1952.

39. Benda, C. E. *Down's Syndrome: Mongolism and Its Management*. Revised ed. New York: Grune and Stratton, 1969.

40. Bender, L. *A Visual Motor Gestalt and Its Clinical Use*. Research Monograph No. 3. New York: American Orthopsychiatric Association, 1938.

41. Berkowitz, Pearl. "Some Psychophysical Aspects of Mental Illness in Children," *Journal of Genetic Psychology Monograph*, LXIII (February 1961), 103–149.

42. Berman, Phyllis W., Waisman, Harry A., and Graham, Frances K. "Intelligence in Treated Phenylketonuric Children: A Developmental Study," *Child Development*, XXXVII, iv (1966), 731–747.

43. Berry, Helen K., Rubinstein, J., and Simon, H.D. "Evaluation of Screening Tests for Phenylketonuria in a Diagnostic Clinic for Retarded Children," *American Journal of Mental Deficiency*, LXVIII, i (1963), 49–53.

44. Berry, Mildred F. *Language Disorders of Children: The Bases and Diagnoses*. New York: Appleton-Century-Crofts, 1969.

45. Berry, Mildred F., and Eisenson, J. *Speech Disorders: Principles and Practices of Therapy*. New York: Appleton-Century-Crofts, 1956.

46. Bialer, I., and Cromwell, Rue L. "Failure as Motivation with Mentally Retarded Children," *American Journal of Mental Deficiency*, LXIX, v (1965), 680–684.

47. Bijou, S. W. "Theory and Research in Mental (Developmental) Retardation," *Psychological Record*, XIII (1963), 95–110.

48. Birch, H.G., and Belmont, Lillian. "The Problem of Comparing Home Rearing versus Foster-Home Rearing in Defective Children," *Pediatrics*, XXVIII (1961), 956–961.

49. Birch, H.G., Thomas, A., and Chess, S. "Behavioral Development in Brain-Damaged Children," *Archives of General Psychiatry*, XI (1964), 6.

50. Birnbrauer, Jay Spencer. "The Effects of Stimulus Pretraining on Discrimination Learning in Retarded Children," *Dissertation Abstracts*, XXIII, vi (1962), 2214.

51. Bitter, J. A. "Attitude Change by Parents of Trainable Mentally

Retarded Children as a Result of Group Discussion," *Exceptional Children*, XXX (1963), 173–177.

52. Blackman, Leonard S. "Research Needs in the Special Education of the Mentally Retarded," *Exceptional Child*, XXIX (1963), 377–383.

53. Blatt, B. "Towards a More Acceptable Terminology in Mental Retardation," *Training School Bulletin*, LVIII (1961), 47–51.

54. Bowes, W. A., Brackbill, T., Conway, E., and Steinschneider, A. *The Effects of Obstetrical Medication on Fetus and Infant.* Monograph of the Society for Research in Child Development No. 137. Chicago: University of Chicago Press, 1970.

55. Bowlby, J. *Maternal Care and Mental Health.* Geneva: World Health Organization, 1951.

56. Boyle, J. A. "Lesch Nyhan Syndrome: Preventative Control by Prenatal Diagnosis," *Science*, CLXIX (1970), 688–689.

57. Brackbill, Yvonne. *Research in Infant Behavior: A Case Indexed Bibliography.* Baltimore: Williams and Wilkins, 1964.

58. Brazelton, T. B. "Psychophysiologic Reactions in the Neonate: Effect of Maternal Medication on the Infant and His Behavior," *Journal of Pediatrics*, LVIII (1961), 513.

59. Brengelmann, J.C., and Kenny, J. T. "Comparison of Leiter, WAIS and Stanford-Binet IQs in Retardates," *Journal of Clinical Psychology*, XVII (1961), 235–238.

60. Bricker, Diane D., and Bricker, William A. "A Programmed Approach to Operant Audiometry for Low-Functioning Children," *Journal of Speech and Hearing Disorders*, XXXIV, iv (1969), 312–320.

61. Bricker, William A., and Bricker, Diane D. "Development and Receptive Vocabulary in Severely Retarded Children," *American Journal of Mental Deficiency*, LXXIV (1970), 599–607.

62. Brody, S. *Patterns of Mothering*. New York: International Universities Press, 1956.

63. Brown, Jose. "Comparative Performance of Trainable Mentally Retarded on the Kraus-Weber Test," *Research Quarterly*, XXXVIII, iii (1967), 348–354.

64. Bryart, P. E. "Verbalization and Immediate Memory of Complex Stimuli in Normal and Severely Subnormal Children," *British Journal of Social and Clinical Psychology*, VI, iii (1967), 212–219.

65. Buchanan, J. G. and Becroft, D.M.O. "Down's Syndrome and Acute Leukemia: A Cytogenetic Study," *Journal of Medical Genetics*, VII (1970), 67–69.

66. Buck, Pearl S. *The Child Who Never Grew*. New York: John Day, 1950.

67. Carey, W. B. "A Simplified Method for Measuring Infant Temperament," *Journal of Pediatrics*, LXXVII (1970), 188–194.

68. Carlson, Bernice W., and Ginglend, D. R. *Play Activities for the Retarded Child*. New York: Abingdon Press, 1961.

69. Carmichael, L., ed. *Manual of Child Psychology*. New York: Wiley, 1954.

70. Carr, J. "Mental and Motor Development in Young Mongol Children," *Journal of Mental Deficiency Research*, XIV (1970), 205–220.

71. Cattell, Psyche. *The Measurement of Intelligence of Infants and Young Children*. New York: Psychological Corp., 1940.

72. Chazan, Maurice. "Recent Developments in the Understanding and Teaching of Educationally Sub-Normal Children in England and Wales," *American Journal of Mental Deficiency*, LXXII, ii (1967), 244–252.

73. Chen, A.T.C., Sergovich, F.R., McKim, J.S., Barr, M.L., and Gruber, D. "Chromosome Studies in Full-Term Low Birth Weight Mentally Retarded Patients," *Journal of Pediatrics*, LXXVI (1970), 393–398.

74. Chess, Stella. "Psychiatric Treatment of the Mentally Retarded Child with Behavior Problems," *American Journal of Orthopsychiatry*, XXXII, v (1962), 863–869.

75. Chess, Stella, and Korn, S. "Temperament and Behavior Disorders in Mentally Retarded Children," *Archives of Genetic Psychiatry*, XXIII (1970), 122–130.

76. Cohen, Pauline C. "Impact of a Handicapped Child on the Family," *Social Casework*, XLIII (1962), 3.

77. Condell, James F. "Parental Attitudes toward Mental Retardation," *American Journal of Mental Deficiency*, LXXI, i (1966), 85–92.

78. Copeland, R. "The Effects of Feedback Modification on Verbal Behavior," *Language Studies of Mentally Retarded Children*. R.F. Schiefelbusch, ed. *Journal of Speech and Hearing Disorders*, Monograph Supplement No. 10., (1963).

79. Crome, L., and Stern, J. *The Pathology of Mental Retardation*. London: J. and A. Churchill, 1967.

80. Cummings, S. Thomas, and Stock, Dorothy. "Brief Group Therapy of Mothers of Retarded Children Outside of the Specialty Clinic Setting," *American Journal of Mental Deficiency*, LXVI (1962), 739–748.

81. Dalton, Juanita, and Epstein, Helene. "Counseling Parents of Mildly Retarded Children," *Social Casework*, XLIV (1963), 9.

82. Daw, J. F. "The Effect of Special Exercises on Body Image in Mentally Retarded Children: A Tentative Exploration," *Slow Learning Child*, XI, ii (1964), 109–116.

83. De Hirsch, K. "A Review of Early Language Development," *Developmental Medicine and Child Neurology*, XII (1970), 87–97.

84. Desmond, M. M., Franklin, R. P., Vallbina, C., Hill, R., Plumb, R., Arnold, H., and Watts, J. "Clinical Behavior of the Newly Born," *Journal of Pediatrics*, LXII (1963), 1307.

85. *Diagnostic and Statistical Manual of Mental Disorders*. Washington, D.C.: American Psychiatric Association, 1968.

86. Diller, L., and Birch, H.G. "Psychological Evaluation of Children with Cerebral Damage," *Brain Damage in Children*. H.G. Birch, ed. Baltimore: Williams and Wilkins, 1964.

87. Dingman, H. F., Eyman, R. K., and Windle, C. D. "An Investigation of Some Child-Rearing Attitudes of Mothers with Retarded Children," *American Journal of Mental Deficiency*, LXVIII, vi (1963), 899–908.

88. DiNola, Alfred, Kaminsky, Bernard, and Sternfeld, Allan. *T.M.R. Performance Profile for the Severely and Moderately Retarded.* Ridgefield, N. J.: Educational Performance Associates, 1963.

89. Dittman, Laura L. *The Mentally Retarded Child at Home: A Manual for Parents*. U.S. Dept. of Health, Education, and Welfare, Children's Bureau Publication, No. 374. Washington: Government Printing Office, 1959.

90. Doll, Edgar. *Vineland Social Maturity Scale*. Minneapolis: Educational Test Bureau, 1947.

91. Downey, K. J. "Parental Interest in the Institutionalized, Severely Mentally Retarded Child," *Social Problems*, XI (1963), 186–193.

92. Drayer, C., and Schlesinger, Elfriede. "The Informing Interview," *American Journal of Mental Deficiency*, LXV (1960), 363–370.

93. Dunn, L. M. *Peabody Picture Vocabulary Test: Manual*. Minneapolis: American Guidance Service, 1959.

94. Dybwad, Gunnar. "Group Approaches and Working with Parents of the Retarded: An Overview," *Challenges in Mental Retardation*. New York: Columbia University Press, 1964.

95. Dybwad, Gunnar. "Who Are the Mentally Retarded?," *Children*, XV, ii (1968), 43–48.

96. Edgar, Clara L., Ball, Thomas S., McIntyre, Robert B., and Shotwell, Anna. "Effectiveness of Sensory-Motor Training in Promoting Adaptive Behavior in Young Retardates," *California Mental Health Research*, III, i (1965), 29.

97. Egg, Maria. *When a Child Is Different: A Basic Guide for Parents and Friends of Mentally Retarded Children, Giving Practical Suggestions on Their Education and Training*. New York: John Day, 1964.

98. Elkind, David, Koegler, Ronald R., Go, Elsie, and Van Davininick, William. "Effects of Perceptual Training on Unmatched Samples of Brain-Injured and Familial Retarded Children," *Journal of Abnormal Psychology*, LXX, iii (1965), 107–110.

99. Ellis, Norman R. *Handbook of Mental Deficiency*. New York: McGraw-Hill, 1963.

100. Erikson, Marilyn T. "The Predictive Validity of the Cattell Infant Intelligence Scale for Young Mentally Retarded Children," *American Journal of Mental Deficiency*, LXXII, v (1968), 728–733.

101. Erikson, Marilyn T., Johnson, N. M., and Campbell, F. A. "Relationship Among Scores on Infant Tests for Children with Developmental Problems," *American Journal of Mental Deficiency*, LXXV (1970), 102–104.

102. Escalona, S. K. "The Use of Infant Tests for Predictive Purposes," *Bulletin Menninger Clinic*, XIV (1950), 117–128.

103. Escalona, S.K., and Moriarty, A. "Prediction of School-Age

Intelligence from Infant Test," *Child Development*, XXXII (1961), 597–605.

104. "Experimental Studies of Child Behavior, Normal and Deviant." *Research in Behavior Modification*. L. Krasner and L.P. Ullman, eds. New York: Holt, Rinehart, and Winston, 1965.

105. Falkner, F., ed. *Key Issues in Infant Mortality*. Bethesda: National Institute of Child Health and Human Development, 1970.

106. Fantz, R. L. "Visual Perception and Experience in Early Infancy: A Look at the Hidden Side of Behavior Development." *Early Behavior: Comparative and Developmental Approaches*. H. W. Stevenson, E. H. Hess, and Harriet Rheingold, eds. New York: Wiley, 1967.

107. Farber, B. "Effects of a Severely Mentally Retarded Child on Family Integration," *Monographs of the Society for Research in Child Development*, XXIV, ii (1959).

108. Fishler, Karol, Graliker, Betty V., and Koch, Richard. "The Predictability of Intelligence with Gesell Developmental Scales in Mentally Retarded Infants and Young Children," *American Journal of Mental Deficiency*, LXIX, iv (1965), 515–525.

109. French, Anne C., Levbarg, M., and Michal-Smith, H. "Parent Counseling as a Means of Improving the Performance of a Mentally Retarded Boy: A Case Study Presentation," *American Journal of Mental Deficiency*, LVIII (1953), 13–20.

110. Freud, A., and Burlingham, D. *Infants Without Families*. New York: International Universities Press, 1944.

111. Friedlander, George H. "A Rationale for Speech and Language Development for the Young Retarded Child," *Training School Bulletin*, LIX (1962), 9–14.

112. Fulton, Robert T., and Lloyd, Lyle L. *Audiometry for the Retarded*. Baltimore: Williams and Wilkins, 1969.

113. Gellner, Lise. *A Neurophysiological Concept of Mental Retardation and Its Educational Implications*. Chicago: Dr. Julian Levinson Foundation, 1960.

114. Gellner, Lise. "Language Studies of Mentally Retarded Children," *Journal of Speech and Hearing Disorders Monograph Supplement No. 10* (January 1963).

115. Gesell, Arnold. *Developmental Diagnosis*. New York: Harper & Brothers, 1941.

116. Gesell, Arnold. *The Embryology of Behavior*. New York: Harper & Brothers, 1945.

117. Gesell, Arnold. *Infant Development: The Embryology of Early Human Behavior*. New York: Harper & Brothers, 1952.

118. Gesell, Arnold, and Ames, L. B. "Early Evidences of Individuality in the Human Infant," *Journal of Genetic Psychology*, XLVII (1947), 339.

119. Gesell, Arnold, and Amatruda, C. *Developmental Diagnosis*. 2nd ed. New York: Hoeber, Inc., 1947.

120. Gesell, Arnold, and Ilg, Frances. *Infant and Child in the Culture of Today*. New York: Harper & Brothers, 1943.

121. Giannini, Margaret J., and Goodman, L. "Counseling Families During the Crisis Reaction to Mongolism," *American Journal of Mental Deficiency*, LXVII (1963), 740–747.

122. Gilliland, A. R. "The Measurement of Mentality of Infants," *Child Development*, XIX (1948).

123. Ginsburg, H., and Opper, S. *Piaget's Theory of Intellectual Development*. Englewood Cliffs, N. J.: Prentice-Hall, 1969.

124. Girardeau, Frederic L., and Spradlin, Joseph E. "Token Rewards in a Cottage Program," *Mental Retardation*, II, vi (1964), 345–351.

125. Goldberg, F. H. "The Performance of Schizophrenic, Retarded and Normal Children on the Bender-Gestalt Test," *American Journal of Mental Deficiency*, LXI (1957), 548–555.

126. Goldberg, I. *Selected Bibliography of Special Education*. New York: Columbia University Press, 1967.

127. Goodman, Lawrence. "Continuing Treatment of Parents with Congenitally Defective Infants," *Social Work*, IX, i (1964), 92–97.

128. Goodman, Lawrence, and Rothman, Ruth. "The Development of a Group Counseling Program in a Clinic for Retarded Children," *American Journal of Mental Deficiency*, LXV (1961), 789–795.

129. Gorton, Chester E., and Hollis, John. "Redesigning a Cottage Unit for Better Programming and Research for the Severely Retarded," *Mental Retardation*, III, iii (1965), 16–21.

130. Graliker, Betty V., Fishler, Karol, and Koch, R. "Teenage Reaction to a Mentally Retarded Sibling," *American Journal of Mental Deficiency*, LXVI (1962), 838–843.

131. Graliker, Betty V., Koch, Richard, and Henderson, Robert A. "A Study of Influencing Placement of Retarded Children in a State Residential Institution," *American Journal of Mental Deficiency*, LXIX, iv (1965), 553–559.

132. Griffiths, R. *The Abilities of Babies*. New York: McGraw-Hill, 1954.

133. Guthrie, R., and Whitney, S. *Phenylketonuria, Detection in the Newborn Infant as a Routine Hospital Procedure*. U.S. Department of Health, Education, and Welfare, Welfare Administration, Children's Bureau Publication 419. Washington: U.S. Government Printing Office, 1964.

134. Haeusserman, E. *Development Potential of Pre-School Children*. New York: Grune and Stratton, 1958.

135. Hallowell, D. K. "Validity of Mental Tests for Young Children," *Journal of Genetic Psychology*, LVIII (1941), 265–286.

136. Hammond, J., Sternlight, M., and Deutsch, M. R. "Parental Interest in Institutionalized Children: a Survey," *Hospital Community Psychiatry*, XX (1969), 338–339.

137. Harlow, H. F. "Love in Infant Monkeys," *Scientific American*, CC (1959), 68.

138. Haskell, Elizabeth N., Woodcock, Dorothy L., Streeter, Helen S., Morton, Mary C., Smith, N. S., and Ervin, E. N. "The First Three Years of a Clinic for Mentally Retarded Pre-school Children," *Journal of Maine Medical Association*, LII (1961), 47–53.

139. Hathaway, S. R., and McKinley, J. C. *Minnesota Multiphasic Personality Inventory*. New York: Psychological Corp., 1943.

140. Haynes, Una. *A Developmental Approach to Casefinding*. Public Health Service Publication No. 2017. Washington, D.C., 1969.

141. Heber, R. *A Manual on Terminology and Classification in Mental Retardation*. Columbus, Ohio: American Association on Mental Deficiency, 1961.

142. Hellmuth, J., ed. *The Exceptional Infant*, Vol. I: *The Normal Infant*. Seattle: Special Child Publications, 1967.

143. Hersh, Alexander. "Casework with Parents of Retarded Children," *Social Work*, VI (1961), 2.

144. Hollis, John H. "The Effects of Social and Nonsocial Stimuli on the Behavior of Profoundly Retarded Children," *American Journal of Mental Deficiency*, LXIX, vi (1965), 755–771.

145. Hollis, John H. "Effects of Reinforcement Shifts on Bent-wire Performance of Severely Retarded Children," *American Journal of Mental Deficiency*, LXIX, iv (1965), 531–535.

146. Horne, Betty M., and Justiss, Will A. "Clinical Indications of

Brain Damage in Mentally Retarded Children," *Journal of Clinical Psychology*, XXIII, iv (1967), 464–465.

147. Howell, R. R. "Phenylketonuria in the General Population," *New England Journal of Medicine*, CCLXXXII (1970), 1486–1488.

148. Hunter, Marvin, and Schucman, Helen. *Early Identification and Treatment of the Infant Retardate and His Family*. Tokyo: Nippon Shoni Iji Shuppan Sha Co., Ltd., 1970.

149. Illingworth, R. S. "Difficulties in Developmental Prediction," *Child Neurology and Cerebral Palsy*, LVIII (1960).

150. Illingworth, R. S. *The Development of the Infant and Young Child: Normal and Abnormal*. 4th ed. Edinburgh: E. and S. Livingstone, 1970.

151. Ireton, H., Thwing, J., and Gravem, H. "Relationships between Infant Mental Development, Infant Medical Data, Socioeconomic Data and Intelligence at Age Four," *American Journal of Orthopsychiatry*, XL (1970), 325.

152. Johnson, Bette M. "Acquisition and Extinction of an Instrumental Response in Normal and Mentally Retarded Children," *Dissertation Abstracts*, XXV, i (1965), 646.

153. Johnson, E. W., Gove, R., and Ostermeier, Barbara. "The Value of Functional Training in Severely Disabled Institutionalized Brain Damaged Children," *American Journal of Mental Deficiency*, LXVII, vi (1963), 860–864.

154. Jones, H. E. "The Retention of Conditioned Emotional Reactions in Infancy," *Journal of Genetic Psychology*, XXXVII (1930), 485–498.

155. Katz, Alfred H. *Parents of the Handicapped*. Springfield, Ill.: Charles C. Thomas, 1961.

156. Kaufman, M. E., and Peterson, W. M. "Acquisition of a Condi-

tional Discrimination Learning-set by Normal and Mentally Retarded Children," *American Journal of Mental Deficiency*, LXIX, vi (1965), 865–870.

157. Kelly, Leo J. "The Sequential Development of Curriculum for Educable Mentally Retarded Children," *Exceptional Children*, XXXIII, iii (1966), 178–179.

158. Kilhara, Hayato, Wright, Stanley W., and Day, Robert W. "Metabolic Disorders in Mentally Deficient Children," *California Mental Health Research Digest*, II, iv (1964), 29.

159. Klatskin, E. H. "Shifts in Child Care Practices in Three Social Classes under an Infant Care Program of Flexible Methodology," *American Journal of Orthopsychiatry*, XXII (1952), 52–61.

160. Knobloch, H., and Pasamanick, B. "Environmental Factors Affecting Human Development: Before and After Birth," *Pediatrics*, XXVI (1960), 210.

161. Knobloch, H., and Pasamanick, B. *The Distribution of Intellectual Potential in an Infant Population: The Epidemiology of Mental Disorder*. American Association for the Advancement of Science Publication No. 60, 1959.

162. Koch, Richard, Graliker, Betty, Bronston, William, and Fishler, Karol. "Mental Retardation in Early Childhood," *American Journal of Diseases of Children*, CIX, iii (1965), 243–251.

163. Kolstoe, O. P. *Teaching Educable Mentally Retarded Children*. New York: Holt, Rinehart and Winston, 1970.

164. Kozier, Ada. "Casework with Parents of Children Born with Severe Brain Defects," *Social Casework*, XXXVIII, iv (1957), 183–189.

165. Kurtz, Richard A. "Comparative Education of Suspected Retardates," *American Journal of Diseases of Children*, CIX, i (1965), 58–65.

166. Labzoffsky, N.A., et al. "Survey of Toxoplasmosis Among Mentally Retarded Children," *Canadian Medical Association Journal*, XCII, ix (1965), 1026.

167. Langan, James G. "A Comparison of Motor Proficiency in Middle and Lower Class Educable Mentally Retarded Children," *Dissertation Abstracts*, XXVII, iia (1966), 396–397.

168. Lanthrom, Wanda. "Music Therapy as a Means of Changing the Adaptive Behavior Level of Retarded Children," *Journal of Music Therapy*, I, iv (1964), 132–134.

169. Lilienfeld, A., and Benesch, C. H. *Epidemiology of Mongolism*. Baltimore: Johns Hopkins Press, 1969.

170. Lipsitt, L. P. "Learning Processes of Human Newborns," *Merrill-Palmer Quarterly*, XII (1966), 45–71.

171. London, Susan Katherine. "The Stability of the I.Q. of Mentally Retarded Pre-School Children," *Dissertation Abstracts*, XXIII, i (1962), 310.

172. Longfellow, Layne A. "Effects of Food Deprivation on Temporally Spaced Responding in Moderately Retarded Children," *Dissertation Abstracts*, XXVIII, viib (1968), 3075–3076.

173. Luria, A. R. *The Role of Speech in the Regulation of Normal and Abnormal Behavior*. New York: Liveright, 1961.

174. Luria, A. R. *The Mentally Retarded Child*. New York: Pergamon Press, 1963.

175. Lyman, F. L., ed. *Phenylketonuria*. Springfield, Ill.: Charles C. Thomas, 1963.

176. Machover, Karen. *Personality Projection in the Drawing of the Human Figure*. Springfield, Ill.: Charles C. Thomas, 1949.

177. Mandelbaum, Arthur. "The Group Process in Helping Parents of Retarded Children," *Children*, XIV, vi (1967), 227–232.

178. Mann, Abby. *A Child Is Waiting*. New York: Popular Library, 1963.

179. Marden, P. N., Smith, D. W., and McDonald, M. J. "Congenital Anomalies of the Newborn," *Journal of Pediatrics*, LXIV (1964), 363.

180. Marquis, D. P. "Can Conditioned Responses Be Established in the Newborn Infant?," *Journal of Genetic Psychology*, XXXIX (1931), 479–492.

181. Martmer, E. E., ed. *The Child with a Handicap*. Springfield, Ill.: Charles C. Thomas, 1959.

182. Masland, R., Sarason, S., and Gladwin, T. *Mental Subnormality*. New York: Basic Books, 1958.

183. Mayer, C. Lamar. "Relationships of Self-Concepts and Social Variables in Retarded Children," *American Journal of Mental Deficiency*, LXXII, ii (1967), 267–271.

184. Mayo, Leonard W. "Education of the Mentally Retarded," *Journal of Rehabilitation*, XXXI, ii (1965), 37–40.

185. McDermott, Ita K. *Public Health Nursing in the Mental Retardation Program*. New York: National League for Nursing, 1960.

186. McIntire, Matilda S., and Kiekhaeker, T.C. "Parental Reaction to a Clinic for the Evaluation of the Mentally Retarded," *Nebraska Medical Journal*, XLVIII (1963), 69–73.

187. McNemar, Quinn. *Psychological Statistics*. New York: John Wiley & Sons, 1949.

188. Metraux, R. W. "Speech Profiles of the Pre-School Child 18 to 54 months," *Journal of Speech and Hearing Disorders*, XV (1950), 37–53.

189. Meurakami, E., Ogino, S., and Tomiyasu, Y. "A Study of Teaching Patterns in Special Classes for the Mentally Retarded," *Japa-*

nese Journal of Educational Psychology, XV, ii (1967), 11–20.

190. Meyer, D. L. "Genetic Counseling Problems Associated with Trisomy 21 Down's Disorder," *American Journal of Mental Deficiency*, LXVII (1963), 334–339.

191. Meyerowitz, Joseph H. "Sociological Aspects of Early Identification and Special Treatment of the Educationally Retarded Child," *Dissertation Abstracts*, XXV, viii (1965), 4858–4859.

192. Meyers, Elizabeth S., and Meyers, C. E. "Problems in School Placement Arising from Divergent Conceptions of Educable Children," *Mental Retardation*, V, v (1967), 19–22.

193. Michaels, Joseph, and Schucman, Helen. "Observations on the Psychodynamics of Parents of Retarded Children," *American Journal of Mental Deficiency*, LXVI (1962), 568–573.

194. Milton, Robert G. "Prediction of Therapeutic and Intellectual Potential in Mentally Retarded Children," *Dissertation Abstracts*, XXVI, v (1964), 3690.

195. Minskoff, Esther H. "Verbal Interactions of Teachers and Mentally Retarded Pupils," *Dissertation Abstracts*, XXVIII, iia (1967), 546–547.

196. Molloy, Julia. *Trainable Children*. Rev. ed. New York: The John Day Co., 1972.

197. Molloy, Julia. *Teaching the Retarded Child to Talk*. New York: The John Day Co., 1961.

198. Monaco, Theresa M. "An Analysis of Operant Conditioning and Learning in Severely Retarded Children," *Dissertation Abstracts*, XXII, viiia (1968), 3077–3078.

199. Moss, Howard A. "Methodological Issues in Studying Mother-Infant Interaction," *American Journal of Orthopsychiatry*, XXXV, iii (1965), 482–486.

200. Myklebust, H. R. *Auditory Disorders in Children*. New York: Grune and Stratton, 1954.

201. Nadal, Robert M. "A Counseling Program for Parents of Severely Retarded Pre-School Children," *Social Casework*, XLII (1961), 78–83.

202. Neser, William B., and Sudderth, Grace B. "Genetics and Casework," *Social Casework*, XLVI (1965), 1.

203. Nipper, William A. "A Comparison of Certain Aspects of Categorizing Behavior in Retarded, Normal and Gifted Children at Two Age Levels," *Dissertation Abstracts*, XXVII, viia (1968), 2563–2564.

204. Olshansky, Simon. "Chronic Sorrow: A Response to a Mentally Defective Child," *Social Casework*, XLIII (1962), 4.

205. Owens, Charlotte. "Parents' Reactions to Defective Babies," *American Journal of Nursing*, LXIV, xi (1964), 83–85.

206. Paine, R. S. "Neurological Examination of Infants and Children," *Pediatric Clinics of North America*, VII (1960), 470–510.

207. Paine, R. S., and Oppe, T. E. *Clinics in Developmental Medicine: Neurological Examination of Children*. Suffolk, England: National Spastics Society in Association with Wm. Heinemann, Ltd., 1966.

208. Pascal, G., and Suttell, B. *The Bender-Gestalt Test Quantification and Validity for Adults*. New York: Grune and Stratton, 1951.

209. Peebles, T. C. "Evaluation of the Routine Physical Examination of Infants in the First Year of Life: Review," *Pediatrics*, XLV (1970), 962–963.

210. Penfield, W., and Roberts, L. *Speech and Brain Mechanisms*. Princeton: Princeton University Press, 1959.

211. Pereira Luz, Nilo. "Aspectos Profilaticos em Psiquiatria Infantel (Preventive Aspects of Child Psychiatry)," *Revista Brasileira de Deficiencia Mental*, II, i (1967), 64–71.

212. Piaget, J. *The Origins of Intelligence in Children*. New York: International Universities Press, 1952.

213. Piaget, J. *The Construction of Reality in the Child*. New York: Basic Books, 1954.

214. Piaget, J. *The Language and Thought of the Child*. 3rd ed. London: Routledge, 1959.

215. Piaget, J. *Play, Dreams, and Imitation in Childhood*. New York: Norton, 1962.

216. Porter, Rutherford B., Collins, James L., and McIver, M. Raymond. "A Comparative Investigation of the Personality of Educable Mentally Retarded Children and Those of a Norm Group of Children," *Exceptional Children*, XXXI, ix (1965), 457–463.

217. Poser, C. M., ed. *Mental Retardation*. New York: Harper & Row, 1969.

218. Provence, S., and Lipton, R. C. *Infants in Institutions*. New York: International Universities Press, 1962.

219. Rajalakshmi, R., and Jeeves, M. A. "Comparative Performance of Normals and Retardates of the Same Mental Age on Certain Psychological Tasks," *Journal of Genetic Psychology*, CVI, i (1965), 39–43.

220. *Recent Demographic Trends and Their Effects on Maternal and Child Health Needs and Services*. Children's Bureau, U.S. Department of Health, Education and Welfare, 1966.

221. Reed, E. W., and Reed, S. C. *Mental Retardation: A Family Study*. Philadelphia: W. B. Saunders, 1965.

222. *Report of the Committee on the Control of Infectious Diseases.* 15th edition. Evanston, Illinois: American Academy of Pediatrics, 1966.

223. Rheingold, H. L., Gerwirtz, J. L., and Ross, H. S. "Social Conditioning of Vocalizations in the Infant," *Journal of Comparative and Physiological Psychology*, LII (1959), 68.

224. Richards, T. W., and Simons, M. P. "The Fels Child Behavior Scales," *Genetic Psychology Monographs*, XXIV (Nov., 1941), 259–311.

225. Robinson, H. B., and Robinson, N. M. *The Mentally Retarded Child: A Psychological Approach.* New York: McGraw-Hill, 1965.

226. Robinson, John S. "Analyses of Perception in the Retarded," *California Mental Health Research Digest*, V, iii (1967), 178–179.

227. Robinson, John S., and Bayley, Nancy. "Behavioral Criteria for Diagnosing Mental Retardation in the First Two Years of Life," *California Mental Health Research Digest*, V, iii (1967), 180–181.

228. Rohrs, F. W., and Haworth, M. R. "The 1960 Stanford-Binet, WISC and Goodenough Tests with Mentally Retarded Children," *American Journal of Mental Deficiency*, LXVI (1962), 853–859.

229. Ross, Leonard E., Hetherington, Mavis, and Wray, Nancy P. "Delay of Reward and the Learning of a Size Problem by Normal and Retarded Children," *Child Development*, XXXVI, ii (1965), 509–517.

230. Rossi, E. L. "Associative Clustering in Normal and Retarded Children," *American Journal of Mental Deficiency*, LXVII, v (1963), 691–699.

231. Rouse, Sue T. "Effects of a Training Program on the Productive Thinking of Educable Mental Retardates," *American Journal of Mental Deficiency*, LXIX, v (1965), 666–673.

232. Salkin, Jeri, and May, Philip R. "Body Ego Technique: An Educational Approach to Body Image and Self-Identity," *Journal of Special Education*, I, iv (1967), 375–386.

233. Sandbank, U. "Infantile Neuroaxonal Dystrophy," *Archives of Neurology*, XII, ii (1965), 155–159.

234. Sarason, S. B. *Psychological Problems in Mental Deficiency*. 3rd ed. New York: Harper & Brothers, 1959.

235. Schaeffer, E. S., Bell, R. Q., and Bayley, N. "Development of a Maternal Behavior Research Instrument," *Journal of Genetic Psychology*, XCV (1959), 83–104.

236. Schiefelbusch, R. L. "A Discussion of Language Treatment Methods for Mentally Retarded Children," *Mental Retardation*, III, ii (1965), 4–7.

237. Schild, Sylvia. "Counseling with Parents of Retarded Children Living at Home," *Social Work*, IX (1964), 86–91.

238. Schmidt, Leo J. "The Affective Cognitive Attitude Dimension of Teachers of Educable Mentally Retarded Minors," *Dissertation Abstracts*, XXVIII, vii a (1968), 2457.

239. Schmiedeberg, Joachim. "Sprache bei Intelligenzgeminderten Kindern (Language in Children with Low Intelligence)," *Heilpadagogische Werkblatter*, XXXVI, v (1967), 237–248.

240. Schreiber, M., and Feeley, M. "Siblings of the Retarded: I. The Guided Group Experience," *Children*, XII (1965), 221–225.

241. Schucman, Helen. "Further Observations on the Psychodynamics of Parents of Retarded Children," *Training School Bulletin*, LX (1963), 70–74.

242. Schull, W. J. "Congenital Malformations, Current Knowledge of Etiology," *Clinical Obstetrics and Gynecology*, IV (1961), 365.

243. Sears, R. R., Maccoby, E. E., and Levin, H. *Patterns of Child*

Rearing. Evanston, Ill.: Row, Peterson, 1957.

244. Semler, Ira J. "Selective Learning in Severely Retarded Children as a Function of Differential Reaction to Nonreward," *Child Development*, XXXVI, i (1965), 143–152.

245. Shannon, Victoria. "When Children Are Born with Mental Defects," *Children* (January-February, 1955).

246. Shield Institute for Retarded Children. *Program for Pre-School Trainable Retardates and Their Parents*, pursuant to Grant #OM-160 from the National Institute of Mental Health, Department of Health, Education and Welfare, Public Health Service (1958 to 1961).

247. Shield Institute for Retarded Children. *Early Identification and Treatment of the Infant Retardate and His Family*, pursuant to Grant #MH-00761 from the National Institute of Mental Health, Department of Health, Education and Welfare, Public Health Service (1963 to 1967).

248. Siegel, Gerald. "Prevailing Concepts in Speech and Research with Mentally Retarded Children," *ASHA*, VI, vi (1964), 193–194.

249. Sigueland, E. R. "Operant Conditioning of Head Turning in Four Infants," *Psychonomic Science*, I (1964), 223–224.

250. Silverstein, A. B. "An Evaluation of Two Short Forms of the Stanford-Binet, Form L-M, for Use with Mentally Retarded Children," *American Journal of Mental Deficiency*, LXVII, vi (1963), 922–923.

251. Simmons, M. W. "Operant Discrimination Learning in Human Infants," *Child Development*, XXXV (1964), 737–748.

252. Skinner, B. F. "Operant Behavior," *American Psychology*, XVIII (1963), 503–515.

253. Slavson, S. R. *Child Centered Group Guidance of Parents*. New

York: International Universities Press, 1958.

254. Sloane, Howard N., Jr., and MacAulay, Barbara D., eds. *Operant Procedures in Remedial Speech and Language Training.* Boston: Houghton Mifflin, 1968.

255. Slobody, L., and Scanlan, J. "Consequences of Early Institutionalization," *American Journal of Mental Deficiency*, LXIII (1959), 971–974.

256. Smith, D. W., and Bostian, K. E. "Congenital Anomalies Associated with Idiopathic Mental Retardation," *Journal of Pediatrics*, LXV (1964), 189.

257. Spock, B. *On Being a Parent of a Handicapped Child.* Chicago: National Society for Crippled Children and Adults, 1961.

258. Stacey, Chalmers L., and DeMartino, Manfred F. *Counseling and Psychotherapy with the Mentally Retarded.* Glen Cove, Ill.: Free Press, 1957.

259. Stafford, Richard L., and Meyer, Roger J. "Diagnosis and Counseling of the Mentally Retarded: Implications for School Health," *Journal of School Health*, XXXVIII, iii (1968), 151–155.

260. Stechler, G., and Latz, E. "Some Observations on Attention and Arousal in the Human Infant," *Journal of the American Academy of Child Psychiatry*, V, iii (1966), 517–525.

261. Stott, L. H., and Ball, R. S. *Evaluation of Infant and Preschool Mental Tests.* Cooperative Research Project No. 1166. Detroit: Merrill-Palmer Institute, 1963.

262. Straus, A. A., and Kephart, N. C. *Psychopathology of the Brain-Injured Child*, Vol. II: Progress in Theory and Clinic. New York: Grune and Stratton, 1955.

263. Stutsman, Rachel. *A Guide for the Administrations of the Merrill-Palmer Scale of Mental Tests.* Chicago: Stoelting Co., 1931.

264. Tereda, Akira. "A Study of the Development of Learning Gains of Mentally Retarded Children," *Tohoku Journal of Educational Psychology*, I, ii (1964), 89–100.

265. Terman, Lewis, and Merrill, Maud. *Measuring Intelligence*. Boston: Houghton Mifflin, 1937.

266. Terman, Lewis, and Merrill, Maud. *Stanford-Binet Intelligence Scale*. Boston: Houghton Mifflin, 1960.

267. *The Role of the Social Worker*. Children's Bureau Publication. Washington, D.C.: U. S. Government Printing Office, 1963.

268. Thormahlen, Paul V. "On-the-Ward Training of Trainable Mentally Retarded Children," *California Mental Health Research Digest*, II, iv (1964), 12–13.

269. Thurston, J. R. "A Procedure for Evaluating Parental Attitudes Toward the Handicapped," *American Journal of Mental Deficiency*, LXIV (1959), 148–155.

270. Travis, L., ed. *Handbook of Speech Pathology*. New York: Appleton-Century-Crofts, 1956.

271. Tredgold, R. F., and Soddy, K. *Tredgold's Mental Retardation*. 11th ed. London: Balliere, Tindall and Cassell, 1970.

272. Twitchell, T. E. "The Neurological Examination in Infantile Cerebral Palsy," *Developmental Medicine and Child Neurology*, V (1963), 271.

273. Van Riper, C. *Speech Correction: Principles and Methods*. Second edition. New York: Prentice-Hall, Inc., 1949.

274. Vigotsky, L. S. *Thought and Language*. Cambridge, Mass.: M.I.T. Press, 1962.

275. Vollmer, H. "A New Reflex in Young Infants," *American Journal of Diseases of Children*, XCV (1958), 481.

276. Waldon, E. *Differential Diagnosis of Speech and Hearing Problems of*

Mental Retardates. Washington: Catholic University of America, 1968.

277. Watson, Luke S., Jr., Orser, Richard, and Sanders, Christopher. "Reinforcement Preferences of Severely Mentally Retarded Children in a Generalized Reinforcement Context," *American Journal of Mental Deficiency*, LXXII, v (1968), 748–756.

278. Webster, Thomas G. "Problems of Emotional Development in Young Retarded Children," *American Journal of Psychiatry*, CXX, i (1963), 37–43.

279. Wechsler, David. *The Measurement and Appraisal of Adult Intelligence*. Baltimore: Williams and Wilkins, 1970.

280. Wechsler, David. *Wechsler Intelligence Scale for Children*. New York: The Psychological Corp., 1949.

281. Wechsler, David. *Wechsler Preschool and Primary Scale of Intelligence*. New York: The Psychological Corp., 1969.

282. Weingold, J. T. "Parents' Groups and the Problem of Mental Retardation," *American Journal of Mental Deficiency*, LVI (1952), 484–492.

283. Wenar, C. "The Reliability of Developmental Histories," *Psychosomatic Medicine*, XXV (1963), 505.

284. Willerman, L., Broman, S. H., and Fielder, M. "Infant Development, Preschool I.Q., and Social Class," *Child Development*, XLI (1970), 69–77.

285. Williams, Charlotte, L., and Tillman, M. H. "Associative Characteristics of Selected Form Classes for Children Varying in Age and Intelligence," *Psychological Reports*, XXII, ii (1968), 459–468.

286. Wischner, George J., and O'Donnell, James P. "Concurrent Learning-Set Formation in Normal and Retarded Children,"

Journal of Comparative Physiological Psychology, LV, iv (1962), 524–527.

287. Witsaman, L. R., and Jones, R. L. "Reliability of the Columbia Mental Maturity Scale with Kindergarten Children," *Journal of Clinical Psychology*, XV (1959), 66–68.

288. Wolfensberger, W. "Age Variations in Vineland SQ for the Four Levels of Adaptive Behavior of the 1959 AAMD Behavioral Classification," *American Journal of Mental Deficiency*, LXVII (1962), 452–454.

289. Wolfensberger, W. "Counseling the Parents of the Retarded," *Mental Retardation*, Alfred Baumeister, ed. Chicago: Aldine Co., 1967.

290. Wood, Nancy. *Language Disorders in Children*. Chicago: National Society for Crippled Children and Adults, 1959.

291. Woodward, Katherine F., Siegel, Miriam G., and Eustis, Marjorie J. "Psychiatric Study of Mentally Retarded Children of Pre-School Age—Report on First and Second Years of a Three-Year Project," *American Journal of Orthopsychiatry*, XXVIII (1958), 376–393.

292. Woodward, M., and Stern, D. J. "Developmental Patterns of Severely Subnormal Children," *British Journal of Educational Psychology*, XXXIII, i (1963), 10–21.

293. Wortis, J. "Prevention of Mental Retardation," *American Journal of Orthopsychiatry*, XXXV (1965), 886–895.

294. Yannet, H. "Mental Deficiency," *Advances in Pediatrics*, VIII (1957), 217–257.

295. Yarrow, L. J., and Goodwin, M. R. "Some Conceptual Issues in the Study of Mother-Infant Interaction," *American Journal of Orthopsychiatry*, XXXV (1965), 473–481.

296. Yates, Mary L., and Lederer, Ruth. "Small, Short-Term Group

Meetings with Parents of Children with Mongolism," *American Journal of Mental Deficiency*, LXV (1961), 467–472.

297. Zigler, Edward. "Rigidity and Social Reinforcement Effects in the Performance of Institutionalized and Noninstitutionalized Normal and Retarded Children," *Journal of Personality*, XXXI, i (1963), 258–269.

Index

About the Authors

Marvin H. Hunter (Ph.D., Columbia University, 1960) is Associate Director, The Shield Institute for Retarded Children, and has also served as Research Director of The National Institute of Mental Health grant "Program for Infant Retardates and Their Families" and other research grants in the area of exceptional children. He is also in the private practice of psychotherapy in New York City. He has served as Research Director and Psychotherapist at Queens County Neuropsychiatric Institute; Research Coordinator-Psychological Service, Brooklyn Veterans Administration Hospital; Senior Research Associate, Research Center for Learning Disabilities, State University of New York; and has taught at Brooklyn College. Author of numerous professional journal articles and convention papers, he is also co-author (with Helen Schucman) of *Early Identification and Treatment of the Infant Retardate and His Family*, published (in Japanese) in Tokyo in 1970.

Helen Schucman (Ph.D., New York University, 1957) is Associate Professor of Medical Psychology, Department of Psychiatry, College of Physicians and Surgeons, Columbia University, and Chief Psychologist, Neurological Institute, Columbia-Presbyterian Medical Center. She has been principal investigator on several research grants and consultant to projects involving various groups of exceptional children.

She has published a Psychological Monograph and articles appearing in *American Journal on Mental Deficiency, Journal of Abnormal Psychology, The Training School Bulletin, Psychological Reports,* and other professional journals. Co-author (with Marvin H. Hunter) of *Early Identification and Treatment of the Infant Retardate and His Family,* she has also written chapters on such subjects as adaptive behavior and psychological testing of children in various edited works.

George H. Friedlander (Ph.D., New York University, 1960) is the Director of the Speech and Language Development Program at The Shield Institute for Retarded Children. He has developed and supervised programs at many schools and clinics for exceptional children. He has served as teacher and supervisor on the secondary, college, and graduate levels in speech therapy and education. He is Director of the Communication Disorders Program at the New York Center for Learning Disorders Inc. He has delivered papers at the state, regional, and national conventions of the American Speech and Hearing Association, in which he holds Clinical Certification in Speech Pathology, and the American Association on Mental Deficiency, in which he holds Fellowship. He is in private practice in New York City.

DATE DUE